Preaching Biblical Wisdom in a Self-Help Society

Alyce M. McKenzie

D1408871

Abingdon Press
Nashville

PREACHING BIBLICAL WISDOM IN A SELF-HELP SOCIETY

This book is printed on recycled, acid-free paper.

Library of Congress Cataloging-in-Publication Data

McKenzie, Alyce M., 1955-
  Preaching biblical wisdom in a self-help society / Alyce M. McKenzie.
    p. cm.
  Includes bibliographical references.
  ISBN 0-687-09050-4 (pbk.: alk. paper)
  1. Wisdom—Biblical teaching. 2. Bible—Homiletical use. I. Title.

BS680.W6 .M35 2002
251—dc21

2002013789

02 03 04 05 06 07 08 09 10 11—10 9 8 7 6 5 4 3 2 1

MANUFACTURED IN THE UNITED STATES OF AMERICA

To my parents, Robert and Beverly Fowler, my first and foremost sages

Contents

Introduction

"Wisdom For Monday Mornings" [1]

"The beginning of wisdom is this: Get wisdom." (Proverbs 4:7)

Lots of pastors take Mondays off. I prefer Fridays. Some Mondays I have wished I could go home, climb back into bed and pull the covers over my head. I remember one such Monday a few years ago when I was serving a local church. I drive to church, still tired from last night's finance meeting. My arms filled with briefcase and folders, I struggle to insert the key in the church's front door, wondering, as I do every morning, why it has to be kept locked when there are people inside. Trudging down the hall to my office, I reason that at least my office door will be unlocked as I had left it last night. I turn the knob, and find that it, too, is locked.

Once inside my office, I set my paraphernalia on my desk and head for the coffeepot. Technically, I gave up coffee six months ago. But a dull headache is already humming in my temples. This is what always happens when I skip breakfast. The phone begins to buzz. First phone call: a church member complaining that the secretary left her announcement about the spaghetti dinner out of yesterday's bulletin for the second time this month. "She has some kind of vendetta against me and my projects." "Vendetta is an awfully strong word," I point out. "I'd call it a sin of omission, but I will draw it to her attention."

A clergy colleague calls lamenting his inner-city Anglo church's negative reaction to a Korean house church's request to use its facilities. "Do you think I should just go over their heads and talk to the bishop?" he asks. "Better make every effort to work it out with them first, or they'll feel betrayed," I respond. I massage my temples with both hands while holding the phone in the crook of my neck. A trustee calls to get my advice on the gridlock among the worship committee, the memorials committee, and the trustees over whether to refurbish the existing organ or buy a new one. "Is there a way to work within our economic limits and still achieve our musical goals?" I ask.

I open up the local paper, already starting my reading for next Sunday's sermon. "Children First to Suffer From Program Cuts" says the headline of an article about the increased demand for food at local food banks and soup kitchens. How can this congregation best address this issue? I ask myself.

A woman who was a visitor at yesterday's 11:00 service is on line one. "I enjoyed your service yesterday very much, but I saw something on the way in that upset me so much I had to call you about it. There was a father who had taken his daughter out in the parking lot. He was angry with her, out of control, yelling. He struck her hard on the side of the face." She goes on to describe them both. "I wanted you to know this so you could take some kind of action," she concludes.

"You were right to call me. Thanks for your concern." I reply. I hang up and begin running both hands through my hair, debating which clumps to pull out first.

I continue flipping through the rest of the paper. Ann Landers is telling a new bride not to tolerate her in-laws' tendency to sit on their hands (not the word used in the letter) while she served them a meal and cleaned up after them. "Dieter's Wisdom," the headline on page one of the Lifestyle section, offers advice on foods to eat that burn fat even if you don't exercise. "Brokers Share Wall Street Wisdom with Local Merchants" reads a blurb in the community events column announcing a forum this afternoon at the Township Building.

A thought congeals in my throbbing head. Wisdom! That's what everybody wants from me this morning. They don't just want the ahhh's and ummm's of reflective listening, a skill I perfected in seminary counseling classes in the late '70s. They want wise guidance, perhaps on Mondays more than any other day. A friend of mine who is a lawyer says Mondays are her worst day, as people who have had really bad weekends jam her e-mail, voice mail, and fax lines. They send messages like "I can't take this anymore" and "You've got to get her to comply with the custody agreement," and "What are you doing to speed this process along?" Gym owners watch their parking lots fill up on Mondays with people who have stepped on the scales earlier in the day and seen the "bottom line" consequences of their weekend fork-lifting exercises.

On Fridays, we thank God it's Friday. Saturday nights are for romance. Sundays are, in theory at least, for rest and worship. Mondays, non-romantic Monday mornings—the day and time of the week you are most likely to have a heart attack—Mondays are for facing reality. And on Monday mornings many people face the truth of the contemporary proverb that "reality bites."

A line from the book of Proverbs pops into my head: "I have taught you the way of wisdom; I have led you in the paths of uprightness. When you walk, your step will not be hampered; and if you run, you will not stumble" (Proverbs 4: 11, 12).

What is wisdom? I sense that it is something I have a measure of now, something I am seeking, and something I need to define before I can spot it and seek it more intentionally. Either that, or start taking Mondays off!

CHAPTER ONE

Wisdom: The Art of Steering

"How Should One Live?"

All pastors have, at one time or another, sat, with head in hands, sunk in the knowledge that everyone needs wisdom from them and they cannot meet these needs with their own resources.

On this particular Monday morning my reverie is interrupted by a call from Jean, a parishioner who, after her mastectomy and bone marrow transplant last year, has gotten the results of a liver biopsy back this morning. Her liver is riddled with tumors. A new drug offers only a 30% chance of shrinking them. "Could you come right over?" she asks with tears in her voice. Seated across from her in her living room, she tells me, "I'm not angry with God. I know these things happen. I don't think it's a punishment. But it doesn't seem right that I should die before I've completed my task of raising Anna—she's only eleven. I guess my task now is to figure out how best to live out whatever time I have left."

Jean had defined the question that drives the human search for wisdom, whether expressed in secular or religious terms—how best to live out the time each of us has left. Socrates, many centuries before, asked, "How should one live?" In times of crisis the question is sharpened. Many decisions lie ahead for Jean: how and when to break the news to her family, what treatment to pursue, and how to balance the demands of daily life with her body's need for rest.

On a daily basis all of us are faced with the need to make wise choices. Yogi Berra, baseball catcher and manager of the New York Mets, once said, "When you come to a fork in the road, take it." His aphorism brings a smile, but we need direction. Should I go to the doctor today or wait and see if I feel worse tomorrow? Should I try to mediate the quarrel my neighbors are having, or stay out of it? Should I preach about homosexuality my first year in a new church or wait until I've gained their trust to tackle controversial issues? Not just individuals, but groups, need guidance.

That's where wisdom comes in. Biblical wisdom in the Old Testament is concentrated in three books sandwiched between the end of the salvation history and the beginning of the Prophets: Proverbs, Job, and Ecclesiastes. The mighty acts of God in Israel's history (the exodus, giving of the law at Sinai, crossing of the Red Sea) are never mentioned in these books. The wisdom writings are primarily concerned with the regularities of ordinary life.[1]

They deal with wisdom, an attitude of mind that enables an observer to see patterns in human experience and an articulation of these observations in forms that can be taught and learned. Taken together they assert that wisdom is attainable in part through human effort (Proverbs 4:5-7), and is at the same time a gift from God (Proverbs 2:6). They also affirm that wisdom in its entirety is unattainable, except by God (Ecclesiastes 3:11; Job 28:23).

Each book in its own way addresses the question of what is good for human beings to do as they live out their brief lives under the sun. Their conclusions vary greatly from one book to another and, at times, from one speaker to another within a single book. While their conclusions about life vary according to their experience of it, their method of inquiry is uniform: reflection on patterns in that experience.[2]

This literature from the Hebrew Scriptures represents insights that span several centuries of reflection by the sages or wise ones of Israel. It has counterparts in the wisdom literatures of other ancient Near Eastern cultures (Sumerian, Babylonian, Persian, and Egyptian).

The sages' counsel comes from varied contexts: field and king's court, hearth and home. It represents a pool of advice on how to be successful in the most important arena of life—not in dieting or investing, but in being faithful to God, the source of wisdom for living in both the safe harbors and the high gales of our day-to-day lives.

In the New Testament, wisdom is found primarily in sayings attributed to Jesus in the Gospels and in Pauline reflection on Jesus' identity in light of his Resurrection. The book of James, replete with concrete guidance for the works that should spring from faith, has also been called a wisdom book.

Wisdom in the book of Proverbs is often described as "the Way" (*derek*) (4:11). This word suggests an action of treading or trampling and calls to mind a path worn by constant use. The implication is that wisdom involves patterns of behavior, not just isolated acts. The purpose of this "way" is the formation of an interior disposition (2:1f, 10; 3:1, 3, 5; 4:4, 21, 23; 6:21; 7:3).[3] Biblical wisdom affirms that the gift of a discernible path of order in nature and human relationships is a manifestation of the guiding presence of God.[4] Wisdom is also described as the Way in several Eastern faith systems. By no coincidence, in the early days of the church, Christians were described as "followers of the Way."

Wisdom is also described as a "tree of life" (Proverbs 3:18). The concept of life includes the notion of health, relative prosperity, and a good reputation, but more deeply, the inward person whose very breath depends on God. At the communal level, life translates into *shalom*, peace with justice. [5]

Wisdom is also described in Proverbs as the art of "steering" (*tahbulot*). "Let the wise also hear and gain in learning, and the discerning acquire skill" (*tahbulot*) (Proverbs 1:5). This description of wisdom as a set of steering strategies is based on ancient Egyptian methods of navigating the Nile River by pulling the ropes on one's boat. Wisdom is "learning the ropes" of life. Navigating a treacherous river that leads to life is a good metaphor for the Monday mornings of our future. Biblical wisdom teachings are the provisions the wise person remembers to bring on the trip of life: the paddle, the map, the food, the compass, and the life jacket.

The Genres of Wisdom

The sages' wisdom insights come to us via several genres. A genre is a group of discourses, whether oral or written, that share common characteristics of substance, style, and situation.[6] These similarities in text (thematic content), texture (language and structure), and context (social setting and function) make a genre a unique form of cultural communication.[7]

The Admonition

Two of the most frequent genres in the wisdom literature are the admonition and the saying. The two are often placed side by side in the book of Proverbs. [8] Biblical admonitions, like those we are familiar with from secular sources, are expressed as do's and don't's. They are imperative and direct. "Honor the Lord with your substance and with the first fruits of all your produce" (Proverbs 3:9); "Do not rob the poor because they are poor, or crush the afflicted at the gate" (Proverbs 22:22). [9]

The Saying

Sayings correspond to what we call proverbs, both in biblical and in contemporary usage. [10] The saying or proverb is a "wisdom sentence expressed in the indicative, based on observation and experience." [11] A good example is, "Those who oppress the poor insult their Maker, but those who are kind to the needy honor him" (Proverbs 14:31).

Proverbs are not expressed as direct do's and don't's. They give advice by being applied to a specific situation by the sage. Proverbs, whether biblical or secular, are devised by the older and wiser to instill traditional values in the generation to come. As I write this I am far from lonely. It is a school holiday and the house is full of children of varying ages. The strains of their music waft under my office door.

> "Just tell your hoodlum friends outside,
> you ain't got time to take a ride.
> Don't talk back, yakkety yak."

Not a bad summation of the social function of proverbs!

Proverbs are by definition anonymous and most often teach traditional values like impulse control, hard work, perseverance, avoidance of evil companions, and respect for the poor. By contrast, aphorisms, sayings whose author is known, often go against the grain, operating on the premise that "rules were meant to be broken," or at least bent! Many modern Western poets and thinkers have embraced the aphorism. [12] "When the gods choose to punish us, they merely answer our prayers" (Oscar Wilde). [13] "No one can make you feel inferior without your own consent" (Eleanor Roosevelt).[14]

Jesus' aphorisms hearken back to traditional religious values. "It is not what goes into the mouth that defiles a person, but it is what comes out of the mouth that defiles" (Matthew 15:11). "Those who find their life will lose it, and those who lose their life for my sake will find it" (Matthew 10:39). He was no rebel without a cause, but a subversive sage, crafting a countercultural life based on radical trust in a God who demands all but, at the same time, gives all.

The Instruction

A third wisdom genre is called instruction. It takes the form of a poem intended to teach a moral lesson, consisting of several lines within which proverbs and admonitions often appear (for examples, Job 6:5-6; Proverbs 2:1-21).[15] The setting is often a court school, the speaker a higher courtier advising his student. The teacher speaks out of experience and tradition, recommending diligence, honesty, reliability, avoidance of bad companions, kindness to the needy, and self-control. Commands and prohibitions are frequent.[16]

The descendants of the ancient instruction genre are alive and well. Roaming the self-help section at Barnes & Noble, you'll find Peter McWilliams' *You Can't Afford the Luxury of a Negative Thought.* There you'll find Richard Carlson's *Don't Sweat the Small Stuff...and it's all small stuff...*, a book filled with admonitions for daily life: 100 of them! After each admonition, the author shares pertinent lessons he and others have gleaned from daily life.

Sometimes we find ourselves preaching to people who know more about not sweating the small stuff than they do about the Sermon on the Mount! There's nothing wrong with advice like "Breathe before you speak," or "Be happy where you are," but they make a shallow substitute for Paul's "Love is patient; love is kind," (1 Corinthians 13:4) and "I have learned to be content with whatever I have" (Philippians 4:11).

The Disputation Speech

Much of the book of Job is in the form of a disputation speech. Job's friends offer him the whys and wherefores of his affliction, using traditional wisdom's preconceptions as their guide. Job disputes their assumptions.[17] The disputation or dialogue format is the ancestor of the question-and-answer strategy in preaching, the dialogue sermon, and the sermon that looks at a controversial issue from all sides and offers an interpretation in light of scripture and tradition.

We can find disputation formats on political talk shows, group interviews with representatives of opposing views on morning news shows, and a plethora of "People's Court" clones on afternoon television.

The Reflection

The "reflection" is another wisdom genre. In Ecclesiastes, Qohelet, the Preacher, takes up various topics such as the value of wisdom and the futility of toil and reflects on them in light of his own experience (Ecclesiastes 2:12-26).[18] The reflection is the ancestor of journal and diary entries, pastors' newsletters, and editorials. The work of Anna Quindlen (*Thinking Out Loud*), and Robert Fulghum (*All I Really Need to Know I Learned in Kindergarten*) fall within the reflection genre.

The Memoir

More extended than the reflection is a genre that abounded in ancient Egypt: the autobiographical narrative. Egyptian kings and prominent officials sought to memorialize their accomplishments and to pass along their wisdom to posterity. Judging from tomb inscriptions, ordinary people, too, were lauded for their exemplary lives. Autobiographical narratives often begin with "I saw...and I have seen." (Ecclesiastes 4:1-8; Proverbs 24:30-34) The autobiographical narrative records for posterity life lessons gained by reflection on experience. It is the ancestor of the memoir and the autobiography.[19]

Over the past five years, the memoir has exploded in popularity. *The New York Times* Best-Seller List regularly includes memoirs in its ranks, and a websearch using the keyword "memoir" reveals over 2,100 sites related to the topic.

Cable television's Biography Channel features a website (www.biography.com) where viewers can summon up profiles of

25,000 of the famous and the infamous. The site includes links to resources on writing biographies and daily journalling. Another site, (www.amillionlives.com), claims to be the largest guide to biographies on the Web and includes links to autobiographies, memoirs, diaries, letters, narratives, and oral histories.[20]

A Gift and a Search

Both biblical and cultural fields are ripe with wisdom for the discerning preacher. The task before today's preachers is to glean in these fields alongside our people. They promise to yield a rich harvest of wisdom for the living of these days. God's gift of wisdom in the midst of daily life reminds me of the "Can You Find?" page in children's magazines. This was a picture in which several items were "hidden." The child's task was to find the carrot, the shoe, the apple, and the baseball bat. The implied promise was that if she looked hard enough, she would find those items.

The Bible's wisdom literature promises that, if we search life thoroughly enough we will find guidelines for attitudes, speech, and conduct. That search will not be an autonomous human achievement, although human effort is an indispensable component. Biblical wisdom affirms that it is God who places the gift of a discernible order in nature and human relationships.[21]

A theological expression of this biblical insight is John Wesley's interpretation that God makes gracious salvific overtures to humankind, but that humans may regrettably resist them. Grace is resistible, and the process of salvation is co-operant between God and us.[22]

Wisdom is not just the effect of God's prior actions, but it is the manifestation of God's presence. Wisdom is not a force immanent and operative in the world apart from God. Wisdom is the power or activity of God manifest in a particular way: namely, as instruction or guidance of the people of God aimed at bringing them to life.[23]

Wisdom scholar Kathleen O'Connor sums it up well, "Ultimately, biblical wisdom is neither innate talent nor disciplined human achievement. It is divine gift. Wisdom is something, or rather someone, to be sought after, to pursue, to pray for, but finally, it is Wisdom who finds us."[24]

Wisdom is presented in Proverbs as a personification of this guiding activity of God—Woman Wisdom. She is present at creation as a "master worker" in the process of creation (Proverbs 8:30). She calls out to passersby to enter onto her path of life. The task of the one who would be wise is to answer her invitation, acknowledge God as the source of Wisdom, and then to be alert to patterns of God's workings in human relationships and nature. The goal and prize of the wisdom process is personal and community harmony (*shalom*) and life.

Proverbs depicts God as a revealing God who offers us clues in daily life for right actions and thought. At the same time, however, biblical wisdom from Proverbs, Job, and Ecclesiastes insists that God is a concealing God. Proverbs affirms the limitations of human knowledge and the sovereignty of our Creator God (30:2-4). Job depicts a God who has no need to justify himself, but does not do a disappearing act when our smooth road becomes rutted with unjust suffering and twisted by tragedy. Qohelet portrays a God who is distant, yet the giver of joy in living.

In the context of the entire canon, biblical wisdom also embraces the subversive sayings of Jesus. These sayings challenge conventional wisdom's advice to listen to one's elders, avoid risk, and live so as to secure good health, a good living, and a good reputation. "You have heard it said, but I say unto you..."(Matthew 5:27). "For those who want to save their life will lose it, and those who lose their life for my sake will find it" (Matthew 16:25). Jesus' lifetime of teaching subversive wisdom culminated in the cross. The cross, as Paul points out, appears to be foolishness when judged by conventional standards. He names it "the wisdom of God" (1 Corinthians 1:18-31). Christianity affirms that Jesus' presence endures, guiding communities of faith to embody the countercultural wisdom by which he lived, died, and lives.

A Resource for Shelter and Storm

This wisdom we encounter in the Bible is a resource for whatever our futures may hold: for both times of good fortune and dark nights of the soul. Biblical wisdom, like that of the ancient Near East in general, falls into two broad categories. They are sometimes called the wisdom of order (Proverbs) and the wisdom of counter-order (Job, Ecclesiastes, and Jesus), or optimistic and pessimistic wisdom.[25] Another way to think of them is wisdom for the harbor and wisdom for the storm. There is a kind of wisdom that helps us order our lives and factor out a degree of chaos, a wisdom meant to shelter us from trouble. We might call it wisdom for the "lee places" of life. In nautical usage, the lee is that side of the ship away from the wind. A lee is a calm or sheltered place, a place defended from the wind. Wisdom that shelters consists of advice that will protect the young from the foreseeable consequences of their own foolishness, avoiding gluttony, greed, lying, extravagance, arrogance, and contention.

The wisdom of Proverbs admit that poverty is sometimes due to injustice rather than laziness (Proverbs 13:23) and that riches can be gained in various evil ways (Proverbs 16:8; 21:6; 28:6). But on the whole Proverbs impresses on the reader that we can make choices that have relatively predictable outcomes in our lives.[26]

Its wisdom promises that it can help us live decently, industriously, frugally, faithfully, obediently, moderately, sensibly, likably, healthily, reputably, and safely. When we say that someone is his own worst enemy, we often mean that he scorns the lee side of life. The community generally benefits from individuals who live by this cautious, industrious brand of wisdom and rewards them with a good reputation. There is a big grain of truth in the proverb "The highway of the upright avoids evil; those who guard their way preserve their lives" (Proverbs 16:17).

Then there is wisdom for the storm. It consists of proverbs and life stories that acknowledge that tragedies strike the wise, injustices oppress the hardworking, and we can suffer from other people's stupidity (and vice versa!). Our best abilities at forging a secure life bump up against three abilities of life to frustrate and disillusion us: the inscrutability of God, the unpredictability of life, and the inevitability of death.

What feel like pains in our necks and hearts are, considered at a deeper level, grains of sand in our world's oyster. These painful realizations are well-disguised blessings. They remind us that wisdom cannot be severed from its origin in God. Certainly one aspect of wisdom consists in responding to patterns of cause and effect that biblical wisdom affirms are gifts of God's ordering presence. At the same time, biblical wisdom exceeds tidy formulas that work best when things are already going well and for people who have the financial resources to create their own reality.

More Than a Set of Principles

Wisdom cannot be diluted to a set of principles that exists apart from God that we can set in operation to assure ourselves of health, prosperity, unimpeded accomplishment, and acclaim. This is precisely the claim of self-help religion, despite its occasional nods to a universal intelligence or force of good. Wisdom is God's self-expression instructing us on "how best to live," through all the twists and turns of our lifelong journey with God.

Human depictions of principles for living are not ends in themselves, to be absolutized and set up both as the goal of living and grounds for judging others. Efficiency at doing things does not guarantee that we are doing the right things. Industriousness lives by the motto "don't just sit there, do something!" By contrast, the vital pursuits of prayer and worship advise us "don't just do something, sit there!" Single-minded devotion to a life goal tends to mellow and multiply when we look on the faces of those we love, guided by the One who loves us all. Moderation can be taken too far, as exemplified by the righteous diners who murmured against the woman who anointed Jesus with nard. And optimism, thank God, is not the same as faith and hope. Biblical wisdom is uncompromising. The end is God. The judge is God.

Biblical wisdom, unlike self-help wisdom, contains the seeds of its own subversion. It is aware of its own pretensions and limitations. It is aware that principles for living are all well and good, except when, as often happens, they lose their flexibility and promote themselves above their competency. Such guidelines need to always be open to unique circumstances that overturn them in service of more ultimate ends: obedience to God and love for others. How efficient is it to allow our list of things to do to be interrupted by a bereaved friend's hour-long phone call? What does it accomplish to take an afternoon off and walk a nature trail? What happens to moderation when we cast our lives on the mercies of God with wholehearted devotion? If we are wise, we will devote ourselves to God first and principles second.

Ecclesiastes, Job, and teachings ascribed to Jesus in the Gospels represent this subversive dynamic of biblical wisdom. Qohelet expresses his disappointment that the facts of life, uncertainty, injustice, and death expose the promises of traditional wisdom for what they really are: wishful thinking. Job expresses his outrage that, from his perspective, God has betrayed the promises of divine retribution. God's response, of course, subverts the facile world-view of traditional wisdom as represented by Job's friends.

Jesus as sage subverts the priorities of traditional religious devo-tion with its emphasis on ritual purity and popular sentiment and with its desire for a political show of strength. His teachings place injustice and the suffering of the righteous in the foreground. His wisdom strategies challenge the status quo of communities built on unquestioned tradition. They encourage followers to leave the judging to God, live in the present, and focus on those on the bot-tom rung of life.

Qohelet, Job, and Jesus are subversive sages. Within Eastern reli-gions the two best-known subversive sages are Lao-tzu and the Buddha. Lao-tzu depicted a "way" that led away from conven-tional values to living aligned with "the Tao" itself. Buddha spoke of "the eightfold path" that led from conventional desires and "grasping" to enlightenment and compassion. In the Western philosophical tradition, Socrates was a wisdom teacher who required Athenians to critically examine the conventions that shaped their lives.[27]

Wisdom, then, is God's self expression, guiding and instructing wisdom seekers in all the varied scenarios of each mundane day. It encompasses, but is by no means reducible to, sensible principles for prudent living. It encompasses the subversion of those princi-ples in service of devotion to God and neighbor. Given this under-standing of wisdom, it makes sense that we would encounter God's presence most poignantly precisely in those circumstances that expose the limitations of cause-and-effect wisdom, the days we can't explain. On such days, we have the opportunity to be most humble and receptive. As for God, well, God has never claimed that the presence of suffering signals divine abandonment. Quite the contrary.

Before long we will embark on an exploration of self-help wis-dom's version of the wise life. A candle is a good thing to take on a journey into shadowy territory. Better yet, a flashlight with a rechargeable battery! We need biblical wisdom's contrasting understanding of the wise life to illuminate our path. According to our biblical tradition, and this goes for both testaments, wisdom is not the attempt to oversimplify life to a set of cause-and-effect principles. Wisdom is not the claim that these principles encompass the fullness of God's wisdom. Wisdom is looking to God for insight and guidance in both the calms and the storms of life.

From the Margins to the Center

For the first two-thirds of the twentieth century, biblical studies largely neglected wisdom in favor of the narrative and prophetic portions of the Hebrew Scriptures. Old Testament scholars focused on the mighty acts of salvation history (Gerhard von Rad) or the theme of covenant (Walter Eichrodt). They viewed wisdom as anthropocentric. It lacked theological substance. It was barely distinguishable from the wisdom literature of Israel's ancient Near Eastern neighbors. It was barely worth a footnote.[28]

Most preachers followed the lead of their biblical teachers, neglecting wisdom texts from the pulpit. There is a dearth of scriptural references to wisdom books in the latest revision of the common lectionary for Sundays and major festivals. The three-year cycle contains only five passages from Proverbs, three from Job, and one from Ecclesiastes.[29]

From the mid 1970s on, an increasing number of biblical scholars began to take an interest in the Wisdom literature of the Bible. Literary criticism fueled this interest, making biblical scholars more sensitive to the varieties of biblical genres and their rhetorical and theological impact. The theological climate was favorable to an interest in Wisdom, a genre that is firmly rooted in daily experience. The understanding of theology as the delivery of unchanging, revealed truth was giving way to an understanding of theology as critical reflection on insights that emerge in specific communities in conversation with our biblical and traditional heritage.

Groups that had been marginalized in traditional theology, women, people of color, and the poor, had begun to interpret biblical traditions out of their own experience. These groups insisted that their day-to-day experience be honored as a locus of God's work in the world. The anguished cry of Job, the innocent sufferer, and the strident aphorisms of Jesus struck a chord with those on the edges.

Feminist thinkers were drawn to a tradition that highlights a female personification of an attribute of God. Woman Wisdom, the no-nonsense prophetess and helper in creation who appears in Proverbs 1:20-33, 8:22-36, 9:1-6, and 31:10-31, embodied the attributes and daily experience of biblical women. She began to be seen as a metaphor for honoring those of contemporary women.

At the same time, postmodernism, across a wide spectrum of disciplines, insisted that what we like to call objective reality is, to a great degree, conditioned by our social setting. Wisdom began to be appreciated as a genre that epitomized what is most helpful in postmodernism for theological reflection: respect for context and openness to a variety of perspectives.

When biblical scholars of both testaments began to take an interest in wisdom, they realized that it has a distinctive theology apart from that of texts that speak of the mighty acts of God who intervenes in a visible, dramatic way in salvation history.[30] Biblical wisdom's theology affirms God the Creator as giver of wisdom and the One who summons us to search for it. It boldly honors the natural world and the ordinary events of daily life as the locus for our encounter with a revealing and concealing God.

Wisdom is a genre that honors the integrity of all creation. The natural world bears the imprint of the presence of Woman Wisdom. She both participates in its creation and delights in all its manifestations, including the human race (Proverbs 8:30). Wisdom is both an agent of creation and now is present throughout its various patterns summoning us to honor them and learn from them. The human community's search for wisdom occurs not apart from but in the context of the natural world in which Wisdom rejoices. These texts provide an early suggestion that ecological and social justice cannot be separated. Neither nature nor other human beings are here to be exploited as mere resources for the projects of those who happen to wield social, political, and economic power.[31]

Wisdom's theological perspective insists on respect for the creation as the realm of both God's presence and human insight. Biblical wisdom offers crucial insights for faith communities in complex times. God is sovereign and, to a degree, inscrutable; while human insights have an important ordering function, human knowledge is limited; and human communities need to have a respect for differing interpretations of God's will in facing the ambiguities of life.

We and our people struggle to find meaning and identity amid an individualistic, violent, consumer culture. Much of the wisdom literature of the Hebrew Scriptures reflects the social turmoil of the Exile and dispersion. It expresses varying approaches to the crises of faith that occur in uncertain times. Biblical wisdom needs to be preached. For, more than any other biblical genre, it faces into the struggles of daily life and offers a variety of responses to its challenges. Proverbs asserts the value of prudent living in an attempt to preserve and vindicate traditional values in a time of turmoil. Job voices the pain of the innocent sufferer and removes our grounds for blaming a sovereign, awesome, but ever-present God. Ecclesiastes views life's sorrows with resignation, attributing them to God. At the same time its author is grateful to God as the giver of our fragile, but precious, portion of life. Biblical wisdom represents the complexity of life and lays out an array of faithful responses. It resists our efforts to oversimplify a complex life and denies our craving for quick fixes. Wisdom is a divine, delightful gift, but it is also a lifelong search. No wonder biblical wisdom is a neglected resource for contemporary preachers in postmodern pulpits! We and our people are told from many quarters that we can have it now and we can have it free of effort. The task of preaching biblical wisdom in our self-help society reminds me of the words to a Rolling Stones song:

"You can't always get what you want.
But if you try sometimes, you just might find
You get what you need."

The Postmodern Pulpit: Uncertainty and Opportunity

Philosopher Ernest Gellner says, "Postmodernism is a contemporary movement. It is strong and fashionable. Over and above this, it is not altogether clear what the devil it is."[32] Postmodernism refers to an insight that has been growing over the past thirty to forty years, that what we call objective reality always comes to us by means of someone else's interpretation. What we "see" depends upon our circumstances. We construct our political, psychological, and even, to a degree, theological realities. This insight, that theology is contextual, has grown to full flower with the advent, over the past thirty years, of two-thirds world theologies, feminist, womanist and mujerista theologies, and theologies indigenous to other ethnic and cultural groups.

Postmodernism's insistence on the influence of social context on individual perceptions threads through a variety of disciplines: linguistics, hermeneutics, sociology, history, political science, psychology, anthropology, legal theory, literary criticism, comparative literature, and even physics!

In the realm of theological discourse, postmodernism has had a strong and irrevocable influence on systematic theology, hermeneutics, and homiletics. With regard to systematic theology, postmodernism challenges the notion of systematic, universal theological schemata, reminding us of the contextual, socially located quality, and accountability of theological truths. Rather than a descent into the abyss of relativity, I interpret postmodernism as the recognition that theological statements arise out of concrete situations and need to be continually placed back into them for both validation and correction.[33]

In the realm of hermeneutics, postmodernism views textual interpretation less as excavation and more as encounter. In modern hermeneutics a reader approaches a text objectively to extract a universally valid interpretation by means of scientific strategies of historical criticism. In postmodern hermeneutics the socially-located reader interacts with and actualizes the text.[34]

Clearly, our postmodern times, like any time of turmoil, offer both insecurity and opportunity for growth. These mingled hopes and fears thread through the experience of a whole generation of young Americans born between 1965 and 1981 who have been dubbed by sociologists "The Postmoderns." Many of them share a sense that absolutes aren't as absolute as they used to be and that they don't want to be religious, they want to be spiritual.[35]

In a climate of religious diversity, people across generations search for a language to honor the uniqueness of our own faith while respecting the wisdom of other faiths. We agonize over injustice and tragedy. The very genre of biblical literature that specializes in such struggles should not be neglected!

Preaching Wisdom and the "New" Homiletic

Our understanding of preaching over the past generation has been deeply affected by postmodernism. In 1976 Fred Craddock published his watershed book *As One Without Authority* in which he criticized traditional, deductive preaching on exegetical, theological, and communicational grounds. His voice was soon joined by a number of others and coalesced into a movement called the "New Homiletic." It shifted understandings of sermon, preacher, people, and text away from standard notions of delivery and reception toward dialogue and participation. The present study of wisdom celebrates and contributes to this fresh understanding of all the components in the preaching event.

The Sermon: Dialogue, Not Monologue

Traditional preaching made preaching a monologue, confused preacherly authority with superiority, and made exegesis into an archaeological dig. As a corrective, Craddock commended inductive preaching, in which the preacher invites the congregation on a journey of discovery of meaning that mirrors the exegetical encounter between preacher and text. Preaching on wisdom texts often means inductive, indirect sermon forms that require congregational participation.

The People: Partners, Not Javelin Catchers!

The members of the congregation were, for Craddock, not "javelin catchers" for the preacher's ideas, but partners in preaching who actively contribute to the actualization of the sermon's meaning. The "New Homiletic" represented a postmodern turn toward the hearer, understanding the preaching event through the lens of the hearer and the listening process. That means that exegesis of the congregation is a key component in interpreting a text and shaping a sermon, not an afterthought we label "application."[36] Our study of wisdom is a vital contribution to understanding contemporary congregations' worldviews and how they both conform to and contradict biblical wisdom's insights.

The Text: Activation, Not Excavation

The New Homiletic not only respects the distinctiveness of congregations, it also extends the same courtesy to the text, in the fullness of its historical, theological, and literary identity. That includes attention to its genre. Texts are not husks that can be tossed aside once the kernel, or the "main idea" for the sermon has been extracted. They are instances of literary communication in which form and content cannot be separated. It makes a difference whether a text is a narrative or a parable, a proverb or an epistle, a psalm or a story. Biblical texts seek not just to impart information about God and the human condition, but also, in different ways, to impact hearers' lives.[37]

Preachers have applied their genre-sensitivity to narrative for over two decades. It is wisdom's turn to have its themes and genres taken seriously in the pulpit.

Preacher and Hearer: An Egalitarian Model

A wisdom focus in preaching yields an egalitarian relationship between preacher and hearer that confers the same title upon both speaker and listener: sage.[38] The preacher functions as a wise observer of life and models that role in the pulpit, empowering listeners to claim that role for themselves as they continue their God-guided search for wisdom in daily life. The sage is a model that honors the wisdom of women, historically barred from formal access to public life. The understanding that sometimes sages need to be subversive of the status quo to be faithful to the gospel empowers traditionally silenced groups to find their voice in the Scriptures and in contemporary life.[39]

The Turn Toward the Church

The New Homiletic instigated an important corrective in its turn toward the hearer. A number of contemporary homileticians are advising the movement that it is now time for a "turn toward the church." Preaching happens in an ecclesial context and bears a responsibility toward it.[40]

The churches within which we preach need a dose of culturally subversive wisdom! Richard Lischer's diagnosis fits many churches today:

> To use sociologist Robert Bellah's terms, the 'community of memory' in which members are nurtured by tradition has given way to the 'life-style enclave' in which convenience and a common mode of consumption are the most important factors. The churches in which we preach too often are not contrast-societies but mirrors of the individualistic culture that surrounds and infects them.[41]

Preaching wisdom is not training people to find meaning for their individual "spiritual pilgrimages" apart from the community of faith. That function is already being filled to the bloating point by others. Christian wisdom preaching offers a version of the good life that challenges cultural versions. It promotes a wisdom that loves the other as much as it loves oneself, a wisdom that is communal and God-centered, a wisdom that knows when to disregard success and personal fulfillment on behalf of the good news of Jesus Christ, a wisdom that looks like folly to the authors of self-help manuals. The goal of preaching biblical wisdom is to form people into a contrast society that exists in distinction from "the world" on behalf of the world. Wisdom preaching sharpens our identity as disciples of a subversive, crucified, and Risen Sage. This reclaims a neglected part of what (Swiss theologian) Karl Barth calls the church's distinctive talk about God.

This book focuses primarily on preaching, but many of the insights it offers are equally appropriate to the teaching office of the pastoral ministry.[42] Historical and biblical efforts to separate the teaching and preaching roles of ministry have been unconvincing. There is a teaching component to preaching as well as to just about everything else a pastor does. This teaching element is present in counseling in visionary leadership of the congregation and in social justice ministries. In Jesus' own ministry, as recounted in the Gospel depictions of his life and work, it is not easy to distinguish teaching, preaching, and acts of healing.[43]

In the face of diverse doctrines and practices in the early years of the church, there was a need for a clearer sense of what constituted the church's teaching ministry. Three central tasks emerged that have abiding relevance for our contemporary ministries.

The first was the determination of the normative beliefs and practices of the church. The second was the reinterpretation of these beliefs and practices in shifting cultural and historical contexts, and the third was and is the formation and sustenance of educational institutions, processes, and curricula for each new generation.[44]

The Preacher's Quest

It's high time for us pastors and preachers to ask ourselves how we are doing in the wisdom department, with regard to both preaching and teaching. Are we naming varieties of cultural wisdom, correcting them where they are self-serving and superficial, and enlisting them to the extent that they can be of service to the gospel?

Are we hearing and, where appropriate, affirming our people's wisdom, including that of our youth and our elderly? Or has our mastery of theological language equipped us to talk to one another while ignoring the innate wisdom of our laypeople? On the other side of the coin, are we challenging attitudes and behaviors that maintain an unjust status quo or undermine the *shalom* of the community of faith? Or has our craving for church growth numbed our conscience and tamed our tongue?

It is time for us preachers to do our field research. In chapters six through eight we will look at biblical wisdom as found in both Old and New Testaments. But first, in chapters two through five, we will train our spotlight on alternatives to biblical wisdom playing on the cultural airwaves today.

Centuries ago, an anguished Job, searching the silent skies, spoke his thoughts out loud. "Surely there is a mine for silver, and a place for gold to be refined....But where is wisdom to be found? And where is the place of understanding?" (28:1, 12). We twenty-first-century preachers owe it to the silent seekers to go on a quest for the answer.

CHAPTER TWO

The Contemporary Search for Wisdom

"I'm Spiritual but not Religious..."

Contemporary preachers across cultural, ethnic, and denominational lines preach to people who have an appetite for spirituality, but distaste for institutional religion. About 94% of Americans say they believe in God or a universal spirit; 60% say they attend religious services regularly, and 53% state that religion is very important in their lives. These figures have not changed significantly since the 1950s. However, in a recent poll 54% of American adults described themselves as religious, while 30% said they were spiritual but not religious.[1]

Our national spiritual quest is characterized by eclecticism in religious views, tolerance of other faiths, inward focus on one's own spiritual journeys and on meeting one's own personal needs. Sociologist Wade Clark Roof points out the proclivity of postwar Baby Boomers toward experimentation and independent thinking. "Choice, so much a part of life for this generation, now expresses itself in dynamic and fluid religious styles," says Roof in his 1993 book on Baby Boomer religion, *A Generation of Seekers*.[2]

There is evidence that trends may be changing among Generation X, those Americans born between 1964 and 1978. Some authors label Generation X-ers as anti-institutionalists who are "uncomfortable" with tradition and obsessed with personal experience. Others counter that Generation X-ers are not so much wary of institutions themselves as they are wary of institutions that don't do what they are supposed to do. Generation X detests hypocrisy. There is a return to traditional morality and traditional religious devotion at work among many under-35's. This is evidenced by an increasing interest in denominational heritage and spiritual direction.[3]

This trend is a hopeful ray of light amid dominant shadows. More than fifteen years after the publication of *Habits of the Heart* by Robert Bellah and his associates, the authors find the results of America's dominant ideology of radical individualism to be more pronounced than ever: its compulsive stress on independence, its contempt for weakness, and its adulation of success. Recognition that identity is both social and personal is still in short supply.[4] We are less likely to belong to the League of Women Voters or the Shriners or to attend a public meeting on town affairs than we were twenty years ago. We are more likely to belong to a support group, a group oriented primarily to the needs of individuals. Such groups make minimal external demands on participants. Sociologist Robert Putnam epitomized our religious individualism in the title he chose for one of his articles: "Bowling Alone: America's Declining Social Capital."[5]

Robert Wuthnow's analysis of American spirituality since the 1950s cites a shift in Americans' understanding of their religious commitments. In the first two thirds of the twentieth century Americans were cradle-to-grave members of their particular religious traditions, experiencing spirituality within the framework of organized religion, its services, teachings, and sacred places. Wuthnow labels this a spirituality of dwelling. It has been replaced, in his view, by a more individualistic spirituality of seeking that negotiates among competing glimpses of the sacred, seeking partial knowledge and practical wisdom. "Now at the end of the twentieth century, growing numbers of Americans piece together their faith like a patchwork quilt. Spirituality has become a vastly complex quest in which each person seeks in his or her own way."[6] "We are becoming less theologically and institutionally grounded and more inclined toward making up our own faiths as we go along."[7]

It's not surprising that, even with all this craving for individual spirituality, we can barely scrape together a definition of wisdom. A recent newspaper article featured a reporter going around town asking people "How would you define wisdom, and who in your opinion is a wise person?" One respondent apparently decided that honesty was the best policy. "I don't know what wisdom is, and I've never given it a thought. Guess you'd have to be a wiser man than me to define it!" [8]

People magazine has yet to run an issue that features cover pictures of "The Fifty Wisest People in the World!" When asked to identify someone who is wise in their lives, many people struggle with the concept. The explosion of technological venues equips us to manage information, not to seek wisdom. Our popular culture tends to showcase and reward those who are financially successful or hold celebrity status on the screen or field more than those who embody the elusive quality called wisdom. We continue to hope that, by virtue of being good-looking and gifted for stage or stadium, celebrities will naturally exude wisdom. What other reason could there be for the steady flow of magazine articles and autobiographies about the wisdom of celebrities? We are looking for wisdom in all the wrong places.

"The Wisdom Smorgasbord"

Alasdair MacIntyre, a moral philosopher concerned with the nature of the good person and the good society, traces this cluelessness with regard to wisdom to the modern liberal individualism that dominates Western societies. He argues that our society has difficulty coming to moral consensus or even engaging in meaningful moral discourse because we have no consistent, shared moral tradition. In the wisdom smorgasbord line, we are people feeding on fragments of philosophies, isolated from the larger systems of moral thought and life to which they originally belonged.[9]

One of the most famous evangelists of the gospel of personal success of this century admitted:

The ideas I stand for are not mine.
I borrowed them from Socrates.
I swiped them from Chesterfield.
I stole them from Jesus.
And I put them in a book.
If you don't like their rules,
Whose would you use?[10]

Some members of our congregations are intentionally moving down the wisdom smorgasbord line that is our culture, choosing wisdom from various secular sources on which to nosh. Members of the business community in my congregation are attending leadership workshops led by nationally recognized motivational speakers. Others are reading Dear Abby and Ann Landers daily, or watching Dr. Laura, Judge Judy, Oprah, and Montel. Several church and community members attend the AA meetings our church sponsors in the basement every Tuesday morning. Still others are reading New Age authors or exploring Zen or Ignatian meditation.

I bumped into an acquaintance from church recently browsing in the self-help section of the local Barnes & Noble bookstore. She was scanning book spines with titles I wish I'd thought of like *Getting Over Getting Older*, *Don't Sweat the Small Stuff*, *Pulling Your Own Strings*, *You'll See It When You Believe It*, and *Manifest Your Destiny*. She was holding a half-dozen copies of *Don't Sweat the Small Stuff: And It's All Small Stuff*. "I give this to everyone I know when they have milestones in their lives, graduations, birthdays, anniversaries," she enthused.

"How about cancer?" I asked.

What about other events that are milestones, though not happy ones? What about the death of a child, a parent fading away from a debilitating disease, or the kidnapping and murder of a youth? They are not small stuff! What can we read to help us as we "sweat the big stuff?"

Lessons in Label-Reading

In an attempt to improve my family's nutrition, I recently attended a class on how to read food labels to find out what's really in the food we buy. Our leader was a man named Jeff, a vegetarian kosher purist, who at forty-one looked twenty-five. His eyes glowed with the righteous indignation of a food zealot. He took a dozen of us on a field trip to the local grocery store. There we learned about the cholesterol, sodium, and sugar content of all my favorite foods. It was both enlightening and depressing. We learned that what we don't know can hurt us. We learned that low fat often means high sodium. We learned that all-natural doesn't mean diddly. We learned to decode attractive, deceptive packaging and labeling. Now when we buy and eat junk food, at least we know what it is!

The label-reading field trip is a good analogy for the preacher's role in improving our congregation's spiritual nutrition. We are deceived all the time by the sweet taste and seductive packaging of cultural wisdom.

The advertising industry through commercials has a clear-cut message of what is most important. It boils down to, "You are what you have and you are what you know." It is the preacher's responsibility to equip people to read the labels in light of the witness of biblical wisdom. Sometimes we will criticize cultural versions of wisdom and sometimes we will commend aspects of them. Paul's question still sounds as a challenge to contemporary proclaimers of the Word: "How are they to hear without a preacher?" (Romans 10:14).

Finding a Method to Manage the Madness

Our task is an exercise in practical theology; and for that we need a workable, faithful method. In traditional depictions of the purpose and structure of theology, systematic theology receives the results of historical investigation; reflects upon their content; tests, refines, and orders them; and transmits the product to the practical field for implementation. Systematic theology is reflection on God's revelation to the church, and practical theology is its application to the fields of preaching, liturgy, pastoral care, and administration.[11]

More recent theological reflection defines systematic and practical theology differently. Contextual concerns are not just an afterthought for systematic theology, but an integral part of its reflections. Practical theology is not a mere receptacle of the insights of other disciplines, but has a role in generating theological insights.[12]

In a profound way, in fact, all theology is practical. For we bring practical concerns to it from the beginning. We come to the theological task with questions shaped by the secular and religious practices in which we are involved. These practices are "theory-laden;" that is, they imply principles and beliefs that are not always clearly understood or articulated.

A helpful recent depiction of the structure of theological inquiry is that of Don Browning in *A Fundamental Practical Theology*. He views the enterprise of theological inquiry as an encompassing discipline called *fundamental practical theology*. Within that larger discipline are four submovements of theological reflection: descriptive theology, historic theology, systematic theology, and strategic practical theology.

The role of descriptive theology is to provide a description of theory-laden religious and cultural practice. Its task is to describe the contemporary theory-laden practices that give rise to the practical questions that generate all theological reflection. It describes these practices in order to discern the conflicting cultural and religious meanings that guide our action and provoke the questions that animate our practical thinking. It gives rise to questions such as, What are we *actually* doing? What *should* we be doing? This leads to a fresh confrontation with normative texts of the Christian faith. The result is guidance as to the sources and norms of practice.

Historical theology is an analysis of those texts seeking such guidance for contemporary communities.

Systematic theology explores general themes of the gospel in response to general questions that characterize present situations. What new horizon of meaning results when questions from present practices are brought into dialogue with the central Christian witness? There is a critical philosophical element to systematic theology. What reasons can be advanced to support the validity of the claims made by this new horizon of meaning? Systematic theology is an orderly expression of general issues and shared themes that run through our practices.

Strategic practical theology asks, What should be our praxis in this concrete situation?[13]

Taken together, for Browning, all four of these submovements of theological reflection make up the encompassing discipline of *fundamental practical theology*. Fundamental practical theology consists of critical reflection on contemporary practice in light of the witness of Scripture and tradition directed toward individual and social transformation. Its steps involve analyzing and describing contemporary practices, consulting historical, biblical, and theological touchstones, reflecting on their themes and implications, and strategizing appropriate actions.[14]

We have all heard sermons in which the preacher, with a haughty wave of his hand, condemned "the world," and consigned the whole ugly lump to hell. But the task of evaluating cultural wisdom in light of our biblical heritage is far more nuanced than that. It involves what Paul Tillich called saying a yes and a no to cultural artifacts. A friend of mine, when a medical student living in New York City, came home one night to find that someone had broken into her apartment, ransacked the entire place, and taken... nothing. She was relieved, but also strangely offended. In the case of cultural wisdom, there are one or two things worth stealing for the Christian life. For example, let's take Stephen Covey's term for a moral compass in life, "True North," and use it to describe the way of Christian Wisdom. Let's take the title of the self-help series "Life 101" and make it the title of a sermon series. Let's look critically at New Age author Wayne Dyer's conviction that our inward thoughts "manifest our destiny," admitting the truth of his insight, but examining its limits and potential abuses if used selfishly. Let's say a yes and a no to the themes and variations of cultural wisdom.

The preacher's task as wisdom teacher requires a method to bring to the surface the assumptions that drive both biblical and contemporary wisdom so they can be analyzed side by side. I find the method set forth by Don Browning in his *A Fundamental Practical Theology* to be most helpful. Browning builds on and adapts the correlational method of Paul Tillich. Tillich's approach to theology asserted that cultural expressions of the human situation imply questions to which the Christian faith provides answers.[15]

Browning and a number of other practical theologians believe that the study of human cultural genres yields not just questions, but implied answers to life's questions. Preaching as a practical theological expression calls for the preachers to analyze the contemporary situation, consult biblical and historical traditions, and point people, including themselves, toward redemptive responses to God's work in the world.[16]

This is our task with regard to cultural bodies of wisdom. For they imply ultimate concerns and strategies for living in keeping with those concerns. As preachers we are called to set secular wisdom's ultimate concerns and strategies next to the tenets of the Christian faith in a two-way correlation. It is one in which both cultural wisdom and Christian wisdom question and answer one another, commend and critique one another.[17]

Preaching, like practical theology in general, is an expression of practical wisdom or reasoning, what Aristotle called *phronesis*. *Phronesis* is reasoning that leads to action. It involves getting clear about our premises in a given situation regarding what we are already doing and what we would like to do.[18]

Aristotle distinguishes between philosophical and practical wisdom, between *sophia* and *phronesis*. Philosophical wisdom aims at truth, while practical wisdom aims at action. Philosophical wisdom involves knowledge of first principles, which are necessary and cannot be otherwise. Practical wisdom, by contrast, is deliberation about what is good and expedient, about what sort of things lead to the good life. Deliberation is about what can be otherwise. It concerns those aspects of concrete situations that can be changed so as to make life better. Practical wisdom yields knowledge about how to improve human lives.[19]

Moral wisdom embodies parts of both philosophical and practical wisdom, seeking knowledge of first principles as they bear on living a good life in the changing contexts of human action. [20]

"Five Alive!"

Practical moral reasoning, whether in secular or religious contexts, according to Browning, operates in five dimensions or levels. He believes that these five dimensions can guide the task of descriptive theology that is the first submovement of a fundamental practical theology. The five levels are these:

Visional
Obligational
Tendency-Need
Environmental
Rule-Role

They yield fruitful insights when employed in exploring various genres of secular wisdom.

The first and most encompassing level is the Visional. This involves the genre's assumptions about what is ultimate in human life and the relationship between the human being and this ultimate. This is what one secular leadership consultant aptly calls the "first things" we need to make first in our lives, the "true north realities that govern quality of life." [21]

Practical reason in a Christian context regards the implied ultimate as a narrative about God's creation, governance, and redemption of the world through the life, death, and resurrection of Jesus Christ. This narrative constitutes the vision that animates and provides the context for practical reason.[22]

The second dimension of practical moral reasoning is the Obligational level. It poses the question, What does the visional level mean for human obligations? What moral principles ought to order our common life? For the Christian these obligations center on *agape* love, mutual regard for the other, and commitment to justice for all God's children. Recent theological reflection has reminded us that our obligations extend to the natural world: the animal world and the care of the earth.

The third dimension is the Tendency-Need level. What central tendencies and needs of human nature drive this wisdom? This level involves vital needs that motivate life including sexuality, the survival instinct, and primal needs for attachment, material acquisition, and group relatedness.

The fourth is the Environmental level. It asks, What social conditions have contributed to this body of wisdom's creation? How has this social context both enriched and limited the usefulness of this wisdom?

The fifth and final dimension of practical moral reasoning to be considered is the Rule-Role dimension. Here the question is, At the most concrete level, what actual practices and behaviors would result from living by this wisdom system?

The five dimensions of practical moral reasoning can be expressed as five basic questions about life's meaning and human behavior. I call them the "Five Alive" questions. When we use them to interview a given body of cultural or biblical wisdom, they bring to life important assumptions that lie beneath the surface. I have reordered them slightly, placing the environmental question first. They are as follows:

Environmental: In what social setting did this wisdom arise? (This question is important because the social setting shapes the vision of what is most important and how we are to live.)

Visional: What is most important in life according to this body of wisdom?

Obligational: Which attitudes and actions get us closer to this vision of ultimacy? (I call these Facilitators.)

Tendency-Need: What acts as obstacles to our attaining this vision of ultimacy? (I call these Obstacles.)

Rule-role: What kind of life (Lifeform) results in living by this body of wisdom?

These are the key questions the preacher needs to ask and answer on behalf of her congregation in preaching on bodies of wisdom literature both in Scripture and in contemporary culture.

Throughout Christian history what I am calling lifeform has been called a "rule of life." A rule of life is a pattern of spiritual disciplines that provides structure and directions for growth in holiness. Patterns in our life refer to attitudes and behaviors that are routine, repeated, and regular. The Christian tradition includes both corporate and personal rules of life. The best known of all corporate rules is that of Saint Benedict, whose rule describes the attitudes and practices for guiding monks in their common life. [23] We will discover that every body of wisdom, both secular and biblical, has an implied or stated rule of life.

The "Five Alive" questions have a narrative shape. And so do the wisdom systems that surround us. It doesn't always look that way. We read book titles like *Ten Days to Self-Esteem*, or *Napoleon Hill's Keys to Success: The 17 Principles of Personal Achievement*, or Joan Lunden's *A Bend in the Road Is Not the End of the Road: 10 Positive Principles for Dealing with Change*. We assume that the wisdom they contain fell down from the sky, packaged as universal, static principles. In reality, wisdom insights are condensations of an underlying, far less tidy narrative of life experience. This is true of both biblical and contemporary wisdom, in whatever genre we encounter it, proverb, instruction, autobiography, parables, riddles, allegories, wisdom psalms, or reflection.

The dynamic of the sages' wisdom was the observation of patterns in repeated events in daily life. These events were seen in the context of larger life-narratives. Imagine the stories behind the insight "A soft answer turns away wrath, but a harsh word stirs up anger!" (Proverbs 15:1) Or how about the contemporary proverb "No gain without pain?" Sometimes authors turn over the tapestry and show the reader the knotted, messy understitching. More often an insight is presented as a painless *fait accompli*. But, as we know from our own life-experience, beneath every fait accompli are the failures and disappointments we have gone through to arrive there.

For Browning, all uses of practical moral reasoning occur within a narrative framework. For a Christian, the narrative framework is God's redemptive dealings with humankind. In that context, there occurs a push and pull between who human beings tend to be (tendency-need level) and who the body of wisdom under scrutiny wants us to be (obligational level). A narrative flow is easily discernible in the "Five Alive" questions we have adapted from Browning. Human beings develop toward a goal of a right relationship with God and others as we struggle with inward obstacles and outward obligations within the limitations of our social settings. This same dynamic can be used to describe the forward movement of faith communities. [24]

There has been much talk in the past twenty years or so of narrative as a fundamental dynamic of human experience.[25] Narrative approaches to ethics, hermeneutics, theology, and preaching abound. We don't have to claim that narrative is the fundamental way people make sense of experience. We can acknowledge that it is a crucial one and use it as a tool for understanding cultural and biblical wisdom systems as they help each of us compose the cradle to grave narrative that is the shape of our days.

Each of us is in the process of composing an autobiographical narrative. There are many narratives circulating in our cultural milieu, offering their services as molds for our lives. Some of them free the self to seek *shalom:* personal and social harmony, and justice. Others shrink God down to size, thereby limiting the self. In effect, when we challenge the wisdom by which contemporary people, including ourselves, live, we're asking them "What's your story?"

Background Checks, Key Texts, Nutshells, and Lifeforms

We will now interview a number of contemporary bodies of wisdom to find out what their story is, and how they answer the "Five Alive" questions (descriptive theology). The selection is by no means exhaustive. The discussion is meant to encourage readers to go far beyond the confines of this discussion to analyze wisdoms that flourish in their congregation.

The discussion of each type of wisdom will be a tour that stops at four ports of call. The order of these stops may vary according to the terrain we are exploring.

One stopping place in this journey will be the Background Check. What is the history and social location of this wisdom? What accounts for its emergence at this time in our cultural history?

Another destination will be Key Texts. Which books most clearly represent the ideas of this form of wisdom? How are we instructed to apply these practices to our lives?

Another stop I call the Nutshell. Here we'll ask the wisdom system to answer the following questions: 1.) What's most important? (Visional); 2.) What are the attitudes and actions that act as obstacles that keep us from life's priority? (Tendency-Need dimension); and 3.) What are the strategies that facilitate our getting closer to this priority? (Obligational dimension)

And finally, we'll visit the issue of Lifeform; i.e., what kind of life is shaped by adherence to this wisdom? (Rule-Role dimension).

CHAPTER THREE

Character Wisdom

"Why didn't somebody tell me this when I was 18?"
(I think maybe they did, but I wasn't listening.)

Stephen R. Covey, in the course of researching his book *The 7 Habits of Highly Effective People: Restoring the Character Ethic*, immersed himself in American success literature published since 1776. He found that the first 150 years of material regarded a "character ethic" as the foundation of success. It advocated integrating basic virtues such as integrity, humility, fidelity, temperance, courage, justice, patience, industry, simplicity, modesty, and the Golden Rule into one's character. It was concerned with social good as well as with personal good. Such a life of virtue directed toward the public good was the definition of a life well-lived; the American Dream was to seize one's freedom to live in such a way.

Shortly after World War I the basic view of success shifted from a character ethic to what Covey calls a personality ethic. It viewed success as a function of personality, public image, communication skills, influence-techniques, power strategies, and positive attitudes. While it accurately identified the power of positive thinking, it suffered from individualism, materialism, and an overblown notion of human control over an unpredictable life. It valued personality more than character. It reduced the American Dream to owning a home in the suburbs. [1]

This personal success wisdom that flourished from the 1950s through the 1980s, from Dale Carnegie to Norman Vincent Peale and Zig Ziglar, is still being produced today. There is no doubt that its admonitions have invigorated many people in pursuing their goals. But a different brand of wisdom is squeezing in beside it on the bookstore shelves. It embodies what Stephen Covey has called the character ethic. It is expressed in a proliferation of recent literature I call character wisdom.

Character wisdom emphasizes community and kindness more than it does efficiency, time management, and goal setting. It insists that to be a successful person is to be a good person. Its focus is a set of basic character qualities that are seen as beneficial for both individuals and society. It reclaims the enterprise of character formation as central to our nation's health and future. A proliferation of organizations and instruction literature devoted to themes of character formation began in the early 1990s and continues today. They commend a wisdom that seems new and fresh, but is really centuries old.

Background Check

A person's character is reflected in the tendency to act, feel and think in certain definable ways. Ethical character refers to a particular cluster of distinctive dispositions that are judged to be positive and to serve as a model for others. Classical and contemporary discussions of character have focused on virtue. A virtue is a disposition, a persistent attitude or "habit" of the heart and mind that results in a consistent pattern of action and expression.[2]

Recent moral philosophy has sought to recover ancient Greek insights into the virtues over contemporary, more superficial understandings.[3] Today, we tend to limit virtue to sexual purity and abstinence from alcoholic beverages and to define morality as a list of things we should not do.[4]

Virtue in classical Greek understanding consists of a cluster of human qualities necessary for personal and social harmony in all the activities of daily life. The four "cardinal" virtues going back to Aristotle and Plato are prudence, justice, fortitude, and temperance. They need translating to overcome their current trivialization.

We think of prudence as caution. For Aristotle it was *phronesis*, practical wisdom that recognizes and makes the right choices in specific situations. It is the master virtue that makes all others possible. *Phronesis* helps us get clear about why we're doing what we're doing in a given situation and what we ought to be doing instead. It is a sort of moderator for the panel discussion among the virtues. It helps us rank the virtues in order of importance as they lead us to action in particular instances. *Phronesis* for Aristotle is both a moral virtue and one of the five intellectual virtues (the others are understanding, science, wisdom, and art). [5]

Justice, as the Greeks thought of it, includes fairness, honesty, and keeping promises. Fortitude means courage, in battle but also in pursuit of justice against all odds.[6]

We equate temperance with moderation or abstinence from alcoholic beverages. For the Greeks it was the self-discipline necessary to minimize life's chaos and to accomplish any worthwhile end. It is the control of the will, the appetites, the temper, and the tongue.

The built-in goal for each individual is to become a responsible initiator of the actions characteristic of the virtues of wisdom, justice, courage, and temperance. For Aristotle these virtues are exercised in a social context. The virtues equip us to overcome the harms, dangers, temptations, and distractions of life by increasing our self-knowledge and our knowledge of the good.[7]

Aristotle emphasizes human friendship as the bond necessary to create the kind of community in which people can flourish and develop the virtues. Friendships can be based on three things: usefulness, pleasure, and virtue. The moral component of friendship is the indispensable basis of a good society by which friends help one another to be more virtuous persons. The goal of friendship becomes to safeguard and further the good of the *polis*, the city-state or society.[8]

This is one of the failings of personality wisdom. It advises us to befriend those who are useful to us in accomplishing our goals. The moral ingredient and the social accountability of friendship are missing. For the Greeks, the appeal of the virtuous life is intrinsic. Much popular self-help "wisdom" blurs the line between moral virtues and skills for success, sometimes called instrumental virtues. [9]

To the classic list of four cardinal virtues, Thomas Aquinas added three theological virtues: faith, hope, and charity (*caritas*, or love). Thomas established a theological context for *habitus*, or virtue. He believed that charity was the form of all the virtues.

Different moral traditions in different societies have emphasized different virtues. The clannish world of Homeric Greece as well as the feudal society of medieval Europe prized loyalty.[10] The wisdom traditions that contributed to the book of Proverbs tended to prize respect for the wisdom of one's elders and self-control, especially mastery of the tongue as means to harmony for individuals and community.

Americans have elevated individualism, personal initiative, and self-reliance into our trinity of national virtues.

The Popcorn Phenomenon

The proliferation of contemporary versions of this ancient character wisdom is an example of the "popcorn phenomenon," when the increasing heat and pressure of the culture creates a rapidly exploding body of literature to address a pressing concern.[11] The pressing concern is the fear that we have lost something we used to have, namely, our character.

What or who is responsible for the erosion of our national character? It depends on whom you ask. Philosophy professor and author Christina Hoff Sommers blames the loss of belief in absolute truth and the assumption that living in a pluralistic society necessitates moral relativism. She diagnoses our problem as "cognitive moral confusion." She observes that, while the young people she works with may engage in behaviors that benefit others and live by a code of fairness, they have no conceptual framework within which to describe or justify their choices. She calls for a "Great Relearning" among children and youth of our moral history and its core values of civility, honesty, consideration, and self-discipline.[12]

Michael Josephson, founder and president of the Josephson Institute of Ethics and The Character Counts! Coalition, diagnoses the problem as "a hole in the moral ozone." Citing the results of a comprehensive national survey on the ethics of young people issued in October 2000 he calls on politicians to recognize the vital importance of dealing with "shocking levels of moral illiteracy" as part of any educational reform package. Says Ron Kinnamon, chairman of the Character Counts! Coalition, "There is a solution: more pervasive and proficient character education at home, at schools, and on the sports fields. Character education is here to stay and it's getting stronger and stronger."[13]

The Grim Reaper

It was early one morning in late October a few years ago. I lay sleeping peacefully, but suddenly felt something trailing across my face. I opened my eyes to see the Grim Reaper standing over me, his face not six inches from my own. He looked just like he did in the pictures and the movies—dark hooded cloak, pale ravaged face, seaweed-like hair sweeping from his head across my pillow. When my eyes fell on the huge sickle he held in his hand, I sat up with a start and a scream. There was a painful clunk as we bumped heads. "Gotcha!" he crowed in triumph. It was my young son, testing the scare-quotient of his Halloween costume.

This time the Grim Reaper was a second grader, and the sickle was plastic, but next time I might not be so lucky. As a wake-up call, it worked for me. And I'm not the only Baby Boomer starting her day this way. Lots of us are waking up, face to face with the specter of our own mortality and fallibility through the challenges of caring for aging parents while raising children. Boomers have tremendous influence on religious life in America today. Many of us are at a critical juncture, looking back on our lives as a means of preparing to move forward. In prime child-rearing years, we evaluate our own characters and the parenting we've done to date and seek to make adjustments in mid-stream. Psychologist John Roschen points out that many Boomers are embarking on a "second journey of the self," in which they inwardly appraise their lives, but also move out toward others.[14] And as we do that, it is natural that we reach for some fundamental qualities of good character that will benefit our inward lives, our parenting, and the future of our common national life.

Character Counts!

In the early '90s a group of educators and philosophers met in the mountains of Colorado and produced the Aspen Declaration. It listed "Six Core Elements of Character" that should be inculcated by all "youth-influencing institutions": trustworthiness (including honesty and loyalty), respect, responsibility (including self-discipline and hard work), fairness, caring (compassion), and citizenship (including obeying laws, staying informed, and voting).

William Bennett, author of *The Book of Virtues*, one of the biggest best-sellers of the 1990s, adds courage and faith to the list. He describes faith as "reverence." Bennett commends the character-shaping value of morality stories drawn from history and the examples of virtuous people. He and others following in his wake believe that there are certain principles of behavior that Americans can agree on, follow, and pass on.[15]

Despite differences in their lists, those concerned with character agree on the importance of character education. Political and civic leaders meeting in the mid-'90s upheld the same six qualities identified earlier by the Aspen Declaration. Naming them "the Six Pillars of Character," they formed a nonprofit, nonpartisan educational program called Character Counts!

In 2000 the organization had over 450 national, regional, and local organizations with school children in over 2,000 schools and hundreds of youth groups learning about the Six Pillars of Character. The recent increase in school violence has brought attention to the problem of low self-esteem and the existence of bullying and raised awareness of the need for such programs.

Character Counts! produces posters, featuring six brightly colored pillars, on which are listed the "do's" and "don't's" of behavior with regard to each character quality.

There is a sense in which, however, from a Christian perspective, the character ethic addresses the "what" without the "why" and leaves many questions unanswered. Should I always be honest, even when it might bring harm to someone? What is the right thing to do? How will I know in every case? Is there ever a time when I should risk my reputation for the sake of, say, justice? Is there a limit to my loyalty to my family, friends, and country? Should it be blind, or is there room for a higher loyalty? What if the rules I am asked to play by are flawed, designed to allow some people to win and others to lose?

What do I do when I make all the right choices and everything goes wrong? How do I decide what I am supposed to do when a strong inner voice urges me to pursue my own talent rather than a more conventional path that others have chosen for me? What does character have to do with people's differing political views? Does having character mean I should automatically take one position or another on, say, school vouchers or the ordination of homosexuals? How do differing faith systems affect decisions about character?

The advocates of this recovery of virtue insist that it provides a baseline morality on which various members of a pluralistic society can agree for our common good.

Opponents charge that it is based on Greek understandings that were fired in the kiln of competitive warfare, and does not do justice to the notions of what are desirable qualities in other cultures and religions.[16]

Contemporary Christian ethicists criticize the naïve appropriation of Greek virtues as a basis for the Christian life, asserting that the deeper implications of a Greek understanding of virtue clash with the essential claims of Christianity.[17]

The Christian virtues represented most strongly by Aquinas offer an alternative that radically challenges Greek notions of virtue. There are significant differences between the Greek understanding of goodness or excellence (*arete*) and Aquinas' charity (*caritas*, or love) For the Greeks, attaining virtue was a victory. The hero vanquished his foes by means of the exercise of his virtues.

By contrast, Aquinas' charitable person is first and foremost a recipient of charity from God. As friendship with God and fellow humans, charity always involves mutuality. Christian charity transcends the model of the person dedicated to the practice and perfection of the virtues of conflict.

According to Aquinas, our true or complete virtue is fundamentally not our own. This is akin to the insight both from Proverbs and from the Prologue to the Gospel of John that wisdom is a divine gift before it is a human search. For Aquinas, virtue is an infusion of God's grace that saves and enables us. Faith generates hope, and hope generates charity. Aristotle's account of virtues being instilled by education and honed by exercise is helpful to Christians seeking a disciplined life of faith. Still, the theological virtues come by the action of God that brings us into relationship with God. In the process our characters are not just formed; they are utterly transformed (2 Corinthians 3:17-18).

The sign and substance of the possession of the Christian virtues is always participation in the Body of Christ. Aristotle's notion of friendship is a relationship among equals who grow ever similar in virtue. By contrast, the metaphor of the church as the Body of

Christ depicts differing members joined in a unity of purpose that is God-given and directed (Romans 12:3-8; 1 Corinthians 12:1-10).[18]

A number of best-selling authors in the past few years have presented us with their versions of an introductory course in Character Wisdom. They form a body of contemporary wisdom literature, whose proverbs and admonitions, in many cases, bear resemblances both to Greek virtues and biblical wisdom themes. In some ways they do justice to neither. The Greek understanding that virtue's reward is intrinsic is lost in the quest for personal fulfillment. When they do commend altruism, their motives are often personal fulfillment and advancement rather than genuine concern for the other.

The biblical view that wisdom is a gift from God to be used for God's glory is absent. Our "Five Alive" questions equip us to analyze contemporary character wisdom from the perspective of our Christian theological context. They equip us to preach sermons that combine theological correction with commendation of secular wisdom. Such sermons shape listeners who are, at the same time, lovers of biblical wisdom and critical consumers of cultural wisdom.

Self-Help Manuals

Self-help manuals combine instruction in the form of admonitions and reflection and are most often written by people with sufficient means to wield a high degree of control over their circumstances. Most often they are people who can afford to view their outward obstacles as "small stuff" that should not be sweated. [19]

Everything I Need to Know I Learned in Kindergarten: UnCommon Thoughts on Common Things by Robert Fulghum. (New York: Ivy Books, 1988) was a best-selling work of cracker-barrel wisdom from the 1980s. Fulghum's lessons from the Sunday school sandbox include admonitions like "Don't hit other people, clean up your own mess, have milk and cookies in the afternoon, take a nap every day, and hold hands when you cross the street." The most important thing in his wisdom's worldview appears to be a life lived in safe and kindly coexistence with others.

The sandbox could prove an interesting metaphor for a faith community. Holding hands when we cross the street holds promise as a metaphor for a community sticking together in a dangerous world. But kindly coexistence is not the *shalom* of the community that is the goal of Proverbs' wisdom. It is not the vision of the kingdom of God that fuels Jesus' radical call for justice. Milk and cookies and holding hands when we cross the street are not the Bread of Life and the Body of Christ.

Memoirs and Reflections

Autobiographies and memoirs are genres that share the fuller life narratives out of which self-help advice and single-sentence lessons emerge. Memoirs invariably contain what I call "wisdom vignettes," reminiscences by the author that are often nutritious for others, either as cautionary tales or windows of transcendence.[20]

The examples that follow offer a window into the variety and sermonic value of this genre.

Reading memoirs that chronicle the experience of injustice can help the preacher articulate social criticism from the point of view of concrete human lives. The blistering memoir *Makes Me Wanna Holler: A Young Black Man in America* by Nathan McCall recounts Nathan McCall's passage from the street to the prison yard and, ultimately, to the newsrooms of the *Washington Post* where, he is now a respected journalist.

Writes McCall,

> Throughout school, except during Black History Week, we were taught more about everybody else than about ourselves. I'll never forget that one of my junior high school history teachers made us memorize all the dynasties of the Chinese empire, from start to finish, in chronological order. Yet the story of Africans brought here as slaves was summed up in our history books in a few short paragraphs, almost as a footnote. . . . that communicated the message that we were less important than everyone else. I wondered how my black teachers could permit such a thing. I understand now that they taught what was approved for the school system, and that while schools had been integrated for blacks and whites, administrators had still failed to integrate the information passed along to us.[21]

The work of Anna Quindlen, *New York Times* columnist turned novelist, and writer Kathleen Norris fall within the genre of autobiographical reflection. Quindlen's is directed toward social and political analysis, while Norris' is shaped by theological reflection.[22]

Says Norris,

> The word "wretch" has taken two paths to arrive at current English usage. The OED tells me that in Old English it had a somewhat romantic connotation, a wretch was a wanderer, an adventurer, a knight errant. In Old Teutonic, however, a wretch meant an exile, a banished person, and it is there that the word's negative connotations begin to haunt us. The word as used today means not so much one who has been driven out of a native land, but one who would be miserable anywhere..."someone exiled from being at peace within the self." It could also mean someone "who is materially poor and unfortunate" or "inwardly hapless and pathetic."... The word "wretch," then, does not paint a picture of who we want to be. Or who we think we are. The word has become so unpopular in recent years, in fact, that people began complaining about its appearance in the first verse of "Amazing Grace"—"Amazing grace, how sweet the sound, that saved a wretch like me." Some hymnals have taken out the offending word, but the bowdlerization of the text that results is thoroughly wretched English, and also laughably bland, which, taken together, is not an inconsiderable accomplishment: "Amazing grace, how sweet the sound, that saved someone like me." Someone? Anyone? Anyone home?[23]

The following is an excerpt from a Quindlen column that appeared July 22, 1992, entitled "No More Waiting."

> From time to time you hear complaints from people of apparent goodwill about how much national attention is being focused on AIDS. What about cancer? say cancer survivors. What about heart disease? And in these complaints there is usually a touch of envy. Many of us whose lives were mangled by mortal illnesses suffered privately, confident that doctors and researchers and the purveyors of government grants were doing their level best to eradicate the scourge. We waited. And waited. And waited.
>
> Then the AIDS activists disrupted hearings and marched down city streets and agitated, agitated, agitated for better drugs, for

speedier approvals, for more research money. Some people think they are too militant. If I could help give someone I loved a second chance, or even an extra year, what people think would not worry me a bit.[24]

Sometimes a memoir will yield an incident or vignette from its author's life that lends itself beautifully to use in a sermon. Writer Anne Lamott offers a combination of reflection, autobiography, and memoir in her books *Bird by Bird, Operating Instructions,* and *Traveling Mercies.* The following is a wisdom vignette from *Bird by Bird* from which the book derives its title.

Thirty years ago my older brother, who was ten years old at the time, was trying to get a report on birds written that he'd had three months to write. It was due the next day. We were out at our family cabin in Bolinas, and he was at the kitchen table close to tears, surrounded by binder paper and pencils and unopened books on birds, immobilized by the hugeness of the task ahead. Then my father sat down beside him put his arm around my brother's shoulder, and said, "Bird by bird, buddy. Just take it bird by bird."[25]

Reading memoirs of people who played pivotal roles in history can be enriching. But so can those of less famous people facing the challenges that, sooner or later, life brings to all of us. *Tuesdays with Morrie: An Old Man, A Young Man, and Life's Greatest Lesson* by Mitch Albom is a book rich with insight into the experience of terminal illness by both the sufferer and his friends and family. Sportswriter and broadcaster Mitch Albom reentered the life of his beloved college sociology professor Morrie Schwartz several months before Morrie died of Lou Gehrig's disease in November, 1995.

Most memoirs set out their purpose and promise in the first few paragraphs, and this one is no different. Mitch opens the book in this way.

The last class of my old professor's life took place once a week in his house, by a window in the study where he could watch a small hibiscus plant shed its pink leaves. The class met on Tuesdays. It began after breakfast. The subject was The Meaning of Life. It was taught from experience...

No books were required, yet many topics were covered, including love, work, community, family, aging, forgiveness, and finally, death. The last lecture was brief, only a few words.
A funeral was held in lieu of graduation.
Although no final exam was given, you were expected to produce one long paper on what was learned. That paper is presented here.[26]

Wisdom vignettes of others can spark our interest in crafting our own for deeper self-knowledge and, when appropriate, for use in sermons. Critical openness to these sources becomes a means by which the Wisdom of God shapes the character of the people of God.[27]

Key Text: *Don't Sweat the Small Stuff*

One of the number-one best-selling books of recent years is *Don't Sweat the Small Stuff...and It's All Small Stuff: Simple Ways to Keep the Little Things From Taking Over Your Life* (New York: Hyperion, 1997). Richard Carlson, Ph.D., therapist and self-help lecturer offers 100 admonitions (with brief commentary) for a more carefree, more humane, more fulfilling life. What is most important in his wisdom is the creation of a "more peaceful and loving you."
We impede our progress toward that goal when we "overreact, blow things out of proportions, hold on too tightly, and focus on the negative aspects of life." To reach this goal, Dr. Carlson recommends that we replace old habits of "reaction" with new habits of perspective. When we do, we will respond to life gracefully, with ease. We will tread "a softer, more graceful path that makes life seem easier and the people in it more compatible." Our actions will be more peaceful and caring. Our lives will become less stressful and more satisfying.[28] Despite the altruism in Carlson's wisdom, its goal is individual benefit rather than service to the community. At the same time, Carlson's admonitions are memorable and lend themselves to being placed in a Christian context.

Key Text: *First Things First*

One of the most widely read self-help manuals of the '90s was a book authored by Stephen Covey, A. Roger and Rebecca R. Merrill entitled *First Things First: To Live, to Love, to Learn, to Leave a Legacy.*

Background Check

The social location of this work appears to be middle class. The examples given throughout are people who have the economic and social resources to control their own destinies.

Nutshell

What Is Most Important?

What is most important in this form of wisdom? To fulfill the four human needs and capacities: to live, to love, to learn, to leave a legacy. They correspond to aspects of life: the physical (to live), the social (to love), the mental (to learn) and the spiritual (to live with an integrity and purpose that leaves a legacy for the next generation). These four needs are interrelated, connected by a powerful synergy. Living in such a way that all four are fulfilled creates a life of true inner balance, deep human fulfillment, and joy. The unifying need, according to the authors, is the need to leave a legacy. "It transforms other needs into capacities for contribution."[29]

Obstacles

What attitudes and actions are obstacles to attaining first things? The authors warn readers of our contemporary "urgency addiction" that keeps us going from crisis to crisis, somehow never finding time to do important planning that might prevent the next "crisis." We have become slaves to the clock, rather than followers of our own inward "compass" which directs us towards the "true north" principles that make for a fulfilling life.

We tend to view others as resources for meeting our goals. Relationships in this model tend to be transactional, rather than transformational, two-way synergistic interactions in which both sides learn and teach.

Facilitators

"The Main Thing is to Keep the Main Thing the Main Thing." Our first priority is to develop and use our inner compass so we can act with integrity in the moment of choice. The endowments of self-awareness, conscience, creative imagination, and independent will are the components of our human freedom: the power to choose, to respond, to change. They create the compass that empowers us to align our lives with true north.

The authors recommend that we practice strategic behaviors to nurture our four endowments. They recommend that we keep a personal journal to heighten our self-awareness, that we learn the true north principles from the wisdom literature of the ages, that we listen to our own and others' experience, that we act in keeping with our own consciences rather than prevailing convention, and that we practice the creative visualization of the future we want in the present.[30]

They encourage us to respect and live by the "law of the farm." This is the author's term for the timeless principle, pointed out in wisdom literature through the ages, that you must sow in order to reap, and that what you sow, you will inevitably reap. Worthwhile goals like integrity, relationships, marriage and parenting, and health and fitness, take time and persistent effort to reap the benefits of joy, community, and energy.[31]

Lifeform

What way of life issues from following Carlson's and Covey's wisdom?

Biblical wisdom in both Testaments offers up some "big stuff'" about which we ought to be sweating bullets and taking Wisdom's hard, narrow path, rather than the softer path of least resistance. The best pulpit use of Carlson would be to challenge listeners to redirect the energy we currently expend being annoyed at small irritations toward working for the kingdom of God.

When we follow Covey's wisdom, we live with more flexibility, more respect for others, more balance, and more joy. We are more concerned with doing the right thing than with doing more things more efficiently. We are empowered to use our endowments to fulfill our basic needs and capacities in a balanced, principle-centered way.[32]

While Covey and company don't define what those principles should be, they point us toward the wisdom literature of various cultures and religions to discover them for ourselves.

Several sayings, phrases, and concepts from Covey are vivid and engaging and would preach well when set in a Christian context. Examples are: "the main thing is to keep the main thing the main thing," "the law of the farm," "True North," and "to live, to love, to learn, and to leave a legacy."

Biblical Wisdom Responds

Character Formation and Justification

I recently conducted a workshop on preaching wisdom with a group of pastors. In the midst of our discussion of character wisdom, one of the participants made an insightful comment. "All this emphasis on virtue is a Greek heresy! We are veering into works righteousness with this talk of character formation. Look at all the people with serious character flaws God chooses and uses in the Bible. We are not saved by our characters!"

The wisdom literature of the Bible heartily concurs with that statement. Its substance is character formation, but not motivated and fueled by the human will alone. When the Biblical wisdom literature recommends various attitudes and actions as "wise," it is always in the context of the prior divine initiative in giving the gift of wisdom. Wisdom is a divine gift before it can be a lifelong human search. This insight of biblical wisdom is honored in the theology of John Wesley. His writings repeatedly affirm that God's pardoning, empowering grace is prevenient (that is, it "goes before" human agency) and is indispensable for human salvation.[33]

As Christians when we talk of character formation it is in the context of divine initiative from start to finish. Character formation is not the same as justification. Rather, it is a result. According to John Calvin, holiness of life, as evidenced by observance of the commandments, is the way God trains those he has previously justified by his grace to be righteous. They are not the way we persuade God we are righteous.[34]

According to Calvin, the use of the law after justification is to warn us of what is right and pleasing in the Lord's sight. However much we may be prompted by the Spirit and eager to obey God, we are still weak in the flesh, and would rather serve sin than God. Concludes Calvin, "The law is to this flesh like a whip to an idle and balky ass, to goad, stir, arouse it to work."[35]

CHAPTER FOUR

New Age Wisdom

"You Create Your Own Reality

Maybe nobody in our congregation is toting crystals, going to past life regression seminars, or asking people to pray for relatives abducted by aliens during the prayer concerns. But before we preachers scan our congregations and say "Nobody's New Age here," we had better think again.

Many of us have attended company-sponsored courses in attaining peak mental performance where we learned techniques of imaging and visualization whose mantra is the New Age self-help slogan: "You create your own reality." Opinion polls show Americans are a lot more willing to consider the credibility of astrology, extraterrestrial intelligence, and reincarnation than we were twenty-five years ago. Television and movies treat themes of extraterrestrial intelligence and occultism. *The X-Files* enjoys tremendous popularity among twenty-somethings. The circulation of *Yoga Journal* is at an all-time high. Courts increasingly use psychics to weed out lying witnesses, pinpoint suspects, and locate missing bodies. New Age publishing is a billion-dollar business.[1]

Background Check

The term "New Age" is an umbrella term that refers to a vast variety of beliefs, practices, and affiliations. The popular sense of the term "New Age," is a primary, though not exclusive, concern with some combination of channeling, reincarnation, extraterrestrials, esoteric aspects of holistic health (psychic healing, herbs, etc), and self-improvement..."[2] These varied beliefs and practices have the same goal: personal transformation of consciousness as a way of ushering in a New Age of Aquarius.

In the New Age scheme of things, the past 2,000 years or so is referred to as the Age of Pisces. War, division, injustice, hatred, mistrust, bigotry, and exploitation of the environment have marred this period. In the 1960s it gave way to an all-encompassing spirituality embracing all manner of religions. Citizens of the New Age, while their beliefs and spiritual practices are diverse, share a common realization of the power of their thoughts to affect outward realities. They assume total self-responsibility for achieving their true potential and creating their own reality, an age of peace, harmony, wholeness, and restoration for all people and the whole universe. [3]

The New Age movement, which has come to prominence in the 1980s and 1990s, is a combination of influences from both the West and the East. It is in part a discovery by Western people of Eastern religions. It is also a recovery of their own Western alternative spiritual traditions that include Gnosticism, Freemasonry, Rosicrucianism, Theosophy, Romanticism, earth religions, Transcendentalism, and spiritualism among others.[4] Elements from these traditions as well as from Eastern mysticism combine with modern psychoanalysis, meditation techniques, and alternative medical therapies to produce a complex maze of pathways to personal fulfillment and wholeness. In general the New Age is concerned with the social, planetary benefits of personal transformation. Many New Agers support political movements that press for social change like Amnesty International and Greenpeace.[5]

Some attribute the popularity of the movement to the shortcomings of organized religions. Others point to the volatility of social conditions and our need for a sense of control. In reality, the popularity of New Age approaches is part of a much larger cultural shift. The New Age movement is a religious manifestation of postmodernity. Postmodernity criticizes the Enlightenment's "modern" scientific mentality for elevating rationality over respect for mystery in the universe and the individual over the community.

New Age thought views Western science, medicine, religion and approaches to the environment as rationalistic, mechanistic, and dualistic. New Agers advocate a holistic perspective that heals what they perceive as the fallacious divide between God and humanity, the physical and the spiritual, and humankind and nature. Most proponents of New Age religion concur that the only way forward will be through a transformational shift in consciousness of cosmic proportions.[6] While it will begin with individuals, its effects will be cumulative and communal.

New Age and Jesus

Many New Agers would assert that Christianity is but one of many inner spiritual paths, all leading to the same goal of cosmic unity. New Agers believe that Jesus was a son of God, but not the only one, and that we can all become one with God as he was. All religions are essentially one. All the founders of major religions, including Jesus, taught the same thing: how to become one with the One. This harmonizing of differences among world religions is called syncretism.[7]

There is a contingent of New Age believers who are Christ-centered, though not in the traditional sense. They believe that Christ has been channeling himself through a number of sources over the past decade or so, attempting to prepare humankind for a dramatic transformation. Channeling is the name for the process by which beings from other planets or the next life supposedly communicate verbatim communications to human beings who are often called "transceivers."[8]

In Helen Schucman and William Thetford's *A Course in Miracles*, the message is one of practical advice and techniques for personal transformation. We too can share the "Christ consciousness" or the "cosmic Christ Spirit" that speaks through the book's lessons. For other authors, Evelyn Gordon and Mary Joyce among them, his message is broader, focusing on historical and moral correction of traditional Christian interpretations.

According to persons who claim to channel Jesus, he is far more concerned with the presence or absence of love in people's hearts than with church attendance or being worshipped. He deeply needs our help in raising consciousness and clearing negativity. He is extraordinarily upset by the atrocities committed in his name by unending war and strife and by the rape of the planet.[9]

Nutshell

To understand what the New Age means to most people who subscribe to its philosophy and theology, it is helpful to look at the main areas of interest and concerns that appear in New Age journals and catalogues. A comprehensive survey of the features of the New Age can be found in *The New Age Catalogue: Access to Information and Sources*, which lists the following eight headings: 1. Intuitive development/channeling, 2. Create your own reality/transformational journeys, 3. Transitions/birth, 4. Spirituality, 5. Holistic healing and health, 6. Bodywork/movement, 7. New lifestyles/communities, and 8. The Planet/planetary visions.

Intuitive Development includes channeling, crystals, divination, astrology, numerology, tarot, palmistry, graphology, and the I Ching, an ancient Chinese method of divination. It also includes the yogic practice of healing through activating the chakras, vortices of energy in the human body arranged along the spinal column. Another tool of intuitive development is aura consultations. The aura is a multi-colored field of energy radiating around the body that reflects changing emotions and state of health. Invisible to the naked eye, the aura can be seen by psychics. A technique involving high freqency, electronic photography (Kirlian photography) claims to be able to capture the aura on film.[10]

Create your own reality includes self-help, subliminal programming, meditation, dreamwork, astral projection, out-of-body experiences, and various schools, institutes, and retreats.

Transitions/birth covers birth, near-death experiences, death and dying and reincarnation and past life regression therapy.

Spirituality includes spiritualism, Native American religious beliefs and practices (such as Shamanism), Women's Spirituality, and Earth Religions (Paganism or Witchcraft).[11]

Holistic healing and health gives special attention to Oriental medicine, homeopathy, herbology, and nutrition.

Bodywork/movement includes various therapies or movements to restore the body to its maximum state of well-being. They include massage, yoga, therapeutic touch, Reiki, Seichem, Rolfing, Reflexology, acupressure, T'ai Chi, and chiropractic therapy.[12]

New lifestyles/communities may be organized as communes or as interest groups that adopt new lifestyles that revolve around natural products and New Age literature, music, art, and socially conscious investing.

The planet/planetary visions area is made up of those who are planetary visionaries as well as those who are knowledgeable about ancient prophecies, and those who maintain the existence of UFOs.[13]

It should be clear by now that New Age is a very broad umbrella—wide enough to cover a variety of ideas and religious expressions. It is beyond the scope of this chapter to cover them all in a comprehensive way. We will have to place many fascinating groups, practices, and beliefs outside our brackets to pursue our homiletical focus.[14]

Our focus will be on New Age thought as a body of practical, daily wisdom strategies as it is expressed in New Age self-help literature. New Age authors convey their life-shaping insights via a number of genres we recognize from the other bodies of wisdom that we have examined so far. The most common genre is the self-help manual. Authors of these manuals include Wayne W. Dyer, Adrian Calabrese, Mary Carroll Moore, Deepak Chopra, Julia Cameron and Mark Bryan, Iyanla Vanzant, Sandra Choquette, Shakti Gawain, and others.[15]

Still other New Age authors use the genre of memoir to instill their insights. Some examples are Stanley Hempf, representative of the New Age Religion Eckankar, psychic and channeler Sylvia Browne, and actress and New Age autobiographer Shirley MacLaine.

James Redfield (*The Celestine Prophecy*; *The Tenth Insight*; *The Celestine Vision*) and Dan Millman (*The Laws of Spirit*, *The Way of the Peaceful Warrior* and *The Sacred Journey of the Peaceful Warrior*) shape their work in the form of fictitious adventure narratives whose plots consist of the discovery of one New Age insight after another.

Conversations with God by Neale Donald Walsch and *A Course in Miracles* by Helen Schucman and William Thetford present New Age insights as Divine Verbatim. *A Course in Miracles* is a self-study spiritual thought system consisting of a three-volume curriculum: a text, a workbook for students, and a manual for teachers. It teaches that the way to universal love and peace is by undoing guilt through forgiving others and ourselves. It focuses on the

healing of relationships and making them holy. It affirms our oneness with God that makes us capable of creating in the likeness of
our Creator. Sickness and death are human creations and can be
abolished through the miracle of allowing forgiveness to fill our
minds and hearts and relationships.

A Course in Miracles purports to have been "scribed" by Dr.
Helen Schucman between 1965 and 1972 through a process of inner
dictation she identified as coming from Jesus. Dr. Schucman was
Associate Professor of Medical Psychology at the College of
Physicians and Surgeons at the Columbia-Presbyterian Medical
Center in New York City. Dr. William Thetford was the head of the
Psychology Department at this same institution. He typed the
material that Dr. Schucman recorded in her notes. There are cur-
rently about one and a half million copies of *A Course in Miracles* in
circulation around the world in twenty languages.[16]

New Age beliefs and practices vary as widely as those within
Jewish and Christian traditions. While no one person or movement
speaks for New Age as a whole, various movements are built on
the same basic assumptions. They share a common vision of the
nature of existence and the purpose of life.

In general, New Agers believe that individual human beings
started out as part of an undifferentiated group of souls. Gradually
this group divided into individualized entities. New Agers believe
that each person has an eternal soul that is part of them and an eternal spirit, that is a part of God. While all New Agers are not rein-
carnationists, most believe that the soul, with the Spirit's guidance,
evolves through a series of incarnations, with each one assimilating, resolving, and integrating experiences. The goal of each of
these incarnations is to make progress toward oneness with God by
assimilating and resolving experiences. Spirit guides the soul into
freewill choices that align with God's will. [17]

Angelic guides are available to assist humans in making these
choices, but their assistance is contingent on human invitation.
Meditative exercises enhance the senses to the point of discerning
those ascended beings for the purpose of sharing in God's work
and of sharing in unconditional love.

Many New Agers believe that each person comes into the world
with a "blueprint" for this particular incarnation that determines
his or her choice of life circumstances and experiences.[18] The blue-

print is a plan for the advancement of the individual's karma in a given lifetime.

Karma, for the New Ager, is "the portfolio of experiences each soul needs to evolve toward God."[19] Karma means, roughly, the moral law of cause and effect. It is similar to Jesus' notion of "As a man sows, so shall he reap." Indian religions tighten the law to the point where it brooks no exceptions.[20] The Hindu notion is that one's past choices determine one's present status in life, and one needs to live a life of contemplation to balance the error of former active choices. Said the Buddha "What you are is what you have done, what you will be is what you do now."[21]

Karma and reincarnation are not punishments for former sins. One's present condition is not a punishment but a consequence. Karma is not fatalistic. It decrees that every decision has an inexorable consequence, but we freely arrive at our decisions. The hand a card player picks up he dealt himself in a former life; now he is free to play it as he chooses.[22]

The New Age view of karma tends to heighten the element of choice in the pre-incarnational period. The events of a former life do not seem to dictate the details of the next one as tightly as in Buddhism and Hinduism. New Agers emphasize the forward looking, active nature of karma. New Age karma is composed of the experiences one needs to resolve unfinished business and unlearned lessons from former lives. We must pursue it actively.

The overriding purpose of reincarnation and karma is personal and spiritual growth toward a state which is either at one with or qualitatively in perfect harmony with the Source from which all things came. The goal of the New Ager's spiritual pilgrimage is unification with God. When we reunite with God, we somehow benefit all of humanity and the cosmos by pulling them a little closer to God. We also enrich the life of God, who depends on our response to grow and evolve.[23] In the process of evolving toward that experience, the entity helps the entire cosmos to grow closer to the Presence of God.

What Is Most Important?

Higher consciousness is the supreme quest of humankind. All our thoughts and actions should be directed toward aligning our consciousness with the creative energy of the universe in which we all partake, of which we all are one. New Age religion affirms monism, the belief that there is no distinction between creation and creator or creating force. Rather than thinking dualistically, New Age views things holistically, discerning a unity between the human realm, the natural world, and the divine. All is One. Furthermore, We are all One. There are not many selves, but one Self. This has been called Cosmic Humanism.[24]

The separate self is an illusion. Reality consists of an even larger Self. This is the New Age God, sometimes referred to as Infinite Intelligence. All is God, and therefore we are God.

The human race is moving toward a glorious, unlimited new order of peace, prosperity, and perfection. Before and after the year 2000, more and more people are evolving toward this higher consciousness. We are on the brink of a major paradigm shift, more dramatic and far-reaching than the Renaissance or the Protestant Reformation. It will be attained as each individual actualizes his or her divine nature and achieves union with the Ultimate Unifying Principle by applying consciousness-changing techniques to body, mind, and spirit.[25]

The New Age contains an apocalyptic dimension that can best be pictured as fitting into three camps. They are: the occult, which seeks personal change through channeling, crystals and magic; the spiritual, which centers on individual growth and trance state attainment through meditation and related techniques; and the social, which emphasizes the development of human potential as a means for collective social change.[26]

More dangerous are brands of New Age apocalyptic teachings that posit an imminent divine intervention by an outside force or figure. On the lips of a mesmerizing religious leader such teachings can turn absurd and often, tragic. Examples abounded in the 1990s. They include the Branch Davidians; the Dami Missionary Church of Seoul, Korea; Elizabeth Clare Prophet's Church Universal and Triumphant; and the Heaven's Gate cult.

Obstacles

Ignorance, not evil, is the chief obstacle to evolving to a higher consciousness. According to New Age thought, the numbing influences of Western culture have caused most people to accept a fragmented vision of self-limitation and failure rather than to know they can be like God. The rational, technology-focused powers of the left brain have overshadowed the playful, creative, intuitive powers of the right brain. We suffer from "metaphysical amnesia." We have forgotten we are one with God and we have infinite potential at our fingertips.[27]

Facilitators

Knowledge, or *gnosis*, is the key to being awakened from our ignorance of divinity. The slumbering "Higher Self" can be roused. Creation and humanity can be "elevated" to divine status through personal transformation. Practices conducive to transformative experiences include meditation, Yoga, chanting, mood-altering music, systems of religious mysticism and knowledge, guided imagery, body disciplines, hypnosis, contemporary psychotherapies, and seminars designed to obliterate former values and inculcate a New Age mind-set.

New Age self-help books agree on several principles for living that form a New Age mind-set conducive for the achievement of a higher consciousness.[28]

Allow your false ego to dissolve and realize you are one with God and all things.[29]
Guilt, poor self-image, denial and fear all stem from the perception of being separate.
What was done can be undone.
We choose what to create out of our lives.
We must accept responsibility for what we create.
We attract situations to mirror what we need to see.
There are often surprises, but never any accidents.
We receive according to our readiness.
Adversity always has a potential "up" side.
We have to decide, and then clearly ask for, what we want.
Access love by letting go of fear.
Give and receive love as unconditionally as you can.
Trust your own feelings and intuitions.[30]

Lifeform

James Redfield's *The Celestine Prophecy* and Wayne Dyer's *Manifest Your Destiny* are two of the most popular New Age books written in the past five years. They have been widely read by people who do not label themselves as New Agers. They summarize key concepts of the New Age as they impact daily living and are thereby representative of a wide spectrum of New Age self-help literature. Interestingly, they each present nine principles of New Age living, but via different genres. Redfield offers readers a fictitious adventure narrative, while Dyer presents a straightforward listing with commentary. Viewed together, they offer an apologetic to readers to adopt the New Age version of the good life for the benefit of both individuals and the planet.

The New Ager's goal is to be a power-filled, self-realized individual. Such people stand poised to enact a "benign conspiracy for a new human agenda on a large scale."[31] Expanded personal awareness leads to planetary transformation, mass enlightenment, and social evolution. This is the theme of James' Redfield's *The Celestine Prophecy: An Adventure.* Setting aside competitive models of relating to others and following our inward intuitions multiplies the synchronicities that happen in daily life, leading us to participate in harmonic convergence.[32]

Key Text: *The Celestine Prophecy*

James Redfield introduces his work in this way,

> "For half a century now, a new consciousness has been entering the human world, a new awareness that can only be called transcendent, spiritual...It begins with a heightened perception of the way our lives move forward. We notice those chance events that occur at just the right moment, and bring forth just the right individuals, to suddenly send our lives in a new and important direction...We know that life is really about a spiritual unfolding that is personal and enchanting—an unfolding that no science or philosophy or religion has yet fully clarified...we know that once we do understand...how to engage this allusive (sic) process and maximize its occurrence in our lives, human society will take a quantum leap into a whole new way of life—one that realizes the

best of our tradition—and creates a culture that has been the goal
of history all along.[33]

Redfield then proceeds to recount, in first person, a fictitious
adventure narrative. It follows the journey of an unnamed narrator through the wilds of Peru searching for an ancient manuscript
written in Aramaic that dates from 600 BC. "The Manuscript," as
the story goes, recently discovered by Peruvian monks, predicts a
massive transformation in human society to begin in the 1960s and
to be achieved when a critical mass of people live by its "Nine
Insights" sometime in the early years of the twenty-first century. So
threatening are these insights to organized religion and political
systems that they are engaged in a conspiracy to suppress the
Manuscript.

The Celestine Prophecy chronicles the narrator's encounters with
proponents and opponents of the Manuscript as he travels through
Peru, and gradually accumulates all Nine Insights, truths about life
that ought to shape our actions, from the reports of its proponents.
He gathers this information in what at first seems to be a haphaz-
ard way, by chance meetings and overheard conversations.

The first insight is that serendipitous coincidences are happening
more and more frequently . . . and they strike us as beyond what
would be expected by pure chance.

The second insight is a respect for the spiritual component of
existence at this time in our history.

The third insight is that the universe responds to how we think
and to our expectations. Our expectation itself causes our energy to
flow into the world and affect other energy systems.

The fourth insight is that we tend to steal energy from others by
controlling them and trying to take over their minds.

The fifth insight is that the universe can provide all the energy
we need if we only open up to it and rely on it.

The sixth insight is that each of us has a purpose that will reveal
itself through our inward, intuitive guidance, and if we follow it,
we will find happiness and fulfillment.[34]

The seventh insight is that dreams hold guidance for our lives
and can be interpreted by comparing them to the story of our
lives.[35]

The eighth insight applies the third insight to our human relationships. It says that when we appreciate the shape and demeanor of a person, we send them energy as well as fill ourselves with energy,[36] and everyone who crosses our path has a message for us. When we have a question, people show up who have the answer. If we are attentive to chance encounters and sudden, spontaneous eye contact, we will be led to energy-enhancing encounters with others.[37]

The ninth insight describes a utopian human existence that is being shaped as more and more people discover and follow the first eight insights. Humans will control their population, respect the environment, curb their consumption, be attentive to intuition, and slow down the pace of life. As a result we will more deliberately savor meaningful interpersonal encounters that increase the energy flow and guide us in positive directions.[38]

Matter is always evolving into a higher state of vibration. The Ninth Insight says that as we humans continue to increase our vibration, whole groups of people will suddenly become invisible to those who are still vibrating at a lower level. While the people on this lower level will assume that the others just disappeared, the groups themselves will feel as though they are still right here, only lighter.

This phenomenon will signal that humankind is crossing the barrier between this life and the other world from which we came before birth and to which we go after death. This is the path laid out for us by Christ. In his lifetime he opened up to the energy until he was so light he could walk on water. In his death and Resurrection he was the first to cross over, to expand the physical world into the spiritual. "His life demonstrated how to do this, and if we connect with the same source, we can head the same way, step by step. At some point everyone will vibrate highly enough so that we can walk into heaven, in our same form."[39]

Christians take issue with many aspects of Redfield's thought. Among them are his identification of our human problem as one of ignorance, his utopian vision of the future, and his assertion that we can walk the same path that Christ walked. Still, a life formed by adherence to Redfield's brand of New Age wisdom would have some positive features. It would be one in which we trusted encounters with others and were attentive to them. It would be a life in which we respected the dignity of nature and other people. Living by Redfield's insights, we would use our thought power to project positive mental energy onto others and stop energy-robbing encounters with them. We would get into the habit of "willing good outcomes through our minds." Our projection of positive energy would attract positive energy into our lives.

Key Text: *Manifest Your Destiny*

New Age author and speaker Wayne Dyer's book *Manifest Your Destiny* is a classic exposition of a key belief of New Age self-help religion: that we create our own reality by creative visualization of desired outcomes.[40] At the outset, Dyer encourages readers to renounce two traditional notions, that God is separate from humankind and that human nature is inherently unworthy of God's regard. Like Redfield, Dyer organizes his ideas in the form of nine insights. The first is this: within us, in our unseen mind, is a divine capacity to become manifesters: to manage the circumstances of our lives to manifest and attract all that we need or desire.[41]

The second insight is that we need to trust ourselves, which is the same as trusting the wisdom that created us. God is an unseen, loving, and accepting power at the heart of everything, allowing us to make our own choices. God is a trusted part of our nature. At our basic core we are not only worthy of trust, but we are the life force that exists everywhere. Everything that we perceive as missing in our lives is a part of the same energy that we are. What we wish to receive is already a part of us.[42]

Says Dyer,

> "In a sense it is like thinking of the things you want as being on a string that is infinitely long, but is nevertheless attached to you in some invisible way. It is only a matter of trusting that you can bring that string to you and that whatever is supposed to come to your life will be there when you have developed the capacity to receive it. But the trick is, you cannot receive it or even come close to manifesting it if you have an absence of trust in yourself as an extension of God. I like to think of God as the ocean and myself as a glass. If I dip the glass into the ocean, I will have a glass full of God."[43]

Prayer, according to Dyer, is inviting divine desire to express itself through us. Our prayers need to be for humane and positive outcomes. Our prayers ought to be for results that contribute to ours and others' highest good. Such prayer opens us to an experience of oneness with divine energy and brings us to a state of peace.[44]

Dyer's third principle emphasizes our oneness with our environment. Dyer criticizes the assumption, with which most of us have been raised—that we are separate from our environment and that our role is to dominate our environment. He wants his readers to sense their connection to their environment, one of mutual cooperation. Once we do, we can realize our ability to draw what we want from it, even as our actions respect and protect it. His motto is "You are not an organism in an environment: You are an environorganism."[45]

His fourth principle is that we can attract to ourselves what we desire. We can use universal energy to bring to us objects of our desire, because the same energy that is in what we desire is also in us and vice versa.[46] Dyer suggests that we recognize that the power even to have a thought is a divine power. With this recognition of its sacredness, we are to form a vision or mental picture. Then we are to hold it lovingly in place with the inner knowledge that the God force that brought everything in the universe into existence also created us. The form that this energy will take will be controlled and directed by your will or your mental pictures. It is waiting to take any direction that you decide.[47] It is something to be nurtured in private and not communicated to others. Revealing your desires to others diffuses the energy of attraction.

The fifth principle is to honor our worthiness to receive. We need to affirm that we are worthy of abundance. Says Dyer, "Thinking that abundance is incompatible with spirituality is a myth that influences many of us and is the largest impediment there is to feeling worthy."[48] "Abundance is the way of creative force in the universe. You are entitled to have abundance in your life, and to radiate prosperity to all that you encounter in your world. Nothing is gained by making yourself small and insignificant other than to manifest smallness and insignificance in your life."[49]

Dyer recommends that we cultivate a knowledge of our worthiness at the cellular level of our being by affirming the following insights: Our self-esteem comes from within rather than from others. We need to replace self-repudiation with self-acceptance and to take full responsibility for the circumstances of our lives.[50] We need to reject guilt in our lives and to embrace the ideal of harmony among our thoughts, feelings, and behaviors.[51]

The sixth principle is to connect to the divine source with unconditional love. Unless we are living the way of unconditional love, eschewing judgmental thoughts and focusing on peace and love, we interfere with our ability to manifest positive outcomes in our lives. We are to pour love into our immediate environment, loving the spirit of others who are unloving, and practicing gentleness in all of our thoughts, words, and actions.[52] It is with unconditional love that we find our true connection to the divine energy that is in all things.[53]

The seventh principle is to meditate using sounds, focusing not on the outcome but on the feelings we are experiencing as we picture our desire manifesting.

The eighth insight is patiently to detach from the outcome, realizing that the manner of how and when what is desired shows up is something we must not try to control. Manifesting is not about making demands of God and the universe. Rather, it is a cooperative venture in which our intention is aligned with the divine intelligence that is in all things and in us at the same time. We are not separate from that which we would like to manifest. Demanding how's and when's from God reinforces the fallacy that God is a separate energy.[54] Placing our trust in our connection with a universal, all-providing intelligence allows us the virtue of patience. Dyer quotes a line from *A Course in Miracles*. "Those who are certain of the outcome can afford to wait, and without anxiety."[55]

The ninth insight is to react to our manifestations with gratitude and generosity. Says Dyer, "The nature of gratitude is the complete and full response of the human heart to everything in the universe." Such gratitude appreciates the energy flowing through all things, and brings us the fulfillment of our desires. Such gratitude recognizes that this fulfillment is not to be taken for granted. It is "a thank you to the God force that is in all things...It recognizes that the spirit within ourselves is the same as that which sustains all life on the planet."[56]

Dyer's depiction of a life well-lived is based on unleashing the power of creative visualization. He does Christians a favor by reminding us of this powerful dynamic acknowledged by prophets in their hopeful end-time visions and by Jesus in his insistence that inward thoughts eventually become actions.[57] Dyer, to his credit, encourages readers to ground their use of this power in unconditional love. But his equation of the human creative impulse with the divine opens the way for the abuse of the dynamic of creative visualization. He encourages us to claim our worthiness to receive abundance. This connection of abundance and worthiness is troubling. It implies that, if we do not receive abundance, it is because we have not visualized it vividly enough. There is no admission that life is unpredictable and beyond our control. Dyer encourages us to take full responsibility for our actions. What recourse do we have when life throws us a curve and, despite our admirable actions and vivid visualizations, we end up embarrassed, rejected, disappointed, and bereft?

The Appeal of New Age Wisdom

The New Age movement has given rise to reactions from many Christian bodies. Evangelical and fundamentalist responses to the New Age movement have generally rejected the New Age as an anti-Christian movement.[58] Mainline Protestant responses have largely been more balanced, pointing out the strengths and weaknesses of the movement, comparing its teachings with major Christian doctrines and hinting that not all New Age beliefs and practices deserve to be condemned.[59] Some Roman Catholic interpretations of New Age, those based on an exclusive approach to non-Christian religions, are critical and suspicious of the movement. Others are based on the more inclusive approach sanctioned by the Second Vatican Council and the work of the Pontifical Council for Interreligious Dialogue. These have been willing to note similarities between New Age and Catholic worldviews and to find in New Age some trends that might be beneficial to the spiritual life of Christians.[60]

It would be easy for us preachers to caricature the New Age movement by highlighting its more eccentric features. We could use our pulpits to talk dismissively about channeling, Tarot cards, astrology, and the purported healing qualities of crystals. We could raise a disdainful eyebrow about past-life regression therapy, the purported existence of attached entities, extraterrestrials and angelic helpers from "the Other Side." But we will be more help to our people if we can understand and articulate the appeal of New Age religion. Then we can bring the insights of biblical wisdom into dialogue with New Age themes and suggest points of similarity and difference.

The key themes of New Age religion have a positive appeal. New Age religion affirms the goodness of nature and our need to respect the natural world, approaching it with an attitude of collaboration rather than domination. New Age religion affirms the essential goodness and worthiness of the human being. Through its interpretation of reincarnation and karma, New Age religion provides a clear explanation for what looks like unjust suffering.

It is hopeful about the future of the human race on this planet, holding out a vision of imminent personal and planetary harmony. It is refreshingly specific about what we as individuals can do to enhance that future. It drafts a blueprint for a mental outlook that contributes to personal and planetary transformation. It specifies a number of spiritual practices that are assured pathways to this transformation.

New Age religion emphasizes individuals' responsibility for their thoughts and actions and their resultant outcomes. It insists that individuals have the ability to take control of their lives and to attain their desires by repeated, meditative visualization of positive outcomes.

It offers a vision of continuity between this world and a spiritual realm where those who have "crossed over" try to assist those still on the earthly plane.

Biblical Wisdom Responds

We preachers can affirm the New Age movement for aspiring to a peaceful, planet-friendly way of life that offers concrete spiritual disciplines that promise to unleash human potential. At the same time, we must assert that biblical wisdom yields insights that are radically different from those of New Age religion and that need to be preached in contemporary pulpits.

The New Age View of God

The New Age view of God is radically different from that of the biblical wisdom of the Hebrew Scriptures. New Age religion denies two of biblical wisdom's key insights into the nature of God: God's transcendence and inscrutability. Biblical wisdom advocates a posture of radical, humble reverence before the otherness of God. New Age religion views the human soul as the spark of God on a journey to reabsorption. God is the ocean and we are the glass. God is ever-evolving, dependent on our human response, enriched by our efforts at reunification. In effect, the self is God for many New Agers. New Age wisdom can legitimately be classified as a form of self-help wisdom, for its monism blurs the distinction between human and divine, Creator and creation, both the human and natural worlds.

This can at times leave New Age religion open to the charge of subjectivity. New Agers like to say "If you truly believe it, it's true for you." There is often the unstated meaning that if something is true for you, then it is as true as it needs to be. Evidence and other beliefs and even criticisms do not need to be taken into account.

The New Age View of Suffering

The New Age handling of the existence of suffering is vastly different from that of biblical wisdom's witness. Biblical wisdom maintains the mystery of suffering in the context of the freedom of the human will and the sovereignty of God. Both testaments witness to the fact that suffering is not a punishment by God, and in the crucifixion and resurrection, God assures us that God is present with us in our sufferings. We are assured that suffering and tragedy will not have the last word on our life with God.

New Agers attribute what looks like unjust suffering to the web of reincarnation and karma and their way of working themselves out in the human community. One message of Job is that unjust suffering is beyond our narrow human categories of cause and effect. But New Agers disagree. They attribute it to the universal cosmic law of cause and effect at work. There are no exceptions to this law. There are no accidents. This is not, as it was for the Reformers, a statement meant to express the all-encompassing sovereignty of God. Rather, it is a statement about the power of human choices in the outworking of human karma.[61]

A New Ager would probably say that Job brought his sufferings on himself so he could accumulate a needed life lesson in service of his karma. But the biblical lesson he learned would never find its way into a New Age primer as one of "nine principles for living." It is that we need to remember our place: that we are human and not God. It is that human constructs are inadequate to contain or explain the complexity of a mysterious life.

My mother had the bad fortune last year to trip and fall in a ditch while hiking. She broke one ankle and sprained the other. As she lay recuperating, a friend visited her with what my mother described as "a vase filled with daisies and a crock full of advice." "I hate to see you in pain, but remember, Bev, there are no accidents!" My mother kept the flowers and pitched the advice.

I attended a New Age church a few months ago. The speaker was a workshop leader from England. His theme was "You draw all happenings to yourself." "If I treat you rudely and you can't understand my actions, it is because you need the lesson that offense produced." I sat in disbelief, my mind spinning objections, then looked around trying to catch someone's eye. They were all listening raptly. I had to restrain myself from leaping to my feet and shouting out something, and it wouldn't have been "Amen."

The New Age View of Evil and Tragedy

New Age religion tends to underestimate the force of evil, and the existence of tragedy in human life. While many Christians continue to blame God for tragedy and evil, biblical wisdom literature discourages this connection. We are encouraged to face tragic events, and, with God's presence to strengthen us, to experience through them a redemptive lesson that could come in no other way. Christ set an example for us by voluntarily choosing to bear the consequences of his life of subversive wisdom. The resurrection confirms God's partnership with Jesus in having the last word on evil and tragedy.

For most New Agers, tragedy and evil are the consequences of unhealthy human thoughts or the outworking of karmic blueprints. We create our illness, and we attract events we need to experience in order to learn the lessons that will advance our karma.

Negative events have an upside that we need to find quickly so the soul can move to the next level. Through disciplined meditation and visualization of our true desires, we can largely factor them out of our lives.

The New Age Denial of Human Limitation

New Age religion denies human limitation. We are one with God, and we can use our thoughts to attain any desirable outcome we choose. We are limited neither by our faculties nor our circumstances. For Christianity, especially as it is nourished by biblical wisdom literature, human limitation is a crucial recognition. Cause and effect is not an overarching, no-exceptions, cosmic principle. It is a human construct that is shown to be inadequate in the face of a mysterious God and a complex life.

New Age religion's denial of human limits may well reflect its social roots. Its obliviousness to limiting circumstances has a decidedly middle class tinge to it, and it may have a hint of wishful thinking as well. It seems likely that one contributor to the popularity of New Age religion is the feeling among many middle class people that they have lost influence and power. Hence the New Age stresses that human beings can control their own destinies.

The wisdom literature of the Bible frees us Christian preachers to admit that we cannot control our own destinies. Many of our cultures define power as the ability to order our lives and those of others by the strength of our individual will. Our Christian understanding of power, nourished by the Bible's wisdom literature, is very different. It involves acknowledging the reality of our powerlessness in the face of life's unpredictable events and our own inward chaos, and placing our lives and futures in the hands of God who has promised never to abandon us. Our power comes in acknowledging the limitations of our humanity and letting God be God.

The New Age View That We Create
Our Own Reality

Jesus acknowledged the power of thoughts to manifest themselves in outward life when he warned his followers that evil thoughts are tantamount to evil actions. He affirmed that to those who have, more will be given. New Age self-help repeatedly insists that thoughts are things, that we create our own reality and that we need to learn to attract our heart's desire to us by meditation and visualization.

"You'll see it when you believe it," goes the New Age proverb. There is enough truth in this principle to open it to good use and to misuse. New Agers throughout the late 1980s and early 1990s held gatherings to visualize world peace. The Hebrew prophets pictured worshippers streaming into the restored temple and banquets in which God gathered all the outcasts to a feast. John of Patmos pictured a heavenly Jerusalem where tears had all been dried. When I am in a writing slump, I visualize a shiny book jacket. It motivates me to get back to it. Whether it sets in motion some more universal force, I am not qualified to say.

We preachers need to think and preach about this dynamic of creative visualization. Repeated visualization of our heart's desire brings it into our lives by a law of universal attraction, say the self-help and New Age gurus. While I would question that sweeping assumption, it seems reasonable that regularly anticipating positive outcomes trains our behavior in ways conducive to accomplishing desired goals.

We preachers can sever the creative visualization dynamic from self-serving goals. We can set it in the context of faith in things unseen, in the vocation of imagining a world that is pleasing to God. There it fuels faithful imagining of the world as God would have it be. The wisdom literature invites us to see ourselves as trees planted by streams of water (Psalm 1), as guests at Wisdom's banquet, and as members of Wisdom's household, cared for and nurtured by her (Proverbs 31).

The prophets modeled the dynamic of creative visualization as they repeatedly painted word pictures of a future world. Often they invite us to imagine a blessed end-time scenario in which food is abundant, all people eat together joyfully and nature joins in testifying to the reign of justice and joy (Isaiah 55). Jesus lived out this banquet in his meal fellowship with society's outcasts and invited us to picture it in several of his parables.

New Age Individualism

The New Ager's emphasis on community encompasses this world and other worlds, past and future. We came from an undifferentiated group of souls, and are surrounded by invisible multi-dimensional helpers, available to help us for the asking. Our goal is reabsorption into God once again. Ironically this emphasis on the oneness of all things does not always translate into a focus on a present-day local community. Much New Age self-help writing focuses on the individual's attainment of desired goals. It tends to view God as immanent and at the service of our heart's desire. The sense of awe conveyed by the biblical notion of "fear of the Lord" is lacking. There is little acknowledgment of the presence of the tragic, chaos, and injustice in life. For the most part, a social message is underdeveloped.

Not all New Age self-help literature lacks a sense of social responsibility, and profiles of New Agers do not fit the socially insensitive stereotype. Subscribers to the periodical *New Age* are four times likelier to be politically active than the average citizen.[62] *New Age Journal* regularly runs major articles on social issues, as do other magazines and newsletters in the genre. Many people who attend New Age workshops also volunteer in homeless shelters or AIDS clinics and write checks to the Sierra Club.[63]

There is a strand of New Age self-help that clearly ties self-healing to the healing of the planet. New Age author Shakti Gawain challenges readers to view their social world as a mirror of their inward lives.

> "If we have the courage to look at the social and political forces in the world as reflections of the forces at work within each of us, we can more effectively take responsibility not only for our own personal healing, but for the healing of the planet.... On the path of transformation we are concerned with not only our own personal process of healing and integration, but with the healing process going on in our world. We recognize the interrelationship between our individual consciousness journey and the evolution of the consciousness of humanity."[64]

What Christian Preaching Can Learn from the Appeal of New Age Religion

The self-help wisdom we have explored are responses to our human fear that we are not in control. Biblical wisdom has the depth to admit that this is a perfectly legitimate fear. Biblical wisdom suggests that our acknowledging the fact that we are not in control could turn out to be our salvation.

Personality wisdom promises us that we can gain control if we assert the strength of our individual will. Character wisdom, with more concern for the communal good, assures us that if we act with integrity we can build a life of satisfying achievements and relationships. New Age wisdom promises us that God is fully on board with the well-intentioned desires of the human heart. More than that, God is in us and we are God. As a result, we can attract the outcomes we desire into our lives by creative visualization.

Taken whole-cloth, these varieties of self-help wisdom exalt a trinity of virtues for living. The first is the strength of will necessary to decide what we want and to pursue it against all obstacles. The second is confidence in our own worthiness to receive abundance. The third is confidence that God's will is indistinguishable from our own good intentions.

Such "wisdom" is not equipped to address human anxiety in the face of life's unpredictability and death's inevitability. It is not equipped to energize us to alleviate the sufferings of others and to acknowledge that they often have a systemic cause to which we ourselves contribute. Such "wisdom" is not equipped to heal the conviction, lodged deep within many of us, that we are not worthy of abundance, that we are not even worthy of love, whether divine or human. Such "wisdom" is not equipped to address the human problem of sin, so much more complex, systemic, and pernicious than mere ignorance.

We preachers need to preach themes of our Christian tradition that are the counterparts of popular New Age themes. We need to preach about the goodness of nature and our responsibility to respect the natural world as stewards of God's good creation. We need to preach on the sacred worth of human beings made in the image of God, body, mind and spirit.

We need to address the phenomenon of unjust suffering, acknowledging the uncertainty of life lived within the certainty of a loving God. We need to preach about the hope we have in Christ for the redemption of the world, a hope that is both already present and yet to come. We need to preach about spiritual disciplines as means of nourishing our relationship with God through

Christ by the power of the Holy Spirit. We need to preach about the connection between personal and social holiness. We need to preach about the communion of the saints, what the book of Hebrews refers to as a "cloud of witnesses" (Hebrews 12:1). This is a communion of holy persons who have lived and died and still live on.

When we recite the Apostles' Creed we state that we believe in the communion of saints, but we Protestants have largely defaulted on preaching this theme. Historically this phrase has had three referents: it can refer to the bond of solidarity between Christians as members of the church and as those partaking in the Holy Sacraments. It can also refer to a communion of holy persons. In the ancient and medieval church this phrase the communion of the saints was taken to refer to communion with the departed saints whose merits were seen as grounding our hope of salvation.

However, the term communion of the saints does not necessarily mean their veneration. We need to preach an inclusive vision of the church as a fellowship both of those present and of those who have gone before. In our fast-paced, ephemeral Western society, it is crucial that we take the communion of the saints seriously, that we reflect on the heritage of the past and engage with the contributions of those who have gone before us. A spiritualist sense of establishing contact with the dead is not in keeping with our biblical witness. But we can attend to those who have gone before with prayers of gratitude and pledges to continue working for the justice that was denied so many of them.[65]

Preaching to the Heart, Not Just the Head

New Age religion challenges us to evaluate our sermonic God-talk. Are our sermons heady and conceptual, time spent talking about God in abstract and generalized terms? New Age religion is often charged with emphasizing intuition at the expense of rationality. Protestant preaching has the opposite failing. It has often tended to be heady and conceptual. The new homiletic with its honoring of emotional logic, metaphor, and story has taken steps toward putting the heart back into Protestant preaching.

Preaching About Spiritual Formation

Do we pay sufficient attention in our preaching to themes of spiritual formation in the Christian life? New Age spirituality is full of specific prescriptions for the use of our thoughts and the management of our emotions. The practicality and specificity of these recommendations are appealing to people trying to form new habits and make the most of their lives. The understanding that salvation affects the whole person in body and soul is a valuable insight for the Christian pulpit.[66]

Many people assume that if they want to learn practices of contemplation, they need to look East. In reality, Christianity has a rich tradition of spiritual disciplines and modes of prayer. An interest in Ignatian spirituality and the Rule of Life of the Benedictine order is blossoming among Protestants as well as Roman Catholics.[67]

Roman Catholic, Protestant, and Eastern Orthodox forms of Christianity offer a cornucopia of disciplines for the spiritual life. These include examination of conscience, meditation, intercessory prayer, spiritual direction, praying with icons, and spiritual reading of Scripture.[68]

The New Age challenges Christian preachers to teach and preach the insights of world religions with a respectful spirit, offering their congregations valuable guidance from other spiritual traditions while affirming the uniqueness of our Christian faith-claims. For example, meditative practices and Christianized forms of yoga and mantra chanting can be quite helpful to Christians, encouraging us to return to the sources of our own rich tradition. Failure to preach about other religions can lead either to their unthinking rejection or the uncritical assumption of beliefs and practices that are contrary to our Christian faith.

One Christian commentator, Vivienne Hull, summarizes four major strengths of the New Age movement from which Christians can benefit.

1. The stress on the renewal of one's spiritual life

2. The affirmation of the sacramentality of the natural world

3. The profession of the value, uniqueness, and integrity of the individual person

4. The understanding of the power of a positive vision, of hope, and love to motivate human beings to be of service to the world.[69]

In the chapters that follow, we will explore biblical wisdom's insights into these themes and their rich harvest for preaching to contemporary people.

CHAPTER FIVE

A Biblical Character Ethic: Wisdom from the Book of Proverbs

"The fear of the Lord is the beginning of knowledge."
(Proverbs 1:7a)

Every couple of years I teach a course entitled "Preaching Biblical Wisdom Literature." My opening question is "When was the last time you preached from the book of Proverbs?" There is often an awkward silence, and then someone will say "Never." And then everyone laughs. A little uncomfortably.

Then comes my second question: "Why do you think many preachers avoid the book of Proverbs?" Through the years, the answers have revolved around three issues: literary form, literary context, and historical context.

"How can I make a sermon out of a one-liner?" is a question preachers often ask about the brief sayings that make up much of the book of Proverbs. The proverb is short by definition, and not every preacher believes this makes it sweet!

The Hebrew word *mashal*, used to refer to a "proverb," is an umbrella term for several genres of wisdom that share the qualities of vividness, connection to daily life, and the ability to evoke ethical reflection. In addition to proverbs, they include admonitions (Proverbs 3:1; 22:22), numerical analogies (Proverbs 30:18-31), and wisdom poems (Proverbs 1:20-33; 8:22-36; 9:1-16; 31:10-31).

The proverb, a wisdom sentence based on observation of experience, is the most common form of *mashal* in the Hebrew Bible.[1] For example, "A soft answer turns away wrath, but a harsh word stirs up anger" (Proverbs 15:1).

Parables, short narrative fictions that illuminate contemporary situations, are also part of the *mashal* family. Their origins can be seen in Ezekiel's story of the eagle (Ezekiel 17:3-10) and Nathan's allegorical warning to David (2 Samuel 12:1-6). Parables become more common in rabbinic exegesis near the end of the first century. They are used to interpret passages of Torah and as explications of traditional practices. Jesus' parables point to the reality of the inbreaking kingdom of God and heighten the tension between its norms and traditional expectations. They are often subversive of traditional interpretations of scripture and ritual practice. They leave the precise application to the mind of the listener.[2]

The word *mashal* has a dual reference: it can connote "to set next to" (to compare) or "to rule."[3] This dual reference describes what proverbs do. They set something we know well next to something that needs illumination. "Like clouds and wind without rain, so is a gift boasted of but never given" (Proverbs 25:14). Proverbs hold out ethical guidance in the complex scenarios of daily life and thereby "rule over" other interpretations. In conversation, public address, and written prose they convey traditional wisdom from one generation to the next.

Not only do proverbs offer specific ethical guidance, they also sum up aspects of our culture's worldviews. "Time is money." "Don't get mad, get even." "Different strokes for different folks." "The sky's the limit." "It's no sin to be rich." "If you need a helping hand, look on the end of your arm." Proverbs both reflect and shape how we experience our world. "The grass is always greener on the other side." "Money talks." "There's more where that came from." These proverbs convey worlds about American discontent, our tendency to reduce everything to its monetary value, and our belief in limitless abundance.[4]

The proverbial form can also be employed to express ethical convictions that challenge our cherished cultural assumptions. "What will it profit them to gain the whole world and forfeit their life?" (Mark 8:36=Matthew 16:26=Luke 9:25). "Why do you see the speck in your neighbor's eye, but do not notice the log in your own eye?" (Matthew 7:3=Luke 6:41).

Proverbs can subvert as well as instill traditional values. "Life is short; play hard" is subverted by "Life is short; pray hard." "Seeing is believing" is subverted by "Believing is seeing." "Wisdom excels folly as light excels darkness" (Ecclesiastes 2:13) is subverted by "Dead flies make the perfumer's ointment give off a foul odor. So a little folly outweighs wisdom and honor" (Ecclesiastes 10:1). "The highway of the upright avoids evil; those who guard their way preserve their lives"(Proverbs 16:17) is subverted by "For those who want to save their life will lose it, and those who lose their life for may sake, and for the sake of the gospel, will save it" (Mark 8:35=Luke 9:24; 17:33=Matthew 10:39).

The proverb's brevity and self-containment are virtues for preaching rather than vices. These qualities are meant to evoke congregational reflection, not reduce it to a one-liner.

Proverbs as Freeze-Dried Narratives: Add Your Life Stories and Stir!

Proverbs can be thought of as freeze-dried narratives, condensations of experiences we add to our own to create a nutritious blend for wise living. The proverb in a literary collection like the book of Proverbs is like a school bus or a tour bus parked in a lot with other buses. They await a driver to get them out on the roads, picking people up, showing people the sights. Proverbs' call to preachers is "Get on the bus!" Get the proverbs out of the lot and out on the roads doing what they were meant to do.

The task of the preacher as sage is to give the proverb to the people as a wisdom tool and send them back out on their daily rounds seeking to discern situations with which this proverb, in their best wisdom, is an apt fit. Sermons on proverbs can take many forms and can include contemporary as well as biblical proverbs. At times contemporary proverbs support biblical wisdom. "If you want to have a friend, you have to be a friend." Or, to quote the Beatles, "Money can't buy me love." At other times, biblical wisdom contradicts our most cherished secular assumptions about life. "The one who has the most toys when he dies, wins!" is contradicted by "What will it profit them if they gain the whole world but forfeit their life?" (Matthew 16:26).

"Don't get mad, get even!" is contradicted by "Love your enemies, do good to those who hate you" (Luke 6:27). A proverbial sermon can focus on a single proverb; it can draw on several proverbs that are related by a single theme; or it can juxtapose two proverbs that appear to contradict one another.

The preacher can choose one proverb that epitomizes a wisdom theme and use it as a spotlight to train across the landscape of life, searching for scenarios that its particular wisdom illuminates.

A sermon drawing on proverbs can also take up a theme and appeal to a number of other proverbs as it develops that theme. This form is sometimes referred to as the "string of beads" form. It was a favorite of the rabbis in their teaching and preaching.[5] Clearly Jesus learned well from the homiletic of Judaism! The contemporary preacher can use the "string of beads" form with good effect to convey a number of the varied themes of biblical wisdom.

They include, among others: the futility of riches; the importance of choosing wise companions; the identity and benefits of wisdom; how to be one's own best friend; how to exercise self-control in speech and sexual matters; and how to live an industrious, reputable life, relating to others with integrity and showing concern for the social health of one's community.

Yet another sermonic form is what I have elsewhere called "dueling proverbs," where the preacher juxtaposes two proverbs that embody opposing worldviews. The preacher can quote a biblical proverb and set a contemporary proverb next to it that challenges it.[6]

Another engaging sermon option is to juxtapose two biblical proverbs that appear to contradict each other, aggravate the tension, then show that they are not universal truths in fierce competition for the job of governing our total lives. Rather, they are partial generalizations that, in differing circumstances, could each be illuminating. For example, a proverb about the advisability of placating speech (Proverbs 15:1) might be juxtaposed with a proverb about the importance of both giving and receiving correction in the form of a spoken rebuke (Proverbs 10:10; 25:12). The preacher challenges the congregation to seek divine wisdom for daily living in determining when to placate by soft speech and when to take a stand.

With all these options for shaping sermons on proverbs, the excuse "I can't make a sermon out of one-liner" loses its force.

Background Check

The Literary Context for Preaching Proverbs

Most of us remember the nursery school song "The Farmer in the Dell." It consists of nine verses. In the first eight, the farmer takes a wife, the wife takes a child, the child takes a nurse, the nurse takes the cow, the cow takes the dog, the dog takes the cat, the cat takes the rat, and the rat takes the cheese.

The concluding verse, verse nine, goes like this

"The cheese stands alone.
The cheese stands alone.
High-ho the derry-o, the cheese stands alone."

In nursery school, when we got to that verse, somebody had to leave the outer circle and stand in the middle all alone while everyone else circled around singing at the poor cheese that no body wanted.

Several years ago, when my younger daughter was in preschool, I noticed tear smudges reddening her face when I picked her up one afternoon. "What's wrong, honey?" I asked. "They sang that farmer song and they made me be the cheese!" she sobbed.

We preachers have sung "The Proverb stands alone" for years. Who chooses a text from Proverbs to preach on? The lectionary doesn't choose them much. We tend to leave the book of Proverbs on the shelf, leaving it alone while we attend to other parts of the canon. We have also assumed that the individual proverbs within the book stand alone, lacking a context. We have assumed that individual sayings lack both a literary context and a historical-social context within the book of Proverbs.

We have assumed that Proverbs is a hodgepodge of fortune cookies thrown in a bag. In reality, it is carefully constructed, intended to be read as the sayings of Woman Wisdom who appears in chapters 1, 8, 9, and 31. A prologue of nine chapters, most likely written sometime after the Exile, introduces the figure of Woman Wisdom and serves as the literary and theological context for several older proverbial collections that make up chapters 10-29. These chapters are attributed to Solomon and other sages. Like the opening nine chapters, chapter 31 also sings the praises of Woman Wisdom and is most likely a later addition to the book.[7]

Chapters 1-9 are a collection of sayings, instructions, didactic narratives, and poetic passages, whose title, "the proverbs of Solomon," also serves as title to the entire book of thirty-one chapters. Chapter 1:1-7 is a kind of course syllabus outlining the course objectives that will be achieved when one enrolls in wisdom's school of life. Wisdom's teachings reflect on the paradoxical nature of wisdom as both divine gift and human search. They command hearers to choose wisdom and her benefits over folly's seductive destruction (chapters 2, 3:1-20; 4, 5). They call readers to trust God and to be loyal to wisdom, accepting the discipline that is a crucial part of learning (Proverbs 3:5-11). These chapters warn readers about the dangers of evil companions (Proverbs 1:8-19), sexual infidelity (Proverbs 5:7f; 6:23-35; 7), and sloth (Proverbs 6:6f-11). They introduce a personification of wisdom as one who had an active role in creation (Proverbs 3:19-20; 8:22f) and who now stands at the crossroads of daily life, calling those who pass by to choose her path rather than the path of folly and death (Proverbs 1:20f; 8:1f). Chapter 31 is a poem in honor of a "woman of worth" or a "strong woman." At first glance, she seems to be the ideal earthly homemaker. We shall see how a closer look at her traits and job description tip us off as to her real identity.

Chapters 10-29 contain three other major sayings collections. Two of these collections are ascribed to Solomon (Proverbs 10:1–22:16; 25:1–29:27). A third (Proverbs 22:17-24:22) shows remarkable similarities to the Egyptian wisdom writing, *Instruction of Amenemope*, written around 1200 BCE. Among its Egyptian relatives, *Amenemope* is known as a particularly humble and contemplative work. Our Israelite author borrowed sayings that emphasize the protection of the poor (Proverbs 22:22-23; 23:10-11), the condemnation of unjust gain, and reservations about the value of wealth (Proverbs 23:4-5).[8] Another similarity between the two sayings collections is the contrast between the silent person and the "heated man" frequent in *Amenemope* and other Egyptian writings (Proverbs 29:22).[9]

The proverbs of chapters 10-15 often take the form of antithetical parallelism. They set two phrases side by side that depict opposing types of behavior, calling one foolish and the other wise. These sayings make sharp distinctions between the righteous and the wicked, the wise and the foolish, the rich and the poor, the diligent and the lazy. For example, "Whoever belittles another lacks sense, but an intelligent person remains silent"(Proverbs 11:12). Sermons based on these texts could begin by pointing out a common pattern of foolish behavior and elaborate on an alternative pattern based on living in response to divine wisdom. It could close by pointing hearers, including the preacher, to God's presence to help us choose wisely in future situations.

Sayings in chapters 16–22, while they contain some antithetical parallelism, are more often marked by synonymous parallelism, in which the second phrase specifies the content of the first. Sometimes these sayings describe foolish behavior. "A fool takes no pleasure in understanding, but only in expressing personal opinion" (Proverbs 18:2). "The highway of the upright avoids evil; those who guard their way preserve their lives" (Proverbs 16:17).[10] "One who is slow to anger is better than the mighty, and one whose temper is controlled than one who captures a city" (Proverbs 16:32). The themes of this section are the importance of the monarch, family stability, and trustworthy, appropriate speech.

The collection in chapters 25-29 may have been originally designed for the training of courtiers. Themes in this collection include social rank and conflict (Proverbs 25:2-27), wise approaches to dealing with fools and sluggards (Proverbs 26:1-16), and advice to a king as the "shepherd" of his people (Proverbs 27:23-27). [11]

The literary context of Proverbs is the interplay between two literary forms: personification and proverb. Personification is a rhetorical device that attributes personal qualities to impersonal things. It is a metaphorical operation that combines a literal subject with a metaphorical predicate, in this case a woman with the function of divine guidance for daily living. As it is used in Proverbs, it generalizes the particular qualities of wise men and women and draws them together into one wisdom figure who personifies an aspect of God's character and relationship to human beings. The rhetorical effect in Proverbs is that readers are assembled from their various walks of life into an audience to hear Woman Wisdom's summons: "Listen to me!"[12]

The function of her genre of choice, the proverb, is to send us back into our daily rounds, to put what we've been taught into action.[13] The interplay of literary genres in Proverbs invites the reader to experience the truth of the saying that "It takes wisdom to use wisdom!"

In self-help wisdom, we attain wisdom by following a list of rules about how we are to think and act. According to Proverbs, we attain wisdom by staying in touch with its source. Wisdom is more than following a set of rules, it is cultivating a lifelong human/divine relationship with a Person.

Employing categories articulated by wisdom scholar Leo G. Perdue, self-help wisdom is an ideology, a body of thought radically geared to the philosophy of self or group promotion. Biblical wisdom, by contrast, is a form of theology, in that it demands that the interests of transcendence take precedence over self-interest. Transcendence becomes a critical force as it challenges and corrects both self-interest and group interest.[14]

The Historical/Social Context for Preaching Proverbs

Some preachers avoid Proverbs because they think it lacks a historical/social context. While it is true that individual proverbs travel light, carrying little or no historical baggage with them, that is part of what makes them useful beyond the original situation(s) out of which they arose. For example, "An estate quickly acquired in the beginning will not be blessed in the end" (Proverbs 20:21). Well, whose estate? Just how quickly was it acquired and how? Where is it located on the map? Inquiring minds might want to know, but such specifics are beside Proverbs' point. They want us to apply them to our lives.

Proverbial wisdom is the wisdom of the people. It grows out of the daily lives of people of all levels of economics, all degrees of education, and all walks of life. References to kings and diplomacy (Proverbs 29:12), agricultural imagery (Proverbs 25:13), and parental instruction (Proverbs 3:1, 2), imply a variety of sages and settings in Israel's history. During the postexilic period sages collected, preserved, augmented, and arranged the sayings into the book of Proverbs.[15]

Its focus is on instructing the young in devotion to wisdom and pragmatic strategies for daily living that result in community harmony and stability. Proverbs contains no mention of Yahweh's covenant with Israel or the milestone events of salvation history: Exodus, Sinai, and the Davidic dynasty. The practical, communal focus of Israelite wisdom is remarkably similar to that of neighboring peoples like the Edomites, and has antecedents in much older cultures of Phoenicia, Egypt, and Mesopotamia.[16] Israelite wisdom was, in fact, part of an international, intercultural, and interreligous movement of thought whose beginnings can be traced to early times in Sumer and Egypt and was to affect both the New Testament and the Talmud.[17] The communal concerns of Israelite wisdom, in part influenced by the wisdom of her neighbors, is part of what distinguishes biblical wisdom from contemporary self-help wisdom with its focus on the individual.

Scholars have long debated the question of the social seedbed of Proverbs. Some have located proverbial wisdom during the reign of King Solomon, a figure connected as closely to wisdom as Moses is to the Pentateuch. According to this theory, proverbs were intended for training young diplomats at court, along the lines of its Egyptian antecedents. Other scholars emphasize the eloquence and artistry of many proverbs, especially those in the didactic poems of the first nine chapters. They insist that wisdom was taught more broadly in schools by a formal class of literate religious experts known as sages.[18] Pointing to the agricultural context and simple structure of many sayings, especially those in chapters 10-30, others have claimed for proverbs an early oral folk wisdom setting.[19]

Are proverbs from clan, school, or court? The answer is yes. Proverbs contains the wisdom of many centuries, from the folk wisdom of the preexilic period to the court wisdom of the monarchic period to the postexilic period with its familial setting, the period in which the collection probably achieved its final form.

The sayings of Proverbs were probably collected, collated, and paired with the figure of Personified Wisdom during the early Persian period (late sixth and fourth centuries BCE) of Israel's postexilic history.[20] This was a time of social chaos when people craved order. It was a time when the traditional male-run institutions of monarchy and temple were in shambles. The language of covenant and chosenness gives way to the more universal focus on God the

Creator's gift of wisdom and its authority in the realm of instruction of the young.[21]

It is no coincidence that a book arose that emphasized a particular aspect of God's character (wisdom) that was not reliant on cult or court for its legitimacy and functioning. Nor is it a coincidence that this aspect of the divine character was personified as a woman, a gender whose realm of influence had traditionally been the home, not the cult or the court.

A number of women scholars, among them Kathleen O'Connor, Claudia Camp, and Carole Fontaine, hold up Woman Wisdom as a positive metaphor for contemporary women seeking to gain confidence in their experience and to influence the public realm. At the same time, they and others recognize the patriarchal limitations of Woman Wisdom.[22] Her book contains misogynist proverbs. Her teachings are exclusively directed to young men. Woman is not only a metaphor for Wisdom, but also for folly, those forbidden desires that threaten family ties and weaken religious identity.[23]

Proverbs served as a kind of postexilic theological *Book of Virtues*, instructing youth in acquiring those qualities of character that result from devotion to God.[24] Its notions of God's character and ordering activity are certainly shaped by its social context. Two convictions prevent Proverbs' depiction of life and God from being mere reflections of the conservatism of its social setting. They are its respect for God's transcendence and its acknowledgment of the limitations of human wisdom. These are the twin seeds of its own subversion by the critical sages.

The ethnic, class, and gender biases of Proverbs are quite obvious.[25] Preachers need to have an awareness of the social origins of Proverbs' wisdom and how they have shaped its depiction of "how best to live." Mindful of God's transcendence and our own limited perspectives, we need to be open to the "critical sages" of that day (Job and Qohelet) and this one.

The Theological Context for Preaching Proverbs

Sayings in the book of Proverbs, then, have both a literary and a historical context. They also have a theological context rich with homiletical insights into the meaning and conduct of life.

Preaching on the theological context of the book of Proverbs reminds me of a *matryoshka,* those brightly painted, beautiful Russian dolls. One opens one of these hollow, wooden dolls only to find a slightly smaller doll inside, and a slightly smaller one inside that, and so on down to the smallest doll of all. So, too, is the theological context of Proverbs. Not only is it bright and beautiful, but it, too, has several increasingly specific layers of reflection.

The most general layer is reflection on the broad canonical context for preaching on Wisdom literature. Then comes reflection on the Wisdom literature as a context for preaching on the Proverbs. The next is the book's theological context, the three theological affirmations that thread through the book and stitch together its disparate parts.

The Canonical Context for Preaching Proverbs

A crucial component of a sermon on any text is theological reflection on the themes of a text as they are in dialogue with other voices in scripture.

Wisdom's themes and those of other biblical genres are interdependent. Examples abound, and what follows are just a few to prime the preacher's imagination. Wisdom's focus on insights for daily living needs apocalyptic's concern with a dramatic divine intervention that will result in judgment and vindication. The Wisdom literature emphasizes that daily life is the realm of our empirical appropriation of the gift of divine guidance. Wisdom's anonymous, ahistorical qualities need the grounding of the longer, connected narratives that undergird both the Pentateuchal and the Prophetic literature. Wisdom's proverbs, parables, and admonitions need the ballast of Israel's covenant history, its recounting of the saving acts of God's dealings with Israel. Parts of Proverbs remind readers that the path of wisdom is paved with respect for the poor. This insight needs the prophets' more direct insistence that the nation's treatment of the vulnerable in its midst is the litmus test of its faithfulness to God.

Apples of Gold in a Setting of Silver: Proverbs in the Family of Wisdom

The book of Proverbs reminds us that "a word fitly spoken is like apples of gold in a setting of silver"(Proverbs 25:11). The book offers the preacher a whole bowl full of gleaming golden apples to choose from.

Our congregations need sermons on Proverbs. Parents struggling to raise children in a competitive, acquisitive, violent, radically individualistic society need sermons on Proverbs. The young and the restless and the just plain restless need sermons on Proverbs. People of all ages facing turning points of decision and temptation need sermons on Proverbs. They need sermons that invite them onto the path of wisdom and into the presence of a God who alone can serve as a reliable guide to the twists and turns of life. They need sermons that proffer precepts for avoiding the foolish actions that bring unnecessary suffering on ourselves and others. They need sermons that hold out the promise of ordering our lives toward auspicious outcomes and community harmony and justice.

An acquisitive, consumer society needs sermons on Proverbs, with itsdepiction of a wisdom that involves respect for creation and moderation of human appetites. As Creator of humankind, God demands respect for the poor.[26]

Our sermons on Proverbs, with its energetic confidence in wisdom's competence to order human life, are apples of gold. But hurting people sit in the pews, and an apple a day does not keep the doctor away. What about the people who, like Job, bring a sense of having been betrayed by life or God with them to church? What about those who, like Job's friends, have fallen prey to the temptation of self-righteousness because things are going well for them? What about those who blame themselves for their illness, misfortune, or abuse at the hands of others? What about those who, like Qohelet, experience God as distant and joy as fleeting? What about those who seethe with outrage or sit cloaked in subdued resignation?

Our proverbial "apple a day" sermons need to be preached in a setting of silver provided by Job and Ecclesiastes. These books major in themes that Proverbs minors in—the limits of human wisdom and ultimately, our need to risk relying on a God who is beyond our control. In the face of an unpredictable life whose paths may well lead us into treacherous and painful places, we can make these predictions about God: God will be generous with gifts we might not think to ask for. God will be present in those places in our futures we would never choose to go.[27]

The Three Theological Affirmations of Proverbs

Proverbs makes three explicit theological affirmations. They clearly differentiate its wisdom from self-help varieties and serve as a context for preaching sermons on texts within the book.[28]

First, wisdom comes from God as a gift to those who will receive it (Proverbs 2:1-15).

The second theological affirmation flows from the first. It is the insistence that the fear of the Lord is the beginning of knowledge. The fear of the Lord in the context of Proverbs does not refer to fear of imminent punishment. Rather, it refers to the acknowledgement that God is the source of all moral guidance for living. It results in a willingness to be alert to and to obey divine instruction in specific situations. The admonition to "fear the Lord " appears throughout Proverbs (1:7; 9:10; 15:33; 31:30).[29] The fear of the Lord is the motivation for following wisdom. If health and prosperity result, they are secondary considerations. The motive for aligning human conduct with wisdom is to serve the purposes of the Creator (16:1, 9; 21:1).

Not the fear of the Lord , but the hope of gain, is the motive in much self-help wisdom. It also tends to inflate the human ability to order and control life to cosmic dimensions, often saying to God, "Thy will be my will."

The third theological affirmation of Proverbs is that those who seek wisdom attain the blessing of an ordered life, a life characterized by good things: longevity, prosperity, harmony, and happiness (3:13-18). This affirmation sounds the closest of the three to the promises of self-help wisdom. Unlike self-help wisdom, however, Proverbs has some checks and balances on its claims for what humans can do to control their lives.

Wisdom comes from God, and acknowledging that source is the first step to becoming wise. From these two convictions flow what some scholars call "the limit proverbs." These sayings acknowledge the sovereignty of God and the unpredictability of life.[30]

Proverbs' theological affirmations offer biblical versions of the most appealing themes of New Age wisdom. One reason for New Age wisdom's appeal is its emphasis on the inward spiritual life. Biblical wisdom in Proverbs invites readers on a lifelong journey of piety that respects God's transcendence as well as God's immanence. The path of Wisdom is a process of intentional seeking of divine guidance in the particulars of daily life that begins and ends with the fear of the Lord .

Another reason that New Age wisdom appeals to many people is because it affirms the sacredness of the natural world, asserting that natural phenomena and ordinary experiences are revelatory avenues to God. Biblical wisdom in Proverbs looks to the realm of nature for insights into the character of God in dealing with humankind. Unlike New Age wisdom, however, biblical wisdom maintains the distinction between Creator and created.

New Age wisdom respects the value, uniqueness, and integrity of the individual. It affirms, sometimes in an uncritical way, the sanctity of intuition and the essential goodness of the human being. Proverbs' brand of wisdom warns its adherents to be suspicious of their own desires and to submit them to God, who is the source of all moral knowledge, the arbiter of human ambitions. It is more realistic about the human tendency to choose foolish, hurtful actions and attitudes.

Proverbs' wisdom does respect the integrity of the human being as created by God and worthy of the determined invitations of Woman Wisdom onto the path of life. It advocates behavior that respects the value of other people as children of God: self-control with regard to speech, sexual behavior, food, drink, and lust for wealth. It upholds the positive values of respect for the poor and marital fidelity.

The New Age outlook holds forth a vision of an Age of Aquarius, an idyllic future to be ushered in by the gradual raising of consciousness of earth's population. Proverbs offers concrete strategies to achieve the reality of a community life infused with righteousness, justice, and equity (Proverbs 1:3).

Nutshell

What Is Most Important?

The goal of Proverbs is remarkably similar to the goal of the character wisdom we discussed in chapter three. It is the moral formation of individuals for the sake of maintaining order in society and the larger community.

Life is both the *goal* and the substance of the wise person's search for order and knowledge. "Wisdom is a tree of life to those who lay hold of her" (3:18). In Proverbs, life encompasses two interrelated levels of meaning expressed by two different Hebrew words, *hayim* and *nephesh*. *Hayim* refers to long years, prosperity, and honor. *Nephesh* is the living inward being whose life resides in breath and blood.

The goal of the wise person is to live responsibly before God, the Creator of Wisdom. When one chooses Wisdom one is assured that she will guard the inward life from harm and that the inward life will manifest itself in an outward life that is a good advertisement for the way of Wisdom. It is this assurance that is questioned by Qohelet and Job.[31]

Obstacles

The fool is wise in his own eyes. Who needs God or wisdom teachers?

The way of folly, in sharp contrast to the way of wisdom, is crooked, not straight; shadowy, not growing ever brighter; it leads to death, not life. If the fear of the Lord is the beginning of wisdom, its lack is the beginning of folly. The wellspring of folly is the fact that the fool hates and rejects Wisdom (1:24-32; 8:36).

What follows are attitudes and actions to embrace if one wants to be a fool, and to eschew if one wants to be wise. The fool fears others (29:25) rather than God. The fool trusts in riches rather than in God (11:4; 28). She is wise in her own eyes (3:7; 26:12) and thinks she has no need of God. She trusts her own wits (28:26) and is pure in her own eyes (30:12). She gives full vent to her anger (29:11). She is filled with pride (29:23; 8:13). She simultaneously disdains others and craves honor (25:27).

Not only does the fool ignore divine instruction, he ignores human guidance from community wisdom figures. He scorns his parents (30:11, 17). He does not listen to his teachers (5:13). He ignores instruction (13:18). He rejects discipline (5:23; 10:17; 12:1).

The fool walks a crooked path. She walks in the way of evildoers (4:14). His path swerves (4:27) according to his own desires and the influence of the evil companions whose company he chooses (1:10-19). Her path is paved with perverse ways (10:9) and worthless pursuits (12:11; 28:19; 29:3). The fool cannot walk freely and uprightly. His feet are ensnared in the iniquities and toil of sin (5:22).

HATEFUL ATTITUDES
TOWARD OTHERS

The result of folly is a constellation of negative, destructive attitudes and actions directed at others. The fool plans harm against the neighbor (3:29). She envies the violent and their gains (3:31). She sows discord (6:14; 11:9). She is covetous (12:12) and jealous (27:4). When it suits her ends, she can be cruel to people (11:17) and animals (12:10). She oppresses the poor (28:3; 30:14). She attempts to conceal her transgressions (28:13).

LACK OF SELF-CONTROL

The fool lacks self-control (25:16; 25:28). He lacks self-control in his sexual appetites (2:16-19; 5:3; 6:24; 7:10f; 9:13-18). He has no control over his anger (12:16; 29:11; 29:22). He is a glutton (28:7). He is greedy (28:25). He is lazy (6:6; 10:26; 12:24; 26:15).

The person who rejects the way of wisdom has no control over her tongue. She has lying lips and a lying tongue (6:6f; 10:18; 12:13, 19, 22; 26:28). Her speech is hasty (29:20), devious (4:24; 4:14), quarrelsome (3:30), and meddlesome (26:17). She uses the gift of speech to backbite (25:23), gossip (26:20), bear false witness, and belittle others (11:12; 11:13).

Facilitators

ATTENTIVENESS TO WISDOM

The wise person listens to Wisdom (1:33). He fears the Lord (1:7; 9:10; 10:27; 14:27). He lays aside immaturity and walks in the way of wisdom (9:6). He heeds the counsel of his community's wisdom figures (1:8, 23; 4:1; 5:1; 12:14, 15; 13:14). He accepts discipline from God (3:11; 12:1; 13:1; 25:12; 28:23). He is humble (3:34; 29:23). Like the young King Solomon, the wise person's life is characterized by a "listening heart." For he listens to God and his wise teachers, alert to patterns of wisdom that are God's self-expression in the world.[32]

Rather than ignoring or neglecting Wisdom, the wise person remembers her (3:1), holds her fast (3:18; 4:3) and keeps her (6:20; 7:1). Chapters 4-9 are filled with the metaphor of embrace for following wisdom. The wise one maintains a stance of loyalty and faithfulness toward God (3:3). He trusts God above all else (3:5; 29:25). For this reason, though Proverbs often promises prosperity as a result of wise living, it also acknowledges that even in riches, moderation is best (30:7-9).

INTEGRITY IN RELATIONSHIP TO OTHERS

The wise person is diligent (12:24). Though humble, the wise person is also bold when the occasion calls for boldness (28:1). He is kind to his neighbor (3:28; 11:17). He lives by love (10:12). He is cheerful (15:15).

SELF-CONTROL: A KEYNOTE OF MATURITY

The wise person is able to control her speech (11:12) and to speak truthfully and to know when to be silent (15:1). She is able to keep confidences (11:13). She also has a reign on her temper (12:16; 13:3; 15:15; 29:11).

Lifeform

What kind of life is shaped by this wisdom? A good way to get at the question of traditional wisdom's life-form is the question, What would we want on our tombstone?

Tomb epitaphs were a common Egyptian wisdom genre in which a ruler or priest left behind a list of his titles and achievements. One telling example is from Neferseshemre, a priest of the pyramid of King Teti from 2340 BCE. It paints a portrait of the kind of life espoused by ancient Egyptian wisdom.

> I executed ma'at for my lord (the deity) satisfied him with what he desired, spoke truly, did ma'at, spoke what was good, repeated what was good, seized the opportune time, wishing that

thereby it might go well with people. I judged between two persons in order to reconcile them. I rescued the oppressed from one more powerful than he as far as I was able. I gave bread to the starving and clothing (to the naked), a means of landing to him without a boat. I buried him who had no son. I made a ferry-boat for him who had none. I was respectful to my father, kind to my mother, and I brought up their children.[33]

Proverbial wisdom would inscribe something like this on our tombstone.

I lived with a listening heart, attentive to God's wisdom all around and within me. With my attention on Divine Wisdom, I was able largely to close my ears to the influence of foolish people and my own unruly appetites. I was faithful to my spouse and controlled my appetites for food and drink. I was industrious, controlled my temper and curbed my unruly tongue. While I came to realize that life contains a measure of mystery and that God is ultimately in charge of things, I focused on those areas of life where, by making wise choices, I could usually ensure auspicious outcomes. I ordered my life so that I knew a measure of peace of mind and worked for harmony in my community. While I respected the poor as those whom God created and loves, I worked to ensure that I would not share their lot. As a result, I secured a reputation for integrity and prudence among my peers.

Key Texts for Preaching

1:1-7 "Your Mission, Should You Choose to Accept It"

Here in the first seven verses of chapter 1 is Proverbs' version of "your mission, should you choose to accept it." It is to love and revere God as the source of all moral knowledge (the fear of the Lord). The first line is better translated: "For knowing wisdom and discipline." The Hebrew word *musar* (here and in verses 3a, 7b, 8a) denotes an authoritative instruction or correction from God or God's agent, personified Wisdom, or from a teacher or a parent. The use of the word *musar* twice in the first two verses sounds a warning note. The acquisition of wisdom is no easy task. It calls for lifelong commitment to discipline.

At the same time, for Israel's sages discipline is a positive concept. One who hates reproof is stupid (12:1*b*). One who hates discipline hates himself (15:32). Many of the sages advocated corporal punishment for sluggish students. In our contemporary context domestic abuse of women and children is tragically rampant. Texts that insist that to spare the rod is to spoil the child are far too likely to be misunderstood.[34] The preacher would be better off to point out that discipline is not an external force applied to make the young do things they don't want to do. It is an interior disposition designed to improve one's character. One who aspires to wisdom must not only receive discipline (8:10; 24:32), but also seek discipline (4:13; 23:23).[35]

The course objectives of the wisdom curriculum are lives graced by righteousness, justice, and equity. The sages "are not just preparing their students for personal success. 'Righteouness, justice, and equity'— these are all relational virtues; they are the elements of the community of the faithful that is hospitable to God's holy presence." [36]

These opening verses address two different groups of people. The first group consists of "the simple" (*peti*) and "the young" (*na'ar*) (verse 4). "The simple" occurs fourteen times in Proverbs and spans a spectrum of meanings: inexperienced, untaught, needing instruction, easily seduced, the opposite of wise. "Simple" can be a parallel term to "fool" (Proverbs 1:32; 8:5) or can indicate one who is "lacking intelligence" (Proverbs 9:4;16). [37]

In wisdom literature, the "simple" or "unlearned" are those who lack sense, that is, the acumen of reasoned thinking, yet who, provided the opportunity, are open to instruction and learning (Proverbs 1:22; 8:5; 9:4, 16). They are those whose gullibility and lack of a disciplined ethic often render them ill-equipped to make prudent judgments and to engage in moral actions (Proverbs 14:15). Untrained in the ways of wisdom, the simple are easily deceived (Proverbs 1:32; 7:7; 9:6; 22:3; 27:12). 38

Verse 5 is addressed to the mature sage. "Let the wise also hear and gain in learning, and the discerning acquire skill." The word "learning" refers to the "received tradition" of the sages. The accomplished sage who hears these words of wisdom may increase his or her own learning and also contribute to the tradition. "Skill" (tahbulot) refers to advice or direction that is well thought out and planned. It is a synonym for counsel (esa).

Says wisdom scholar Leo Perdue, "This inclusion of accomplished sages among the audience of students indicates that wisdom is not obtained once and for all but rather is to be pursued, cultivated and deepened throughout life. This wisdom is not simply the knowledge of the intellect but the fiber of the soul."[39]

Proverbs, in its first few verses, acknowledges that it addresses two different groups of people. So do we preachers every week. That is a helpful fact to keep in mind. It will take wisdom for us to not underestimate our congregation's wisdom. It will take wisdom for us not to assume knowledge and experience they may be lacking.

We have been told in verse 2 to expect instruction. The first piece of advice we receive comes in verse 7a. "The fear of the Lord is the beginning of knowledge." This is, as we have seen, the cardinal teaching in all the biblical wisdom literature. The fear of the Lord is the only security that life holds. When we fear the Lord we have no need to fear anyone or anything else.

The fear of the Lord, willingness to obey divine instruction, is the beginning, or prerequisite, of knowledge. Elsewhere in the Hebrew Bible, the word used in Proverbs 1:7 for beginning (*reshit*) refers to firstborn (Deuteronomy 21:17) and firstfruits (Exodus 23:19). The giving of one's "first," whether of offspring or crops, represents the giving of all we have to God. A part stands in for the whole. Similarly, when Proverbs says "the beginning of wisdom is the fear of the Lord," we are being encouraged to give the first of our attention and obedience to God, with the understanding that the fear of the Lord is not only the origin of the wisdom process, but that it forever and always informs and influences the process.[40]

Proverbs is peppered with injunctions to fear the Lord (1:7; 9:10; 15:33). (See also Job 28:28 and Psalm 111:10). Fear of the Lord also appears in Proverbs 31:30 as a kind of conclusion to the book. Fear of the Lord had many meanings in the Hebrew Bible. It can refer to the awareness of the gulf between the human and the divine, as exemplified in Isaiah 6, the cultic piety of the psalms, or the covenant loyalty of Deuteronomy. In Proverbs its meaning is the basic recognition that commitment to God is the source of insights for daily life.[41]

Fear of the Lord involves developing the habit of making choices that do not merely reflect our own self-interest or the mood of the moment. It means putting God's preferences before our own. It involves a reversal of our natural priorities, what the Bible calls humility, which is linked in several proverbs with fear of the Lord (15:33; 22:4).[42]

Key Texts for Preaching

Three Portraits of Woman Wisdom

I have chosen to deal with three texts from Proverbs that depict personified Wisdom, the agent of God. We have seen how secular wisdom emphasizes principles for successful living, while biblical wisdom emphasizes a relationship with a faithful God. In each of the biblical books we will explore, I have chosen as "key texts for preaching" passages that deal with God as the source of wisdom in relation to humankind. This focus on God as the giver of wisdom forms the context for understanding the specific guidelines for living that each book commends.

THE WARNING: WISDOM'S FIRST SPEECH (1:20-33)

Woman Wisdom's speeches are a passionate portrayal of her invitation to those wandering on the highways and byways of life. She stands at the gates to the city, the hub of commerce and government. She speaks to all but focuses on the inexperienced, the not-yet wise. How telling that Wisdom's first speech is addressed to those most likely to refuse her! We soon find out that these youth have a history of ignoring her instruction (verses 24-31).

Her tone is harsh and matter-of-fact, with no sugarcoating. Wisdom does not threaten her hearers with any punishment beyond the consequences of their own foolish choices.

As novelist Robert Louis Stevenson once said, "Eventually, everyone sits down to a banquet of consequences." [43]

Woman Wisdom will lose no sleep at the prospect of their getting their just desserts (verse 32). She will laugh when inevitable disaster descends (verses 26-27) and will simply not be present (verse 28). She ends by contrasting the fate of the foolish with that of those who heed her warnings and embrace her teachings. "For waywardness kills the simple, and the complacency of fools destroys them; but those who listen to me will be secure and will live at ease, without dread of disaster" (1:33).

The invitation to respond to God's Wisdom has an RSVP deadline. One of the motifs of Old Testament wisdom traditions that became prominent in apocalyptic literature was the rejection of Wisdom and her withdrawal to heaven as an event that would signal the last times.[44]

This is a theme we will hear again in the New Testament. Jesus was viewed by many early Christians as having been Wisdom-In-person. His teachings, like those of Woman Wisdom, have an RSVP deadline. Those who reject him and his subversive wisdom teachings now, will be rejected by him when he returns to judge the earth as Son of Man (Mark 8:27-38).

Who is this person who calls us into relationship with her? What kind of God does she represent? She is one who places herself at the center of secular life. She will not be confined to specific sacred places and days. She pulls no punches, bluntly confronting us with the consequences of rejecting her. She exudes a sense of urgency. Three adjectives that describe this no-nonsense prophetess are proactive, confrontational, and urgent.

Woman Wisdom is offering us an urgent ultimatum: step onto the pathway that leads to a relationship with God that is life itself, and do it today. Or don't, and watch what happens.

This first speech of Woman Wisdom challenges us preachers to urgently exhort our congregations to choose wisdom. She dares us to claim our confidence in her, our sense of clarity about her teachings, and our commitment to our calling to preach. She enjoins us to warn our people of the consequences of not choosing her way. She dares us to convey to them how much there is to gain by choosing God's wisdom and how much there is to lose by rejecting it.[45]

THE PROMISE: WISDOM'S SECOND SPEECH (8:22-36)

The first speech of Wisdom was an extended warning with a concluding one-line promise (1:33). Her second speech is an extended promise capped off with a one-line warning (8:36). Her address is public and universal. In her first speech Wisdom has bluntly warned the young of the consequences of ignoring her call. In this second speech, she switches tactics. Now she speaks persuasively of the benefits of following her. She speaks first of the virtues and values of her words and instructions. Her first claim is the honesty and integrity of her message, in contrast to the words of the smooth talking, "strange" woman of Proverbs (2:16, 5:3; 6:4; 7:21). She propounds truth and justice (8:7-8). The credibility of her message lies in her connection with the Lord, who is truthful and just.

Since the sages believed that words have the power to shape the character of the people, she is assuring would-be followers that her words are righteous, directed toward the stability, success, and well-being of the cosmos and of the government of the people through its rulers.[46] Her qualities of counsel, strength, and understanding are what enable her to be the basis for royal rule. These qualities are divine, according to Job 12:13, and in Isaiah 11:2 they are gifts of the Lord 's spirit to the messianic figure. As is often claimed in the wisdom literature, Wisdom's teachings are said to yield rewards more precious than worldly wealth (8:19-21). [47]

In the first twenty-one verses of this second speech, Wisdom has been answering the unspoken question, "Why should a disciple trust and believe in her?" In verse 22, she weights her words with the authority of her relationship with Yahweh. Wisdom asserts that she was created before anything else, a theme that is repeated several times and points to this precedence as a mark of the highest honor. She was with Yahweh, beside him, during the creation.

The word translated "master worker" (*amon*) remains somewhat mysterious. It may refer to a "crafts (wo)man" assisting in the work of creation or it could connote a child playing. It may ultimately derive from the Akkadian *ummanu*, "sage, or artisan" The term refers to the venerable sages who lived after the great flood of Mesopotamian lore who brought the human race culture and specialized knowledge. Chapter eight applies the term to Wisdom, a heavenly being giving beneficial knowledge to the human race.[48]

We are to understand that Woman Wisdom, a sage seeking disciples, is also a heavenly being who wishes to form a relationship with disciples modeled on her relationship with Yahweh. She was daily his delight and she rejoices (plays) before God and the created world. She also delights in the human race. What form did this playful rejoicing take? Was it like the joyous singing of the morning stars, when God created them (Job 38:7)? Was it, as O. Keel suggests, similar to the figures who are represented doing cartwheels in the processions of Egyptian divinities in Egyptian iconography? Whatever form this playful rejoicing took, Wisdom operates joyfully before both God and the human race.

At the close of these joyous verses, Wisdom does not spoil the mood by offering specific admonitions. After this exalted statement of her pedigree, Wisdom, in general terms, affirms her role as the one who summons human beings to blessedness and happiness (8:32, 34).[49]

Says Old Testament scholar Roland Murphy, Wisdom is "the revelation of God. She is the divine summons issued in and through creation, sounding through the vast realm of the created world and heard on the level of human experience" (Proverbs 8:31).[50]

Carole L. Fontaine affirms Woman Wisdom eloquently: Wisdom is like "some primal energy acquired by Yahweh before creation and seeded into every part of it" (8:22-31)—a sort of cosmic will-to-harmony. She is knowable; she is near; and she is willing to love those who love her (8:17)....A striking anomaly within Israel's patriarchal worldview, the figure of Woman Wisdom is the most unique and expressive answer to the question of the meaning of wisdom in the book of Proverbs.[51]

The poem ends (verses 32-36) with an appeal to the youth to wait at Wisdom's door as a loving disciple. "Happy is the one who listens to me, watching daily at my gates, waiting beside my doors." The Wisdom of Solomon, an apocryphal wisdom book probably written in Alexandria during the last of the first century BCE, reverses the picture, with a poignant portrait of Wisdom waiting at the disciple's door. "Wisdom is radiant and unfading, and she is easily discerned by those who love her, and is found by those who seek her. She hastens to make herself known to those who desire her. He who rises early to seek her will have no difficulty, for he will find her sitting at his gates" (Wisdom of Solomon 6:12-14).[52]

This portrait of Wisdom in the eighth chapter of Proverbs has echoes in subsequent literature. The apocryphal book The Wisdom of Jesus Ben Sirach (Ecclesiasticus) written about 190 BCE depicts Wisdom leaving her heavenly home and finding a new dwelling in Jerusalem, in the book of the covenant of the Most High God. Jewish tradition identifies Wisdom with the Torah. In the New Testament, the first chapter of the Gospel of John alludes to Proverbs 8:22, "In the beginning was the Word, and the Word was with God, and the Word was God" (1:1). John combines into one term "the Word" (Greek *logos*) from Genesis 1 ("Then God spoke, 'Let there be...'") and wisdom from Proverbs 8.[53]

What about this portrait of Wisdom forms a context for our preaching on her specific teachings? She actively seeks out followers, standing at the city gates, the center of law and commerce. She speaks to everyone, not just the simple. Her teachings are trustworthy and lead to great benefit. This trustworthiness is grounded in her relationship with Yahweh. She loves God, God's creation, and human beings. This is no pale, static love, but an active delight, a playful, sportive love. Wisdom seeks us out because she loves us. And she seeks us out because she loves God. There is some mysterious delight to the life of Wisdom that involves the love of God, humankind, and Wisdom in a kind of circle dance.

Have we preachers progressed far enough in the life of Wisdom ourselves to be able to speak concretely about her delights? Can we persuasively invite people into a way of life that brings increasing satisfaction, spiritual nourishment and dawning insight with each passing year? "The path of the righteous is like the light of dawn, which shines brighter and brighter until fully day" (Proverbs 4:18). Can we speak from experience about the integrity of her teachings and the righteousness of her counsel? Do we know what it means to affirm that Wisdom's yield is better than choice silver? Do we know what it is to be attentive to Wisdom and not neglect her, to listen, watch, and wait for Wisdom? Can we affirm that listening to and keeping the ways of Wisdom is a wellspring of happiness in our lives? Despite the adversities and drudgery of our lives, do we rejoice in attending the school of life? Do we delight in God's unfolding gift of Wisdom?

Ralph and Gregg Lewis, authors of *Inductive Preaching: Helping People Listen*, put it well: "Practicing what we preach involves much more than rehearsing our sermons."[54] Our lives are the most persuasive inductive sermon we will ever preach!

THE WOMAN OF WORTH: FINAL ODE TO WOMAN WISDOM (31:10-31)

This last poem of Proverbs is traditionally called "A Poem to a Woman of Worth." It opens with a rhetorical question. "A strong woman, who can find?" (31:10). The Hebrew expression (*eset hayil*) used in this verse means literally "a strong woman," or "a woman of military strength." It has most often been held up as the description of the ideal homemaker, the ideal wife whom the young man should choose to enhance his future. There are several clues that have caused recent scholars to suspect that someone else may be its referent.

There are a number of uncanny resemblances between this woman of worth and Woman Wisdom. Both shed light on the way of those who follow her (compare 31:18b with 13:9). Both are worth more than precious jewels (compare 31:10 with 3:15, 8:11, 16:16). Both bring prosperity, protection, and honor upon those who trust in them (compare 31:11, 12 with 4:5, 8, 9). Both honor the poor and fear the Lord, hallmarks of the seeker of wisdom in Proverbs (1:7; 9:10; 15:33). Throughout Proverbs we have been told that the fear of the Lord is beginning of knowledge (1:7, 9, 10; 15:33). The woman of worth, in the closing verses of Proverbs, is described as a "woman who fears the Lord." While spending her days in serving others, this woman's works praise her in the city gates.[55]

The suspicion dawns that this woman of worth is Woman Wisdom herself. This description is not meant as a model for daily accomplishment for actual women then or now. It is, however, infused with the skills and positive qualities of postexilic Hebrew women. Woman Wisdom is the source of the identity of the household, as were women in postexilic Israelite society. As we have seen, in this period, the activities of women in running households and teaching wisdom to the young became crucial for the community's survival.

However, no woman of ancient Israel held such a high place in family, society, or economy as the poem imagines. No woman held such authority or responsibility, even as an ideal. No woman was viewed as the cause of her husband's honor; rather, the reverse. This woman's activities, informed to a degree by women's roles, summarize the behavior of Woman Wisdom toward her disciples.[56]

Surely this woman of worth is Woman Wisdom herself! Coming at the very end of Proverbs, this acrostic poem is part heroic poetry, part hymn of praise. It sums up the qualities of Wisdom and commends her benefits to potential followers. Woman Wisdom, who earlier in Proverbs has come out of her home to challenge the young to enter the path of wisdom, now invites them into her home, a place graced by lovingkindness (31:26), industry, and care for the poor of the community. The message is clear for the readers of Proverbs:

Become members of this woman's household! If you do this, you will gain every measure of happiness.[57]

CHAPTER SIX

Job: Witness to Pain and Presence

"But where shall wisdom be found? And where is the place of understanding?" (Job 28:12)

Background Check

> Once upon a time, in a faraway land, there lived a man, just and wise, humble and charitable...Through the problems he embodied and the trials he endured, he seems familiar—even contemporary. We know his history for having lived it. In times of stress it is to his words that we turn to express our anger, revolt or resignation. He belongs to our most intimate landscape, the most vulnerable part of our past.[1]

Thus begins Elie Wiesel's essay entitled "Job Our Contemporary."

Job wrestles with the question of innocent suffering, a theme that has echoes in writings throughout the ancient world.[2] As we shall see, it has implications for how a human being is to relate to others, to the community, and to God during such times. How can the community best relate to persons in distress? Can we offer empathy without imposing judgment? How can one speak of and relate to God in times of deep and undeserved suffering? Can we speak of and pray to God without blaming God or ourselves for our misfortune, and without demanding compensation for our suffering?

In his undeserved suffering, Job represents the experience of many of our people who suffer emotionally and physically from illness and loss. Job's experience also makes him the spokesperson for those who suffer from social injustice. Central American theologian Gustavo Gutiérrez points out that the book has a unique relevance for "readers in a continent where the suffering of the innocent is a massive reality."[3] It does the book an injustice to privatize and overly spiritualize its message. It is a response to the spiritual crisis of an entire nation.[4]

So it has relevance today for both individuals and communities. Whatever the economic circumstances of our people, wherever in the world we are, Job has a message that is both universal and particular. When we understand the background and purpose of the book, we can better preach Job's much-needed wisdom on behalf of our people.

Based on the language, most scholars date the composition of the book of Job in the exilic (587-539 BCE) or early postexilic period. The book does not explicitly mention either the chosen people or the covenant.[5] The sacred name of Yahweh appears only in the Prologue and Epilogue and is rarely mentioned in the great debate (12:9 is an exception). The events of Israel's history are not referred to. Nevertheless, Job is a book of Israelite wisdom and stays within the perspective of wisdom.[6]

The Wisdom Connection

Job is a unique work that defies classification in any one literary genre. It is a combination of forms: wisdom, prophecy, psalm, drama, contest, lament, legal disputation, theodicy, history, and allegory, fused in the crucible of genius into a one-of-a-kind work.[7]

Job also has elements of an answered lament, a literary form common in the ancient Near East in which an innocent sufferer utters a complaint in which he describes his distress (29-31), asserts his innocence (31), and receives a divine response and restoration.[8] The speeches of Job and his friends, as well as the Lord's response to Job, are disputation speeches, which employ genres both of law and wisdom.[9]

Like Ecclesiastes, Job brings to the foreground issues that are in the background in the traditional, optimistic book of Proverbs. These include the suffering of the innocent, the limitations of human wisdom, and the inscrutability of God. There are several wisdom themes interweaving the dialogue that are integral to other wisdom books as well. They include a preoccupation with creation, the importance of the name or memory, life as burdensome, the tradition of the fathers, personification of Wisdom, and the problem of retribution.[10]

Job is not an anti-wisdom book, as some have claimed. Rather, it is a book that represents the profoundest dynamic of biblical wisdom, the ability to recognize the limitations of human constructs. What was acknowledged in the "limit proverbs" of the book of Proverbs comes front and center in the Book of Job: the limitation of human knowledge and the inscrutability of God.

Job's most positive teaching is at the same time negative: the traditional theory of divine retribution is not relevant to Job's situation. It is even wrong. The Lord's verdict in Job's favor against his friends makes this clear (42:7). This does not mean there is no truth in the traditional theory. The very fact that Job is restored in the end (42:10-17), while not the main point of the book, upholds the author's belief in the traditional goodness and justice of the Lord.[11]

Then and now, Job represents both the situation of the struggling believer and the struggling community. In later rabbinic commentary on Job he is compared to the Jewish people. Israel too is alone; its best friends are ready to commiserate in its misfortunes but will do nothing to help. Israel too has been accused of acting against God, forcing him to resort to punishment.[12] The book does imply that suffering can be redemptive. Job's experience of loss and death upturn his religious faith, shake his certainties, and collapse his relationships. But in that dark night he meets his Creator and the whole world is transformed.

Much of the Bible, including the major strand of Proverbs and Deuteronomy, affirms that the righteous person will prosper. Proverbs concedes that since God is mysterious and human life is unpredictable, the rule does not always apply. It stays in the major key, though, insisting that, for the most part, good deeds lead to life, which is understood as health, reputation, and community harmony. Qohelet deals with the phenomenon of innocent suffering by presenting God as distant and removed from human life, the source of calamity and good fortune alike. His mood is one of melancholy acceptance of the way things are. This is a far different emotional tone from the outraged Job who calls God onto the carpet for having transgressed the divine laws!

If everything is to be attributed to God, and God makes the righteous person prosper, then how do we account for the sufferings of the righteous? Is it, as Job's friends assert, that they really are not as righteous as they would have the world think? Or are we to attribute it to divine caprice? Job's message is that the phenomenon exceeds the rubrics we fashion to explain it, and that a personal God speaks out of the whirlwind. This God reminds us, on the one hand, of who is God and who is human. On the other hand, God reminds us of the divine intention to restore us to fullness of life with God. The human stance in all of this is disinterested piety. We are to love God for God's own sake and not for hope of reward or fear of punishment. The whole drama of Job began with the Satan's challenge to God over whether this kind of devotion existed at all. Job's life and response to God throughout his affliction proves that it does.

A common theory of the book of Job regards the Prologue-Epilogue (chapters 1-2; 42:7-17) as an original folk tale that describes the suffering of an innocent, righteous man who is rewarded by God for his patience. The twenty-eight-chapter dialogue between Job and his friends, in which Job is thoroughly impatient, was added later, the theory goes. It was meant as a theological correction to the original to address the issue of innocent suffering.[13]

More recent interpretations insist that Job is structured in such a way that the final narrative form is coherent as it stands and should be read with all the pieces in place and in just these places. The message of the book is conveyed not just through individual passages but through the design of the book as a whole: Prologue, three rounds of dialogues, Elihu's speech, Job's reply, God's reply, and Epilogue.

Kathleen O'Connor insists that the structure of the book is itself part of the message. The disjunction between prose and poetry, the dialogues that disintegrate into bitter monologues, and the introduction of things that don't get developed and mar the symmetry of the book are like the real life it is trying to describe. In her view, "the book of Job is a sophisticated, carefully crafted masterpiece, designed to entangle the reader in the ambiguities and uncertainties of Job's suffering."[14]

Four Wisdom Visions

One way to enter into the book as readers is to envision it as four interwoven or entangled wisdom visions: that of God, Job, the Satan, and the three friends. Our four questions: what is most important, what attitudes and behaviors act as obstacles, which as facilitators, and what kind of life results need to be asked of all of the characters in the drama. The result is an intriguing tangle of confusion, contradiction, and insight.

THE SATAN

The Hebrew word for Satan is not a proper name for a person, but a noun best translated as "prosecutor" with a definite article. As such it becomes a title—"The Prosecutor." He turns up elsewhere in the Hebrew Bible. His most notable appearance is in the third chapter of Zechariah where he functions much as he does at the beginning of Job.[15]

By the Common Era, Satan had become a proper name for the Devil. In Job 1-2, the Satan is a heavenly prosecuting attorney, roving the earth bringing malefactors to justice. While unfriendly, the Satan of Job is not evil. He is just doing his job. To identify the Satan in this text as the Devil, a principle of evil, or, in a dualistic system, the principle of evil, is anachronistic.[16]

The Satan implies that Job has ulterior motives for his seemingly upright behavior, for his extraordinary sacrificial diligence. Perhaps his sacrifices for his offspring were conducted to protect his honor as head of the household and to keep God at bay from his possessions. Was Job's reverence for God motivated by self-interest?[17]

Apparently this was a question God was wondering about as well. Nobody has much nice to say about the Satan in commenting on Job. But he does us a favor by asking an unpopular question we and our people would rather ignore; i.e., Do humans simply serve God because they are rewarded by prosperity in terms of health, family well-being, a degree of material comfort, and reputation in the community? His question gets at the heart of motivation which is at the heart of wisdom. It is at the heart of the difference between a desire to help ourselves and a desire to be in relationship with God.

The Satan's object of desire is ambiguous. On the surface, he seems to want to uphold God's honor. It is wrong that any human being should only honor and serve God out of desire for reward. He will uncover hypocrisy and defend the divine honor. If, in the process, he enhances his own career as super prosecutor and stirs up dissension between God and human beings, is that such a bad thing?

GOD

Job challenges both our faith and our credulity in its depictions of God. How are we to respond to this depiction of a God who allows a mortal to be stripped of home, possessions, family, health, and friends? Does God strike deals like this in the heavenly council? For what reasons and on what grounds? God allows the Satan to test Job because God wants to know whether humankind worships God for reward alone. The description of God as tester is common throughout Hebrew Scriptures. God tests Abraham's obedience in Genesis 22. In Psalm 26, a lament, the psalmist petitions God to test his "heart and mind" (26:2) in order to vindicate him against an unspecified challenge to his integrity.

We get a glimpse of God's inward turmoil in Job 2:3 where he expresses his sense that he has allowed Job to be tested "for no reason." In Genesis 6:6 God is said to be sorry for having created humankind. So this verse in Job may hint at a remorseful God. The Satan is not satisfied that the test has been strenuous enough, and, it would seem, God's compassion loses out to God's desire that Job's character, and by association, his own, be vindicated.[18]

How to preach such a tangled web? Nowhere in our scriptural tradition or in our experience does God promise that our earthly lives will be entirely free from suffering and challenges. Our expectation that it is our right to have it easy sprouts from our natural distaste for pain and deprivation of any kind.

I do not believe God hands out misfortune and illness and loss. God does not have to. Such experiences are woven into the fabric of everyone's life. With some exceptions, they cannot be attributed to our shortcomings: wrong thinking or failure to live by cosmic principles of success. They are simply a part of life. We could argue that God set life up this way, so it is God's fault. But ascribing blame seems like a futile waste of energy. Besides, could it be that

God knows something that we do not? Could it be that we cannot receive the good in life without the bad?

When Job's wife suggests that he abandon his integrity, curse God and die, he says "Shall we receive the good at the hand of God and not receive the bad?" (2:10). Misfortune and sorrow always feel like an unwelcome test, a pop quiz for which we are not prepared. But they serve a mysterious, nutritious, formative role in human life. Why it is or must be so is a mystery beyond the discernment of our human minds that "see in a glass but darkly."

God in the book of Job wants human beings to give God that which God cannot coerce: our devotion, obedience, and love without regard to the benefits such a life will bring. The God of the whirlwind is a free God whose range of concerns both includes and transcends human beings. The God of the storm neither explains suffering nor accepts responsibility for it, but does claim to be a God of justice (38:15).

We have asked the question of other bodies of wisdom, What facilitates our living in keep with its insights? In the case of Job, the answer is our own attitudes toward God. God puts boundaries on evil, but not on the unbounded freedom we have to trust, or not trust, God. God does not coerce our devotion and obedience. Offering it is our choice.

By the same token, our own assumptions and attitudes can act as obstacles to our relationship with God and others in times of suffering. Among those attitudes and assumptions are the following:

> Our assumption that bad luck is divine punishment and good fortune is divine reward.
>
> Our tendency to distance ourselves from or judge those who suffer.
>
> Our assumption that the presence of pain means the absence of God.

THE FRIENDS

When we ask the question "What is most important to the friends?" we must take into account their shifting tactics. In round one of the dialogue, their aim is to motivate Job to call on God for help. At this point they emphasize Job's chances for restoration by a just God if he will call out for mercy (4:6, 7; 8:20, 21). In round two, their aim changes to motivating Job to admit his own sin that must have caused this drastic suffering. It seems that what is most important is defending traditional "act-consequence" wisdom which they affirm is evidence of the justice of God.

The obstacle to Job's living a life in line with that justice is his self-righteousness. Bildad, even more acerbic than Eliphaz, asserts that God is just and therefore cannot be the cause of suffering. If suffering does occur, it is God's chastisement for human sin. If Job will live uprightly and turn to God, God will reward him. Escape from this suffering is possible, but everything depends on Job.[19]

Zophar is convinced that if Job will "direct his heart rightly" and "put iniquity far away" (11:13, 14), security and joy will return and his "life will be brighter than the noonday" (11:17).[20]

The friends set forth several strategies that they believe will facilitate one's arriving at that blessed state. We need to be mindful of the teachings of our elders, says Eliphaz, the eldest, in advice that is reminiscent of Proverbs. Remember that suffering comes from human activity and it is divine punishment for wicked living (4:8-9). Sometimes suffering is divine discipline, a temporary warning for which we should be grateful and by which we should be motivated to turn to God (5:17).

We should repent so that suffering will not happen to us and before even more suffering happens to us. We should think twice before sinning. The prospect of punishment for sin that inevitably awaits us ought to be a deterrent from sin. If we live as we should, God has no choice but to reward us.

A lot of self-help literature seems to have been written by Job's friends. It assumes that we create just about all of our own suffering. It preaches that if we would refrain from certain thoughts and habits, our lives would roll along to the destination of our heart's desire smoothly, or at least a whole lot more smoothly than they do right now. There is enough truth in those statements to make them alluring and dangerous.

JOB

What is the driving purpose of life for Job? At the outset Job is a man in desperate pursuit of vindication from God. He is the prophet in reverse, relentlessly pursuing God with a call to duty and justice.[21] In grief and outrage Job tells God what he thinks God should have known for a long time, that something was amiss in the universe. The just are punished for no reason, the criminal rewarded for no reason.

From another angle, Job is concerned to maintain his integrity. Job is twice described as "a blameless and upright man, who fears God and turns away from evil" (Job 1:1, 8; 2:3). The key word that most sharply describes Job's character is *tam*, usually translated "blameless," along with the cognate term (*tumme*), "integrity." Integrity "denotes a person whose conduct is in complete accord with moral and religious norms and whose character is one of utter honesty."[22] One who is *tam* is one whose life is coherent and consistent in the ways he or she makes ethical choices within the life of the community.[23] *Tumma* denotes a wholeness or coherence of character. Two of the fundamental virtues of the sage are justice and piety (Proverbs 1:3). Job is unwilling to relinquish these.

Another of Job's virtues is that he fears the Lord. We are familiar with this crucial starting point of wisdom from Proverbs. It is the acknowledgment that God is the source of all wisdom (1:7). In the Prologue we are repeatedly told that Job "feared God and turned away from evil" (1:1,8; 2:3). As readers we know that Job is not suffering because he failed to fear the Lord. Yet, Eliphaz, in each of his cycles, uses the words "fear of God" implying that Job has fallen short of that wisdom ideal (4:6; 15:4; 22:4). In the Wisdom poem of chapter 28, which sounds more like something out of Proverbs than from the lips of Job, we are told that "Truly, the fear of the Lord, that is wisdom; and to depart from evil is understanding" (28:28). God vindicates Job in the Epilogue. This is an ironic indication that Job, by being faithful to his own experience of innocent suffering, has been true to God. He has thereby opened himself up to receive a deeper, nonconventional wisdom that comes from God.[24]

From Job's perspective, what constitutes the obstacles to his aims in life? At first Job regards God's indifference and silence as obstacles to his vindication. Eventually Job comes to view his own misunderstanding of his place in the universe as the obstacle to his relationship with God.

"What constitutes facilitators to the attainment of Job's purposes?" The answer shifts as we journey through the book. At the outset, these would be the confidence to ignore the bad advice of others, however widespread their views and determination in regard to calling God to account.

After his encounter with God, Job's view of what gets us closer to right relationship with God is recognition of the limitations of our human wisdom and knowledge and trust in God's faithfulness in all the challenges of life.

Nutshell

What Is Most Important?

No thing, no person, and no suffering, has the power to erode the connection between God and us. While God is a mystery to us in many ways, God is always near in our sufferings.

Obstacles

As readers, we need to ask the question, "What constitutes the obstacles in our lives to receiving good as Job perceives it?"

We allow suffering to turn us against God.

We serve God for the benefits of prosperity, health and eternal rewards, not for love of God. Interestingly, this is a motive that is unashamedly put forth as valid in a lot of self-help literature.

We assume that our sufferings are the result of our sinfulness.

We assume it is our mission in life to interpret others' lives for them in an officious way that accuses them of wrongdoing based on their current luck.

We assume that the older are necessarily the wiser.

Facilitators

As readers, we also need to ask the question, "What attitudes and actions facilitate our arriving at our good?"

While it is probably absurd to reduce Job to a series of insights to live by, I take that risk to point out how vastly different Job's wisdom is from self-help wisdom.

Remember that sometimes the path of wisdom lies in flying in the face of the best advice of your most respected peers.

Be aware of our human wisdom's limits.

Serve God because we love God, not out of hope of better health, better business luck, better relationships, and a better reputation. ("Seek ye first the kingdom of God.")

Be mindful of God's sovereignty, but also of God as a personal God.

Be comforted by the knowledge that this God will not allow suffering to preclude our relationship with him and the fullness of life that it brings. God sets limits on how much damage chaos and suffering can wreak on our inward lives.

Offer help and comfort to those who are suffering, not brainstorming what they have done to warrant its intrusion into their life. ("Judge not that ye be not judged.")

Recognize the limits of our wisdom as human beings and the sovereign freedom of God.

Key Texts for Preaching

God Responds to Job

GOD'S FIRST RESPONSE TO JOB (38, 39)

Job had uttered seven curses on creation in his opening soliloquy in chapter 3, an attempt to turn the world back to darkness and chaos. God responds with a celebration of the beauty and orderliness of the universe. Although the speeches seem to sidestep Job's questions about his suffering, they do represent a response to him in two ways. In response to Job's challenge to God to "justify his ways to humans," the speeches affirm that there is order and purpose in God's creation. But it is impossible for the human mind, using human language and concepts, fully to understand or "explain" God and God's actions. The speeches assert divine freedom and honor the mystery that separates a transcendent Creator from mortal creatures. Second, God's appearance is a response to Job's demand for an audience.[25]

God's speeches encourage us to preach ecological stewardship, for they push us, like Job, to place our lives in the context of the mysteries and gift of the creation, not view it as a resource to be exploited for human gain. God's speeches also encourage us to preach against ethnic and economic stereotyping that measures human worth by a yardstick of economic prosperity.[26]

"Then the Lord answered Job out of the whirlwind" (38:1). The name used for God is Yahweh, the God who acted and spoke in the Prologue, the God revealed in Israel's saving history. Yahweh is used only in the Prologue, Yahweh's speeches, and Epilogue (with one exception, 12:9).[27] Yahweh the Wise Teacher takes the offensive and interrogates Job, his complaining servant. Job's questioning has led him to challenge the traditional belief that God governs the world in justice (chapters 21 and 24). Without presenting a self-defense against these accusations, Yahweh opens by putting Job in his place with a question that casts doubt on Job's insight (38:2). Without discounting Job's moral integrity, Yahweh challenges Job's perception of his governance of the world. He then embarks on a series of questions designed to lead Job to abandon his position.[28]

In his first speech (chapters 38, 39), God accuses Job of "darkening design," that is, Job has challenged the basic design of the cosmos, accusing God of mismanagement. Job makes these accusations without knowledge and so obscures the reality of God's ways in the world (38:2).[29] Now Yahweh launches into an answer to Job. It is not the answer to the questions Job has been asking. Job has been asking "How could you do this to me?" God speaks as if Job has been asking "Why should I have confidence in you in light of my undeserved sufferings?"

A LESSON IN METEOROLOGY

Rather than answer Job directly, from 38:4-38, Yahweh asks him a series of questions that come in the context of a lesson in ancient meteorology. Each of the questions has a simple answer: "nowhere," "I don't know," "only you," and "no." What is the point of these questions?

At first glance this first part of God's address to Job appears to reveal God as a blowhard, more concerned with divine majesty than with human anguish. Biblical scholar and homiletician John

Holbert concludes that a closer look reveals several positive features about this passage. The fact that God comes to Job at all is positive. His friends predicted God would not deign to speak to Job, or, if a meeting occurred, would destroy him. Second, God's tone is harsh, but it needs to be to grab Job's attention. Job has uttered ten harsh speeches of his own. With each speech Job places himself and his concerns more and more directly in the center of creation and moves God farther and farther away from the center.

God's harsh tone decenters Job, moves him out of the spotlight of the cosmos. This is the purpose of the meteorology lesson. God has concerns more important than the alleged injustices of one person. The world does not revolve around Job and his plight, but around God and the complex world God has created and is sustaining.

A Catalogue of Animals

The catalogue of the world's animals serves the same purpose of decentering Job (38:39–39:30). The creatures listed, with the exception of the great war horse, are those who have little or nothing to do with human beings. The catalogue of animals challenges Job and his friends' simple view of life: the good receive good and the bad receive bad. Would a simple world include a bizarre creature like the ostrich, whose wings flap but don't fly, and who leaves its eggs on the ground to be stepped on? (39:14-15). Would a simple world include the raven whose young depend on the blood of corpses for life? If death is necessary in this complex cosmos in order to foster life, are questions of righteousness and wickedness the right questions? They certainly are not simple questions!

God is the source of mind-boggling creativity, not one who is preoccupied only with human affairs. Job is prodded to view his experience in the broader context of the natural world. Human history takes place in that context and not vice versa. God's speeches offer us a cosmological rather than an anthropological perspective.[30]

"The actions of God are not, in fact, centered in conventional responses to wickedness and righteousness," says John Holbert. "The universe is, in fact, filled to the brim with mystery and surprise and wonder. The theology of Job and the friends provided for none of these. God's answer to Job is: 'Think again, Job. Open your eyes wider to the whole of the cosmos. Redirect your attentions away from what you have done to what I am doing.'"[31]

Do You Have to Make Me Wrong
So You Can Be Right?

In Job's response in 40:1-5 Job is terse and seemingly sullen. It is as if God's words have gone unheard. And so God speaks again. Verses 6-14 are a turning point. God asks Job, Do you have to make me wrong so that you can be right? (40:8). This is a response to Job's earlier statement "Far be it from me to say that you are right; until I die I will not put away my integrity from me" (27:5). Now God asks if that is the only way to formulate the problem of the pain of the universe: "If I am righteous, then God must be wicked."

Job and his four friends have missed out on the same crucial insight. Job can be righteous. And God can be righteous. And there can still be undeserved suffering and evil in this complex world.

Robert Wise cautions us against blaming our suffering on the will of God. "God's will becomes a drape to throw over problems we don't want to explore. The divine shroud is dropped over the issue to stifle and avoid any in-depth encounter with the hard side of life. General usage implies, 'Don't think, just accept.' ...If all the terror is God's will, then what kind of God do we have?"[32]

God is inviting Job to look beyond his circle of pain and reflect on the ordering of the cosmos. Job and the friends believe that God punishes the wicked and rewards the righteous. God challenges Job, saying if this is what he thinks God should do, then he [Job] should do it, using his El-like arm to deal with the wicked as he thinks God should.

This divine challenge accomplishes two important things. First, it shows how ridiculous Job and the friends' notion of how God acts in the world really is. God doesn't go about crushing the wicked. Job wishes God would, so he, by being righteous, could get the rewards he would then deserve. But such a God is a human invention. Second, if God doesn't punish the wicked, the burden of proof is not on God to show either that Job is wicked or to admit that God is wicked.[33]

Job's demand that God show him the sins that brought on the divine attacks is completely off base. God does not act like that at all. The actions of God are not all reactions to human behaviors. We can no longer suppose that life events are signs of God's approval and favor or God's punishment. God is shown to be free. Our attempts to control God are exposed as futile.[34]

GOD'S SECOND SPEECH (40:6–41:34)

Now God focuses Job's attention on two primordial beasts, Behemoth (40:15-24) and Leviathan (41). Behemoth may find its mythological origins in one of the two monsters of chaos of an ancient religion. Leviathan was identified with the sea while Behemoth was consigned to the wilderness. In the intertestamental books of IV Esdras and the Apocalypse of Baruch, these two beasts are named as the fish to be eaten at the great messianic banquet which will celebrate God's final victory over the forces of chaos and evil.[35] God's point here is that Behemoth is as much a creation of Yahweh as Job is. God wants Job to look at the beasts and learn that evil and chaos exist in the world of God.[36]

The name Behemoth is the plural form for beast or cattle. This huge land monster is God's handiwork (39:15) and is not independent of God nor a threat to God's power.[37] Job needs to learn that both he and Behemoth have common origins and are therefore bound up together in the world created by Yahweh. Yahweh will not destroy Behemoth so Job can live free in a neat and tidy world. The existence of Behemoth and his creation by Yahweh suggests that the cosmos is messier and more mysterious than Job had imagined. In a universe where the fearsome Behemoth lives, how can we posit a mechanical view of divine actions?

The same principle applies to Leviathan. This twisting serpent of the sea, ever ready to rise and destroy the world, could have free reign to destroy the world without the power of a vigilant God.

These creatures, like Job, find their place in the complex world of God.[38] None of the myths of the ancient world tell of the ultimate destruction of chaos. Rather, the god who is equal to the battle and able to conquer the enemy merely restrains it. Constant vigilance over this captive threat is vital for the continued safety and harmony of the universe. Job had accused Yahweh, using his own suffering as evidence, of having lost this control.

In his response to Job, Yahweh portrays Leviathan as a creature like the crocodile, a ferocious menace. Can Job snare and repress him? Yahweh asks. Cajole him like a domesticated pet? Train him and lead him around as a showpiece? In effect, Yahweh has been able to do this. While the animal may pose a threat to Job, he certainly does not pose a threat to God in any way. The fact that Yahweh has bridled the monster of chaos indicates that divine control is exercised in each and every realm of creation, mythological, material, or moral. No human has the capacity to confront Leviathan. It stands to reason, then, that no human can challenge the monster's captor. God is beholden to no one, and has no equal to question divine governance.[39]

Behemoth shakes the earth with his step and Leviathan slithers through the oceans. God forces Job to acknowledge their fearsome existence. Why? In order that he can see firsthand that chaos and mystery are a real part of God's complex creation. Job's questions have not been dismissed. Rather, they have been put in the context of a cosmic reality that makes them ultimately irrelevant to the real world revealed by Yahweh.

The two beasts are evidence that God does not destroy the wicked out of hand, though God continually acts to control them, both at the human and the cosmic level. In a world where Behemoth and Leviathan stomp and swim, how could we hold the notion that God easily controls the forces of chaos without struggle? How can we hold to a notion of simple rewards and punishments?[40] There is evil in the complex design of Yahweh's creation, and yet Yahweh is somehow involved in it. Rather than defend a world that does not exist, we need to busy ourselves with the comfort of those who have suffered appallingly in that real world.[41]

Job emerges from his encounter with God with a different worldview and a different understanding of God than that of traditional wisdom. Says wisdom scholar Leo Perdue,

> It is grounded in the understanding that the creator engages in a life and death struggle with a chaos, embodied in two mythological monsters, intent on bringing creation to an end. Justice as a life-giving power is not a guaranteed given in the nature and operation of the cosmos, but rather an agent at work in the character and active rule of God. And this God, though powerful and wise, is not omnipotent. While evil may not have gained the upper hand, it still infringes on the world and causes great suffering. Job learns that the ongoingness of life is ultimately

dependent on Yahweh's power and wisdom in bringing mighty chaos and its mythical incarnations to their knees. This active struggle for the continuation of threatened life is divine justice.[42]

Lifeform

As a result of making our way through the varying threads of this narrative, what shapes the lifeform we are to live by?

The book of Job is not a unified wisdom system for harnessing spiritual principles in the service of attaining our heart's desires. In fact, its major premise undercuts much of contemporary motivational and self-help wisdom's assumption that if we follow certain principles of attitude and behavior, we will be accomplished and successful, in whatever field of endeavor matters to us. Only God can put a ring in the nose of the mighty beasts of sea and air that symbolize evil and chaos and swim and strut across the created order. But in contemporary motivational wisdom, the Behemoths and Leviathans of modern life can be tamed by mind training—positive thinking and imaging.

Such wisdom has the achievement of a desired end or human goal as the motivation for religious devotion. It is functional, pragmatic, utilitarian, self-help. Nowhere does it ever ask, Shouldn't we love God for the sheer joy of loving God and the satisfaction it brings? Shouldn't we love God even if that love means failure or even censure in the eyes of the world?

Legend recounts the following dream by sixteenth-century Spanish mystic St. Teresa of Avila. She was walking down the street of a town and saw coming toward her a prophetess carrying a torch in one hand and a bucket of water in the other. Why do you carry these things? she asked the prophetess. "With this torch I will burn down the halls of heaven, and with this bucket of water I will douse the flames of hell. Then people will worship God, not for hope of heaven or fear of hell, but for God's sake alone."[43]

Both Job and his friends share the same assumption, the tenets of traditional wisdom with which they grew up. That is; if they live righteously and wisely, things will go well for them. And if they live wickedly and foolishly, their lives will be filled with suffering.

From the Prologue we know that this suffering was allowed, not caused, by God. For most of the book, Job and his friends are left to draw their own conclusions. The friends conclude that since Job is suffering, he must be evil. Job concludes that, since he knows he is righteous and he is suffering, God must be evil. As it turns out, both conclusions are in error.

At the beginning of his *Summa Theologiae* Thomas Aquinas states what he believes to be a basic principle governing theological reflection. "We cannot know what God is but only what God is not."[44] Reading through Job offers a stringent session of reality therapy around the issue of who God is and is not. The God who created and maintains the universe is well-qualified for the job. Our individual lives are not at the center of the universe, as we assume by our total absorption in our sufferings.

Our traditional formulas of "divine" retribution are far more human than they are divine. There is mystery at the heart of the universe beyond our human categories. There are no grounds for seeking to place blame, either on ourselves or on God.

When Our Friends Suffer

Perhaps we ought to give the friends the benefit of the doubt and assume they intended to console Job. Perhaps on the way there they discussed pastoral strategies. Perhaps there was something about seeing his suffering up close and personal and seeing it continue day after day, that turned their consolations into accusations. The friends begin by offering up the traditional notion that suffering is God's disciplining of the righteous to perfect them still further. It is temporary, says Eliphaz, and Job will be restored and strengthened if he can endure this trial (5:17-27). But like us, his vicarious pain threshold is low. That is why the disciples slept while Jesus prayed in the garden of Gethsemane. That is why, after an appropriate interval, we want to hear bereaved people respond to our "How are you?" with a cheery "Much better, thank you!" That is why the care of a loved one during a prolonged illness is one of the most taxing assignments life can hold. We hold a vigil that is a strange emotional mix, a stew of concern, empathy, anger, sorrow, and irritation. Perhaps that is why Job's friends shift from consolation to accusations.

It is reported in a late Rabbinic text, *The Fathers According to Rabbi Nathan*, Chapter 14, that when the son of Rabban Johanan ben

Zakkai died, each of the rabbi's five disciples came to comfort him. Four of them successively compared Rabban Johanan's loss to the respective losses suffered by Adam at the death of Abel (Genesis 4:8), Job at the loss of his sons and daughters, Aaron's loss of his sons Nadab and Abihu (Leviticus 10:1-2), and King David's loss of the unnamed love child born to him by Bathsheba (2 Samuel 12:19). To each of these four would-be comforters who, as they say, "meant well." Rabban Johanan asked, "Is it not enough that I grieve over my own, that you remind me of the grief of (someone else)?!" However, Rabbi Eleazar son of 'Arak told his teacher Rabban Johanan how very special was the latter's deceased son who studied all of the Torah "and departed from the world without sin. And you should be comforted since you returned (to God) your trust unimpaired."[45]

The difference between Rabbi Eleazar son of 'Arak and the other disciples is that he alone relates directly to the issue at hand—the unique loss of Rabban Johanan's son. It is he alone who chooses to validate and to empathize rather than to trivialize the matter at hand. The disciples of Rabban Johanan could have done much worse, they could have done what Job's friends did: marginalize and blame the sufferer.[46]

We all know people who send cancer patients books which suggest that they brought the disease on themselves and that they have it in their power to reactivate their immune system. One of the very basic elements of grief is anger, some of which is turned on the suffering person him/herself by family and friends.[47] Mingled in with grief and anger is fear, for the suffering of another is an unwelcome reminder that, if it could happen to them, it could happen to us.

Job teaches us to face into our own fears for the sake of one another.

Says liberation theologian Gustavo Gutiérrez "In the book of Job, to be a believer means sharing human suffering, especially that of the most destitute, enduring a spiritual struggle, and finally accepting the fact that God cannot be pigeonholed in human categories."[48]

Gutiérrez articulates the core questions to which Job is a response.

How, then, is a human being to speak of God and to God in the situation Job must endure? We ask the same question today in the lands of want and hope that are Latin America. Here the masses of the poor suffer an inhuman situation that is...undeserved. Nothing can justify a situation in which human beings lack the basic necessities for a life of dignity and in which their most elementary rights are not respected. The suffering and the destructive effect on individuals go far beyond what is seen in a first contact with the world of the poor. In such a situation, what content can be assigned to the "Abba, Father!"... that the Spirit cries within us (Galatians 4:6)? How are we to proclaim the reign of love and justice to those who live in an inexplicable situation that denies this reign? How are we to bring joyous conviction to our utterance of the name of God?[49]

He concludes that "[talk] about God... leads to a living encounter with God in specific historical circumstances. It requires... that we discover the features of Christ in the sometimes disfigured faces of the poor of this world. This discovery will not be made apart from concrete gestures of solidarity with our brothers and sisters who are wretched, abandoned, and deprived."[50]

Sometimes, people are hesitant to visit friends and family members who are suffering because they "just don't know what to say." The truth is, some of the things we think of to say do more harm than good.

"It is God's will." "God wanted another little angel in the heavenly choir." "Everything happens for a reason." "Have you heard about the relationship between cancer and stress?" "If you have enough faith, you can receive a healing." These kinds of comments slip out of our mouths when we come face to face with the misfortune of another. I hear them in the grocery aisle, the funeral home, and the fellowship hall at church. They are meant to be kind words, words that have the power to heal by conveying our faith in God's will, our struggle to figure life out, and our empathy for God's children. We want to reassure people that God will fix things, or that they can fix themselves, that, whatever the bereavement, they will eventually "get over it," and recoup their losses.

In their attempt to offer consolation, Job's friends trivialized his sufferings and plastered over, or whitewashed, some disturbing reflections. Imagine a wall on which some painful facts of life are scrawled. "All suffering cannot be avoided or banished by our right thoughts and faithful prayers." "God's will is vastly more complex than the straightforward doling out of good and bad events to punish, reward, and teach human beings." "Life's misfortunes have the power to do us damage. None of us escapes unscathed."

Job expresses his reaction to his friends' attempts at pastoral consolation with these angry words, "As for you, you whitewash with lies; . . . All of you are worthless physicians" (13: 4). Our comments, meant to heal, because they are rooted in falsehood, do more damage than good.

However, we ought not avoid our suffering loved ones because "we don't know what to say." But rather than spout such fallacies, it would be far better to sit down next to them and put our arm around their shoulder.

That would have been Job's preference with regard to his friends. His friends' finest moments were the seven days and seven nights that they sat with him and kept silent (2:13).

Could it be that actions are the most important form of consolation in the face of inexplicable suffering? A friend of mine, during a recent illness, became irritated by the number of people who said to her "If there is anything I can do, let me know." "Why do they say that?" she demanded. "They don't really mean it! Suppose I really called them up and told them something I wanted them to do for me. Like, come over and paint my house. Cut my toenails. Clean out my garage. Detail my car."

"Well," I replied, "what would you rather they said?"

"I'd rather they would call and ask if they can come over. I'd rather they show they care by their presence. Instead, they put the burden on me to call them and tell them if there is anything they can do for me. I'm not going to pick up the phone, call them, and tell them what I really need them to do for me. Because if I did that, here is what I would say: 'I feel alone. I'm scared. I feel vulnerable. Please come over.' Who wants to get an invitation like that?"

There is a story that appeared in *Guideposts* magazine in 1981 about a young mother who received word that her brother and his wife, her sister, and both the sister's children had been killed in a car wreck. She goes on to tell how she was numbed by the news and was having difficulty accomplishing the necessary tasks to prepare for their flight back to Missouri to be with her family. At that point, a friend stopped by and simply said he was there to polish their shoes. In response to her surprised look he recounted how during a family tragedy it had taken him over an hour to polish all the family's shoes. Watching this friend sitting on the kitchen floor polishing all their shoes reminded her of someone else sitting on the floor washing people's feet, a simple act of presence and service. She writes, "Now, whenever I hear of an acquaintance who has lost a loved one, I no longer call with the vague offer, 'If there's anything I can do…' Now I try to think of one specific task that suits that person's need—such as washing the family car, taking the dogs to the boarding kennel, or housesitting during the funeral. And if the person says to me, 'How did you know I needed that done?' I reply 'It's because a man once cleaned my shoes.'"[51]

"If only you would keep silent, that would be your wisdom!" says Job to his friends in 13:12. We need to reflect on the consolation we can offer another by our intercessory prayers on their behalf in the privacy of our own chambers. We need to reflect on whether at times it might not be best to sit in silence with a suffering friend, embodying God's consolation by our presence and our compassion.

Instead, Job's friends blather on with variations on the same theme that Job must have sinned or he would not be suffering. In chapter 16, Job once again rails at his friends for their poor comfort, saying "Miserable comforters are you all. Have windy words no limit? Or what provokes you that you keep on talking?" (16:2-3).

Perhaps they keep talking because their empathy has given way to irritable, fearful accusations. Job imagines what he would like to say, were he in their shoes and they in his. "I also could talk as you do, if you were in my place; I could join words together against you, and shake my head at you. I could encourage you with my mouth, and the solace of my lips would assuage your pain" (Job 16:1-5). Job's friends should keep their day jobs. "Your maxims are proverbs of ashes, your defenses are defenses of clay" (13:12).

They have been unable or unwilling to hear Job's pain, his raw experience, and to include that experience in their understanding of the way things really are. Job's experience is not compatible with their theological platitudes. Job does not exist for them; they consider his account of his life experience to be invalid and not worthy of a hearing because it does not match their own. As preachers we need to remind ourselves and our people that our world most certainly does include Job and his sufferings, no matter how inconvenient his experience may be for our tidy conception of the way things are.[52]

Job's friends cannot be called wise, because they have abandoned the very criterion for wisdom, namely, a deep and faithful reflection on life with all its joys and sorrows. Wisdom scholar Dianne Bergant characterizes the friends in this way: "There is no evidence that these men preach one thing and live another. They appear to be fundamentally good men who, according to Job's accusation, have been spared the ambiguities of life and mistake the tranquility of their situation for virtue."[53]

A student of mine once recounted how, as a novice preacher, she took her sermons to her mother who was in the hospital in the last stages of cancer. Saturday nights she would take her manuscript and read it to her mother. Her mother had always been one to speak her mind, and now was no different. She was not content to let any saccharine generalizations about God's love solving our problems, or the power of faith go unchallenged. "Blanche," her mother would say, "I'm lying here dying, what does this mean to me?" After the fifth or sixth interruption, Blanche said, "Mama, I know you're lying there dying, but you still know how to drive me crazy!"

We preachers need to allow Job to interrupt our easy assurances about how faith solves everything, how turning our lives over to Jesus means an end to sin and sorrow in our lives. He represents the voices of suffering people in our community and world, "We're lying here dying, what does this mean to us?" Don't tell us what we ought to feel when we are suffering. Don't tell us how we could have avoided our sufferings. Tell us something good and realistic and specific. Tell us what God's presence means for us while we are suffering. Tell us how we can speak of and to God in such pain.

On the one hand, Job offers a cautionary tale—it points toward Job's friends and says to us, "There but by the grace of God go you." On the other hand, it is a positive encouragement to hear and accept the sufferings of others, to offer empathy, not judgment, compassion, not accusations, and helpful, practical companionship, not tidy platitudes.

There is a social dimension to the guidance Job gives us on how to treat our friends. It equips us to preach about our congregation's perspective on the suffering of marginalized social groups. Dianne Bergant says Job makes several claims in this regard. First, deprivation is no indication of ethical inferiority. Second, conventional systems of understanding sometimes treat nonconformity as moral deviance. Third, God condemns such prejudicial thinking. Good and upright people do, in fact, fall victim to misfortune. Honesty and personal integrity demand that injustice be unmasked regardless of who the perpetrator seems to be. Solidarity with the oppressed is a religious as well as a humanitarian responsibility.[54]

When We Suffer

There is no circumstance in human life that makes it more difficult to accept the freely given love of God than our own experience of suffering, especially if the suffering is unjust. We have seen how Job's friends, worn out by the intense and unrelenting quality of his suffering, shift from consolation to accusation. Job undergoes a shift in his response to his own suffering. He begins with resigned acceptance of his plight from the hand of God. As his sufferings deepen and show no signs of letting up, his emotions shift gears. His initial acceptance (2:10) shifts to cursing the day he was born (chapter 3). He then transitions to a dogged defense of his own integrity that makes such suffering an affront. His final phase is a recognition of his own human limitations and the greatness, presence, and mystery of God (42:1-6).

Resignation, anger, defensiveness—these are all emotions we experience in times of suffering. The book of Job does not help us explain the impenetrable mystery of suffering, rather it sheds light on how we are to speak of God in the midst of suffering. Job equips us to preach alternative responses to undeserved suffering in our own lives: sturdy acceptance of life's bitter pills, stubborn expectation of spiritual blessing as an outcome of our suffering, and surrender of our plans and hopes into the hands of God.

How will Job speak of God in this situation? Will he reject God? Have his piety and uprightness perhaps been really based on his material prosperity? Will he curse God for having destroyed all that prosperity? Are we, when suffering, able to enter into an authentic relationship with God and find a correct way of speaking about God? If the answer is yes, then it will be possible to do the same in other human situations. If the answer is no, then in less profound and challenging situations we may only appear to accept the freely given grace of God's love and only claim to love God for God's own sake. In reality, we may be practicing barter religion, offering devotion to God as long as God blesses us with health, prosperity, and good fortune.

Homiletics professor Ronald Osborn once read an announcement in his local paper that a new preacher was coming to town who had won an award in "pre-aching" while she was in seminary. Osborn was puzzled. Was this award for exemplary advance empathy toward people's pain? Finally it dawned on him that it was a typo and that she had won a preaching award, not a preaching one![55] There is, however, considerable truth in that typo. Our preaching has an important preparatory function.

Before the next crisis strikes, during that pre-aching period, we are called to help prepare people spiritually for times of anguish. Now is the time to challenge our people to evaluate the depth of their faith. Now is the time to face the facts of an unpredictable life. Now is the time to introduce them to a mysterious yet gracious God. Now is the time to teach them that the presence of suffering and evil in the world does not signal an absent or malevolent God.

Now is the time to preach sermons that reframe the statement "It must be God's will" for our people. Many of them apply that sentence narrowly to times of unexplained and excruciating suffering, to times when the physical healing we begged for didn't materialize. What about all the positive and redeeming outcomes that are said to be God's will in Scripture? In the Wisdom literature, God's will is that we find guidance, peace, joy, light, harmony, and eternal life. Why do we reserve the statement "It must be God's will" for tragic moments and forget to utter it during times of celebration and hope? How about a sermon series on the positive applications of the concept of the will of God?

We have allowed Job's friends to write our scripts for too long. God seems to think so, anyway. For in the end, God agrees with Job that the only good thing about his friends' advice is that it is free. He says to Eliphaz the Temanite, the last speaker, "My wrath is kindled against you and against your two friends; for you have not spoken of me what is right, as my servant Job has" (42:7).

How has he spoken of God what is right? He is not right about God and God's actions in the world. He has just recanted those comments in his final address of 42:1-6. Yahweh appears to mean simply that the words that Job directed to God were judged to be truly spoken.[56] What God affirms is Job's refusal to deny the pain and reality of his sufferings, even though they did not fit with traditional formulations. Job has refused to compromise his integrity. He has presented to God the full range of his sorrow and outrage at the sufferings of life. Job scholar Norman Habel says "the blunt and forthright language of Job from the depths of his agony are far closer to the truth of things than those conventional unquestioning pronouncements of the friends."[57]

When we suffer, we need continually to come before God offering the wide spectrum of our emotions, the raging anger, the melancholy, the hurt, and the disappointment. When others suffer we need to hear their experience without judgment but with compassion, offering the consolation of our presence and active assistance. That is the path to restoration for individuals and communities.

Preaching Restoration

The restoration in chapter 42 of Job has long puzzled students because it seems to undermine the lessons of the poems. But the restoration is not simply a return to how things were before. Job is changed and so is his world. Job's restoration is tied to his intercessory prayer for his friends. When we are suffering, our tendency is to draw within ourselves, consumed by our physical and emotional pain. Part of that pain can be the result of holding in negative, accusatory feelings toward others for the ways they have wrongly responded or neglected to respond to our situation. They said the wrong thing. They dropped by at an inconvenient time. They never came to see me. No one from church called to see how I was until I'd been in the hospital for three whole days! It might be very healing to pray for others when we are suffering ourselves. We might find, as Job did, that extending forgiveness to others, realizing we are not the center of the cosmos, can open up a path of liberation and spiritual restoration.

The restored community shares a communal meal, an act of hospitality that cemented relationships among people in that culture. They offer Job comfort and consolation. Rather than whitewash the reality of suffering in the world, they comfort one who is in pain. We are told that Job gives his daughters as well as his sons an inheritance. It seems as if his experience of suffering has led him, the head of the household in a patriarchal society, to a new vision of God working toward *shalom* through both men and women. (42: 15). We are told that Job died old and "full of days." This is a sign of God's favor reminiscent of the patriarchs Abraham, Isaac, Jacob, and Joseph. God favors Job for his truth-telling, for his refusal to blame himself and other sufferers for their own misery. God favors Job with a personal audience.

There is an African-American saying that we are always going into a storm, in a storm, or coming out of a storm. In all these places, our people, us included, need to meet the God Job met. We need to come before this God telling the truth about the depth of our pain and our disappointment in our own and others' lives. This God may not turn out to be the God to whom we have been praying or the God we were raised to expect. This is not the God who promises prosperity and protection. This is a God for grownups. This is the God who cares enough to show up. This is the God who has enough respect for us to give us the harsh, but liberating truth, right between the eyes. Thanks be to God!

CHAPTER SEVEN

Qohelet: Face the Truth, Find the Joy!

When times are good, be happy; but when times are bad, consider: God has made the one as well as the other.
(Ecclesiastes 7:15)

Background Check

What a pity that Christian preachers don't preach on Ecclesiastes more often! When we flip past it, assuming it is depressing and pessimistic, we miss a book that is just what the doctor ordered for contemporary congregations. We skip over the work of a seasoned sage whose realistic joy can help equip us for the drudgery of everyday life and the dreaded day when illness, accident, or bereavement strikes.

Ecclesiastes offers us the vision of someone who, like today's self-help authors, wrote out of a context of social uncertainty. He is someone, however, who presents us with a diametrically opposite message and purpose to the varieties of cultural wisdoms. In my imagination I picture Qohelet reading Napoleon Hill's *Think and Grow Rich* or sitting in the audience at a self-help seminar. I have no doubt he would be shaking his head and rolling his eyes.

It would be just like Qohelet, were he around today, to advertise a seminar of his own with a crowd-drawing title like "Face the Truth: Find the Joy!" I can picture the wry old sage standing next to his laptop with a PowerPoint presentation going on the big screen. The morning session would be devoted to the topic "Your Limitations: Live with Them!" The first afternoon session, by which time half the participants would have left, would cover the topic: "The God You'll Never Know." The two people who stayed until the final session would be treated to the topic: "Life Is Unpre-dictable Except for Death."

So much for our hopes of ever seeing Qohelet's face on a Barnes & Noble bag! No wonder we don't preach much from Ecclesiastes. We aren't used to such a potent dose of reality therapy. Contemporary Christian preachers are not the only ones who have had trouble embracing the bracing message of Qohelet. When the Council of Jamnia met in 90 CE to establish the Hebrew canon, the rival schools of rabbis, Shammai and Hillel, differed over the status of Ecclesiastes. The House of Shammai rejected its claim to be an inspired book because of its radical perspective. The school of Hillel approved it out of appreciation for the same. Ecclesiastes remained a book on the margins of the canon, but eventually its authority was acknowledged by a majority of Jews and Christians.[1] Martin Luther said we should read "this noble little book" every day, precisely because it so firmly rejects sentimental religiosity![2]

We contemporary Christian preachers need to embrace Qohelet's collection precisely because of its radical perspective. Far from being an unorthodox spoiler, Qohelet affirms an insight that is at the heart of biblical wisdom. That is the acknowledgment that human limitation and divine transcendence shape the context in which all our efforts at wisdom are conducted. As we have seen, this insight is touched upon in Proverbs in the "limit proverbs" (16:1, 2, 9; 19:21; 20:24; 21:30-31). For Qohelet, risk, humility, recep-tivity to the precarious joy of the present moment, and gratitude become the virtues of the wise life.

The same rabbis who attributed Proverbs to the young King Solomon viewed Ecclesiastes as the reflections of the years when his hair had turned the color of almond blossoms. Though the author never mentions Solomon explicitly in the book, the text intends to evoke the memory of the king in its autobiographical confessions of a royal figure who collects both wisdom and wealth.[3] The book is a collection of wisdom teachings cast as an autobiography of a king.[4]

His work is a parody of ancient Near Eastern royal inscriptions that recount the great deeds of kings of the past so that those who pass by will remember their great wisdom and achievements. It is a parody because Qohelet's greatest accomplishment is the recog-nition of the vanity of human ambition and efforts at gaining immortality through one's great deeds. Ecclesiastes represents what wisdom scholar James Williams has called "an aphoristic wisdom of counter-order." Others have labeled the book's brand of wisdom "a bleak and cynical strain" in ancient Near Eastern wisdom literature. Ecclesiastes has distant cousins among writings from Egyptian and Mesopotamian wisdom literature.[5]

Scholars have proposed dates of composition ranging from the tenth century BCE (on the assumption that Solomon wrote it) down to the first century BCE. Specific historical references are absent, but linguistic clues point to the Persian period.[6] Ecclesiastes was most likely written between the second half of the fifth and the first half of the fourth centuries BCE during the period of Persian rule.

Qohelet was likely a member of what Leo Perdue has called the "critical sages," a group who were critical of the priests, prophets, and traditional sages who had wealth and political influence. These traditional-minded groups had aligned themselves with the political agenda of the Persian authorities and were heavily invested in maintaining the economic and political status quo. The critical sages were not themselves poor, dispossessed, and uneducated. They were from responsible families with means, if not with power, and were well-educated intellectuals. They became increasingly pessimistic about the transformation of the current social order. Some became apocalyptic visionaries, nurturing a hope that God would bring a dramatic ending to the current state of things and refashion a new social and political order.

Others, like the sages responsible for Job and Qohelet, held no such hope. According to Qohelet, "there is nothing new under the sun" (Ecclesiastes 1:9*b*). These critical sages focused their energies on challenging the conventions of conservative wisdom teachers and the priests with whom they had aligned themselves. They reached pessimistic, skeptical conclusions about the evils of the current cosmic and social order and its glaring injustices.[7]

Qohelet's concerns and themes are consistent with this time of economic and social uncertainty. The economy of this period had changed from the subsistence agrarian culture of preexilic Judah to a competitive commercial atmosphere. The Persians introduced coinage, and money became not just a convenient medium of exchange, but a commodity. Inscriptions of the period are full of references to money in connection with taxes, wages, rent, loans, fines, inheritance, and the prices of goods and services. Money was used in everyday business transactions both large and small, given as gifts and bribes, and hoarded.[8]

Commerce was no longer primarily a royal enterprise, but was democratized and privatized. Qohelet's warnings about the limited satisfaction and protection offered by money reflect his context: a competitive commercial environment.[9] Finding analogies between his time and our own hardly stretches the homiletical imagination.

The Persian system of land grants to favored individuals was a feature of Qohelet's social setting that influenced his view of both life and God. Those who received such grants were responsible to collect the taxes from their domains, but they could also retain a portion of that collection.[10] Proprietors sublet their properties to smallholders who in turn rented them to tenant farmers who in turn employed workers. This system has shaped the way Qohelet expresses life's opportunities: as a portion (*heleq*) (5:18-20).

In this view, life is like a portion that one receives as a grant from the divine sovereign. It is like a lot that is limited in time and space. In this lot the grantee toils, but it is also possible to enjoy the fruits of one's toil from that lot (5:18). In this grant from God there is both the inevitability of toil and the possibility of enjoyment. So when one has a portion, however imperfect that portion may be, one had better make the most of it, for that portion can be enjoyed only while one is alive. No one can take the portion along with him or her when death comes. No one has a portion that lasts forever (9:6).[11]

The social setting in which Qohelet wrote has also affected his view of God. Qohelet's experience of the arbitrariness of the Persian rulers colors his view of God. The divine sovereign can be just as arbitrary as the Persian ruler who issues royal grants. We live our lives in the context of an inscrutable and distant God. We receive whatever portion the divine sovereign chooses to give us. Wisdom pleases God, but it is no guarantee of a large and lucky portion (2:24-26).[12]

"Life in General, Mostly Dogs"

When I teach Introductory Preaching classes, the first session I hand out an index card to each student. I ask them to write down their name, phone number, denomination, preaching experience, what they hope to learn from the course, and their greatest anxiety about preaching. A couple of years ago, I followed this procedure in my morning class. That evening, after the children were in bed, I sat at my desk in my home office going through the cards. Under the "greatest anxiety" category, a couple of students had written: "speaking in front of a group." I could help them with that. Another had written "coming up with new ideas every week." I could help with that. Still another had written "dealing with controversial topics." I could help with that.

When I got to the last three cards I discovered that my directions on how to fill out the cards must not have been sufficiently clear. Not everyone had gotten the message that what I was looking for in the anxiety category was specific: what was their greatest fear *about preaching*.

For under the "greatest anxiety" category, one student had written "aging." Not much I could do for them there. A second had written, "death." There I felt even more helpless. And one dear soul, in a spurt of honesty, had scrawled, "Life in general, mostly dogs."

Any good preacher analyzes the anxieties as well as the complacencies of her intended audience and shapes her message to assuage and confront as needed. We can watch and learn from Qohelet in this regard. His economic setting is one which, like our own, lends itself both to economic exploitation and economic opportunity (5:8-9). Poorer people could accumulate assets by borrowing, hiring themselves out as substitutes for others in mandatory military service, or by pooling capital with others in joint ventures. With ambition, however, came risks of loss and injury. Qohelet's audience lives with the possibility of improving their lot, but also with the fear of poverty. Qohelet's comments about envy (4:4, 6) and the vain pursuit of wealth (4:7-8) reflect his social setting.

He knows his audience well: they are people who are not secure with what they have. They are constantly toiling to acquire more and more, and they are worried about losing what they have. They are not society's wealthy, not the nobles, the princes, and the rich (10:16-20). They are in the middle, the commoners, the smallholders and homesteaders, the middle class. Accidents and mishaps in the workplace threaten them. They are perfumers (10:1), hunters, farmers, woodcutters, and quarry workers (10:8-10). They are criticized by their servants (7:21) and in turn criticize their social superiors (10:20).[13]

In Qohelet's competitive economic culture people are driven by envy to strive for success and cannot seem to be satisfied (4:4-8). Those suffering from injustice have no one on their side (4:1-3). The evil of human greed is portrayed in terms of a gaping mouth (6:7-9). There are people willing to do anything in order to get ahead, and the rich are circumventing the law at the expense of others (8:11-14). The ordinary citizen is at the mercy of rich and powerful proprietors, provincial judges and other officials, and the government with its hosts of spies (10:20).

This social setting shapes Qohelet's depiction of humanity as helpless before the whim of the sovereign deity (Ecclesiastes 6:10). His world was unpredictable, full of opportunity but also of risk. It was a world of money, commerce, and investment, but also of loans, mortgages, and foreclosures. For the smallholder, the homesteader, and the worker, there was much room for anxiety and little room for certainty. In the economy of the Persian period, members of Qohelet's audience were helplessly caught in the tides of swift political and economic changes. Many of Qohelet's teachings critique their responses of anxiety, envy, and greed.14

Nutshell

What Is Most Important?

One fall, a couple of years ago, I was asked by a religion professor at a small Christian college to come and speak on the message of Ecclesiastes to his freshman "Introduction to the Bible" class. I gave the assignment a lot of thought. I wrote and rewrote the introduction several times. In my first draft, which I entitled, "Traditional Wisdom: Hope and Frustration in Theological Context," I began with a quotation from a commentary on Ecclesiastes:

> The subject of Qohelet's reflections is human life lived in the context of a cosmos that is in the power of a deity who determines all.

It is an existence that, at every hand, frustrates human expectations and over which mortals have no control (7:13-14).[15]

Too heady for college freshmen, I decided, deleted it and tried again. My second attempt, which I called "The Theological Anthropology of a Realistic Sage," went like this:

> Qohelet presents us with a theological anthropology, an account of human life lived before God. Like most wisdom writers, Qohelet takes humanity as his starting point. God is not mentioned in the statements that frame the work (1:2; 12:8), nor does God appear in the preface (1:2-11). But a depiction of an inscrutable, distant God, responsible for good and bad alike, generous yet formidable, looms over the entire book.

Too lofty. Too general, I decided. In the spirit of Qohelet, better cut to the chase.

I typed up my final introduction, did a spell check, printed it out and popped it in my briefcase. I figured it could go one of two ways: three strikes you're out, or the third time's a charm. And there was, as always, only one way to find out.

Since the college was two hours from my home and the class started at 8:00 AM, I got up early to get ready. I poured my travel mug of coffee and set off. Two hours later I stood before a lecture hall packed with fresh-faced eighteen-year-olds.

And so I began. "The title of my talk this morning is 'The Facts of Life.'"

I went on, "Ecclesiastes wants us to face three facts of life we would rather not face: 1. Life is unpredictable; 2. God is unknowable; and 3. Death is inevitable." Having told them what I was going to tell them, I began to tell them. I began by quoting the eloquent words of 9:11-12 that express the unpredictability of life.

> Again I saw that under the sun the race is not to the swift, nor the battle to the strong, nor bread to the wise, nor riches to the intelligent, nor favor to the skillful; but time and chance happen to them. For no one can anticipate the time of disaster. Like fish taken in a cruel net, and like birds caught in a snare, so mortals are snared at a time of calamity, when it suddenly falls upon them (Ecclesiastes 9:11-12).

After appropriate elaboration, I moved on to Qohelet's second point, the inscrutability of God, quoting relevant verses.

> Just as you do not know how the breath comes to the bones in the mother's womb, so you do not know the work of God, who makes everything (11:5).
>
> Consider the work of God; who can make straight what he has made crooked? In the day of prosperity be joyful, and in the day of adversity consider; God has made the one as well as the other, so that mortals may not find out anything that will come after them (7:13, 14).
>
> I have seen the business that God has given to everyone to be busy with. He has made everything suitable for its time; moreover he has put a sense of past and future into their minds, yet they cannot find out what God has done from the beginning to the end (3:10, 11).

Seeing some distressed looks, I worked in a few jokes, and I even mentioned that Qohelet has been called by some scholars "a preacher of joy," for his emphasis that, despite the drudgery and injustice of life, there is joy in our portion. Still, by the time I reached Qohelet's third point, the inevitability of death, a boy on the back row looked pale as a sheet. As I launched into a dramatic reading of chapter 12, I noticed a glistening tear running down the face of a girl halfway back.

By the time the silver cord had snapped, I realized they were all at the end of their ropes. I wrapped it up and sat down. The religion professor stood up, cleared his throat and said, "Thank you, Dr. McKenzie, for that very, uh, enlightening talk. We would love to have you back sometime." The students filed out. Most of them were looking down. One or two cast sullen glances at me. I went home and waited by the phone for two years, but the professor never called back!

I had flopped before when giving sermons and talks. But I had flopped in this case because I had in some way failed to do what I thought I *had* done in that freshman religion class: present biblical truth concisely, clearly, and vividly. Maybe it was my fault. Maybe I had presented the death and limitation stuff more compellingly than the joy theme. Maybe I could blame them: maybe they were just too sheltered to handle the truth! I could only hope that, while I never got a call back, maybe Qohelet did. Maybe they open their Bibles now and then to the realistic yet joyful words of the sadder-but-wiser sage.

"What is most important" or "What is the goal of the life well lived" according to Qohelet? It comes in two parts. First, we face the facts of life we would much prefer to ignore. Only then can we do part two, which is to live each present moment aware of our human limitations and the precious, if precarious, joy an inscrutable God has granted us as our portion in this unpredictable life (3:9-14).

Obstacles

For Qohelet, the highest value is to live gratefully and content-edly in the present moment, acknowledging human limitations and divine mystery. Ironically, he believed that buying into key tenets of traditional wisdom is the chief obstacle to genuine, clear-eyed wisdom. There are three tenets of traditional wisdom that Qohelet is out to debunk. The first is that the "fear of the LORD is the beginning of wisdom." The second is that wisdom leads to a generally fortunate, orderly life characterized by health, prosperity, and many children, and to a community that is characterized by harmony and equity. The third is that wisdom is a gift that God gives us that holds the key to understanding how human life is to be ordered and conducted in relation to God. To base one's life on these three traditional tenets, in Qohelet's view, is to preclude the possibility of enjoying one's portion in the presence of a distant, yet generous God.

In Proverbs we are promised that wisdom holds great benefits for us. When we trust God's wisdom, God makes straight paths for our feet (3:5-8), paths that lead to life (3:13-18). Folly's path is crooked (2:15) and leads to death (8:32-36). By contrast, Qohelet insists that the pursuit of wisdom leads to vexation (1:18) and that "what is crooked cannot be made straight, and what is lacking cannot be counted" (1:15). No amount of wisdom can straighten and order the tangle. Qohelet attributes this to the agency of a mysterious God. "Consider the work of God; who can make straight what he has made crooked?" (7:13). Proverbs personifies both wisdom and folly as inviting women, but Woman Wisdom strengthens the youth to resist the siren call of Woman Folly. Qohelet asserts that he is pursued by folly personified as a woman as he searches for a wisdom that is not to be found (7:23-26).

Qohelet grudgingly acknowledges a couple of positive features of wisdom. Wisdom is better than folly (2:13, 14), wisdom is a gift from God to the one who pleases God (2:26), and God will somehow judge between the righteous and the wicked (3:17).

But close on the heels of each compliment to wisdom comes a reality check. Though wisdom is better than folly, the same fate befalls both the wise and the fool (2:14b). Though God judges between the righteous and the wicked, all die just like the animals with no knowledge of what comes after (3:16-22).[16] Though wise words are better than foolish ones, "one bungler can destroy much good...(9:18b) and "a little folly can outweigh wisdom and honor" (10:1b).

His observations and experience compel Qohelet to divorce the pursuit of wisdom from gain or benefit. There is no profit (*yitron*) in wisdom or toil. Death awaits both wise and fool (2:14; 4:16; 9:2, 3). No matter how hard one works, you cannot rest assured that deserving people will inherit the fruits of your labor (2:21). Among the living, wise conduct does not always result in reward (8:14).

Facilitators

ACCEPT YOUR HUMANITY

Qohelet recommends attitudes and actions that are the subversive flip side of traditional wisdom's tenets. He does not preach that "the fear of the LORD is the beginning of wisdom" as does Proverbs. He does not believe that a canny alertness to life will yield secrets of successful living. Rather, he tells us to "fear God!" Recognize that we are human beings with God-given limitations. Recognize your limitations and be humble and silent before a distant, powerful, and inscrutable God. Do not live your life assuming you can know God (3:9-22; 4:1-3; 5:1-7; 8:16, 17).

EXPECT TO BE DISAPPOINTED

Wisdom has certain powers. It enables one to attain practical goals (9:13-15). It can bring wealth (7:12). It fosters good judgment in personal behavior and practical affairs. The wise person's speech is pleasant and careful (10:12), his face cheerful (8:1*b*). He senses the right time and form of behavior, particularly in the presence of authorities (8:5). The sensible man's softly spoken speech is more effective than a ruler's shout among fools (9:17). The wise person refrains from the frustration of futile inquiry (7:10). The mind of the sensible person is his blessing, the fool's is his bane (10:1).[17]

Despite wisdom's beneficial influence, it fails in several key respects. It is overwhelmed by fickle fortune (9:18; 10:1); it is overwhelmed by death (2:16); and its pursuit leads to pain, for wisdom reveals the limitations of human knowledge and the absurdity of life (1:13; 7:15).[18]

Qohelet does not buy traditional wisdom's assurances that wise living leads to long life, health, many children, and prosperity. Qohelet does not experience life as a predictable, orderly, rewarding experience. Rather, he is continually bumping up against three realities that we would rather ignore: the unpredictability of life, the inscrutability of God, and the inevitability of death. The continual frustration of traditional wisdom's expectations he labels *hebel*. He had hoped the traditional wisdom of cause and effect would help him gain security and profit, but it proved itself to be unreliable, an investment that guaranteed no return.

The literal and probably original meaning of *hebel* is "breath" or "breeze" (Isaiah 57:13). Sometimes *hebel* means "ephemeral," (Proverbs 21:6, Job 7:16; Psalms 39:12; 144:4). It is also used to indicate inefficacy (Isaiah 30:7; 49:4; Job 9:29). It is also used to mean "deceitful," in the sense that something or someone does not do what they are supposed to do (Zechariah 10:2; Psalms 62:10; Job 21:34). In these cases *hebel* refers to a "deceit" or a "lie." The implication of inefficacy and deceit makes *hebel* a fitting epithet for false gods (2 Kings 17:15; Jeremiah 2:5, 8:19, 14:22; Jonah 2:9).[19]

Scholars have suggested a variety of words as the meaning of *hebel* in Qohelet. Some have suggested "vapor," but its connotation of transitory or fleeting does not fit many of the uses of *hebel* in Qohelet (2:23; 6:1-2; 8:14). "Vain," in the sense of trivial and "incomprehensible" have been suggested as renderings of *hebel* in Qohelet, but they prove inadequate as well.[20]

No single English word corresponds exactly to the semantic shape of *hebel* as Qohelet uses it. The best suggestion comes from

Michael V. Fox who argues cogently that the term that most adequately gathers up the connotations of Qohelet's use of *hebel* is "absurdity." He understands absurdity as a disparity between two phenomena that are supposed to be joined by a link of causality but are actually disjunct or even conflicting. The absurd is irrational, an affront to reason understood in the broad sense of the human faculty that seeks and discovers order in the world around us. The quality of absurdity does not inhere in a being, act, or event in and of itself. Rather, it describes the tension between a certain reality and a framework of expectations. [21]

Says Fox,

> Basic to Qohelet's thinking are certain assumptions about the way reality should operate. His primary assumption is that an action and a fitting recompense for that action are cause and effect; one who creates the cause can justly expect the effect. Qohelet identifies this expectation with the reasonableness he looks for in the working of the universe. At the same time that he cleaves to this expectation, he sees that there is in reality no such reasonableness, and his expectations are constantly frustrated.[22]

Qohelet uses *hebel* to refer to human existence and experience but not to God or the cosmos in general. *Hebel* is not something that cannot be understood or that is meaningless. It is something that is absurd, something that actively violates our existing categories of what is meaningful. It represents the varied and continual frustrations of traditional wisdom's expectations. The song lyrics insist, "I beg your pardon, I never promised you a rose garden." Qohelet begs to differ. Traditional wisdom makes all sorts of promises that, in the face of the facts of life, it cannot keep. *Hebel* is the lifelong letdown he experiences along with this painful insight.

ACCEPT YOUR PORTION

A final theme of traditional wisdom that Qohelet debunks is that wisdom is an all-encompassing gift from God that leads to discernment and joy (Proverbs 3:13-18). Because wisdom's tenets do not square with a harsh reality, Qohelet believes its pursuit generally leads to frustration (Ecclesiastes 1:18). Hence Qohelet's repeated question, "What does it profit a man—to exist, to strive, to seek, to achieve?" To this question the answer comes through clearly. There is *no* profit. There is no profit for the human being in his existence, but there is, nevertheless, a "portion" (*heleq*), a share in the world which cannot be preserved, but simply enjoyed at the right time, as God gives the right time in an inscrutable way.[23]

Life holds a gift for human beings, but it is much more modest than the key to an orderly personal and communal life that Proverbs promises. Wisdom's gift is the gift of a portion, or our lot in life, with its measure of irritation and pain, but also with an inherent measure of joy (2:10; 3:22; 5:12, 18; 8:15; 9:9).

Key Texts for Preaching

I can imagine preaching a series entitled "When You Don't Get the Rose Garden You Were Never Promised," following the attitudes listed above that Qohelet believes spring from genuine wisdom and lead to contentment: accept your humanity, expect to be disappointed, and find enjoyment in your portion.

Week One: "Deal!"
(3:9-22; 4:1-3; 5:1-7; 8:16, 17)

Deal! The focus of this first sermon would be on accepting our humanity.

A common phrase these days is "deal with it!" sometimes abbreviated to one word, "deal!" It's used in two primary settings: times when we need to shut up and accept some trivial inconvenience and times when we need to assert self-discipline and hard work to solve a problem. "We have Diet Pepsi, not Diet Coke (or vice versa, depending on your preference.) Deal with it!" "There are no direct flights. You'll have to change planes in Cincinnati. Deal with it!"

Other times, "deal with it!" means asserting self-discipline and elbow grease to find a solution to a problem. "They want the documents by tomorrow. Deal with it!" "You're going to have to start eating better and exercising more if that cholesterol is going to come down. Deal with it!"

Self-help material insists that we "deal with" the challenges of daily life, both big and small, by denying our human limitations. "Know your limits, then exceed them!" says the self-help admonition.

The advice works well in some circumstances. But at other times, we cannot so easily silence our anxieties, and a peppy admonition leads to guilt. "You're going to die. Deal with it!"

"You are only one person. You are not going to accomplish all you might like to in life. Deal with it!" "You cannot know the future. Deal with it!" "You will not be young and healthy and good-looking forever. Deal with it!"

Easier said than done!

Qohelet rubs our noses in the fact that not all limits can be exceeded by the exertion of human will and optimism. We are all limited in time, energy, lifespan, control of certain circumstances (the actions of others and earthquakes, to mention two), and knowledge of God.

Qohelet believes that true wisdom lies in acknowledging our limitations and turning to the One who put them in place. His melancholy resignation is tinged with serenity. What seems to be bad news is actually liberating. We are limited because this is the way God has set things up. It is the divine-human "deal." God will be God and we will be human. We stand before God with appropriate humility. We allow God to be God.

Week Two: "What Ben Franklin Knew"

Recently I toured my son's sixth-grade classroom. On a bulletin board in the corner was a display of "Quotable Quotes." The students had been assigned to write to celebrities and ask them to send back an autographed picture and their favorite quote. There were glossy photos of the governor, sports figures, and local newscasters, all inscribed with upbeat quotes. A photo of a local anchorwoman beamed from the board, inscribed with the saying, "If you can conceive it and believe it, you will achieve it." My son, a big Beatles fan, had written to Paul McCartney and gotten no response, so on an index card pinned to the cork near the bottom of the bulletin board, he had scrawled the following, "Expect the worst and you'll never be disappointed." Ben Franklin. I confronted him with his droll saying when I got home. "I like it. It works," was all he would say, but he said it with a grin.

In this second sermon, the preacher could talk about all the things that disappoint us in life. I asked a group of laypeople at a workshop recently what disappoints them most about life. Among the answers were the following: "child abuse," "human nature," and "having a chronic illness when I'm only 44."

Qohelet's list includes the inevitability of death for wise and fool alike (2:12-17), the fact that earthly toil doesn't lead to lasting profit (2:18-23), the uncertainty and unpredictability of life (6:1-6), and the oppression of the weak by the powerful (4:1-3). Most of us cherish a deeply rooted hope that good behavior should lead to good luck. Gradually, as we proceed through life, we may come to suspect, as Qohelet did, that this construct says more about human beings than it does about God. Maybe the notion of divine retribution was not invented by God!

We need to face into our disappointment with life and God because our lives have not unfolded according to the script we wrote. In the script I wrote, God rubber-stamped all my ambitions and justified all my actions. In my screenplay my good habits led to good health, and my cooperation and kindness to others is reciprocated without fail. In my autobiography, the future is no mystery. Rather, my planning and common sense lead to an orderly, altogether admirable life! And now, at mid-life, I come to find out that, while I have conceived it, and at times even believed it, I have not thoroughly achieved it.

So I wonder what tact to take now. I don't want to live my life expecting the worst so as never to be disappointed. I want to live my life realizing that tidy human constructs, however comforting, are inadequate. I want to live, staying open to the growth that comes from both tragedy and triumph.

I want to accept my humanity so that I can enter into the mystery of the divine presence, not mouthing the particulars of my heart's desire, but with a listening heart. I want to accept the limitations of cause-effect thinking now, with no need for further evidence. For that acceptance enables me to turn my attention from wishful thinking or shrill recriminations to the stubborn stem of joy sprouting up through the concrete of life's challenges.

A few weeks ago I sat in a consulting room at Johns Hopkins Medical Center in Baltimore with my older brother Wade, and our parents, Bob and Beverly. And a liver specialist. The four of us sat in chairs along one wall looking at the doctor who sat on his little swivel doctor's chair drawing a picture of my father's blocked bile ducts on a yellow legal pad. Behind us a gloomy, hazy, late-May afternoon made its presence known through a large window. On the wall opposite us there was a mirror. It framed the four of us in a family portrait whose setting none of us would have chosen. "The tumor has to be removed whether it is benign or malignant. I won't know until I get in there if it is cancerous and how far it has spread," the doctor was saying. I had sat in many such rooms with other people's parents, a solid pastoral comfort. But this was *my* father, my tall, still dark-haired, vigorous father, who walked daily and had been watching his cholesterol like a hawk for twenty or more years. In that moment I discovered some good news: that I hadn't saturated my mind and heart with the Bible's wisdom literature for over a decade for nothing. For someone came to comfort me in that moment. It was none other than the clear-eyed old sage himself: "For everything there is a season, and a time for every matter under heaven: a time to be born, and a time to die; a time to weep, and a time to laugh; a time to mourn, and a time to dance" (3:1, 2, 4).

The doctor was asking my brother and me our blood types and instructing us to go down to the lab to give a pint of blood each for the surgery. He was saying he would have his secretary schedule the operation for the next week and call us in the morning to confirm.

We trudged downstairs and gave our blood. Then, since the sun was shining again, we decided to walk across the street and have crab cake sandwiches.

We sat at an outside table, overlooking the harbor, and enjoyed the delicious food and one another's company, two parents, two grown children, and one old (invisible) guy with hair the color of almond blossoms. His contribution to my thoughts almost brought a half-smile to my lips.

> This is what I have seen to be good: it is fitting to eat and drink and find enjoyment in all the toil with which one toils under the sun the few days of the life God gives us; for this is our lot. Likewise all to whom God gives wealth and possessions and whom he enables to enjoy them, and to accept their lot and find enjoyment in their toil—this is the gift of God. For they will scarcely brood over the days of their lives, because God keeps them occupied with the joy of their hearts (5:18-20).

Week Three: Portion Control

Qohelet's message, on the surface, sounds much like a character wisdom dictum that we ought to be grateful for our blessings because it makes them multiply. A contemporary self-help message states this motivation well.

> Be thankful for this day, and you will fill it with joy. Be appreciative of those around you, and they will bring much value to your life. Be grateful for your opportunities, and you'll find yourself making the most of them.
>
> Be thankful for what you have, and you'll get more from it. Be grateful for the challenges, and they will help you become stronger. Appreciate the dark, cloudy days and they'll instantly become brighter. Appreciate the sunny days, and you'll enjoy them even more.
>
> Those things you take for granted will fade from usefulness as you forget they're even there. By contrast, those things for which you're thankful remain readily available and will grow even stronger as a result of your appreciative attention.
>
> Consider how very fortunate you are. Consider it often. The more you count your blessings, the more there will be to count.[24]

Qohelet repeatedly exhorts us to enjoy our portions and be grateful for the blessings of food and drink, work, and conjugal love. His reason is not because gratitude multiplies our blessings, but because our portions, joy and all, are a gift from God.

Qohelet repeatedly urges us to enjoy life. He repeatedly urges us to remember the inevitability of our death. In fact, he links the two. Acknowledging that we will someday die intensifies our enjoyment of our portions. He reminds us that our portions are not all the same, and encourages us to focus on the joy in our own plot of life rather than bewail that we do not have as much land as our neighbor. Qohelet was someone who expected to exercise a degree of control over his own life because of his wealth and personal authority. He is the perfect messenger for contemporary people in similar positions. His message is that human beings are dependent on structures and systems that are beyond our control. There is not a definite correlation between behavior and the circumstances of life. We need to keep this insight in mind when we are tempted to judge others or ourselves.

Our circumstances are not wholly the result of our choices and actions. Life is threaded through with ambiguity. Neither guilt nor judgment is a productive response to the failure of the humanly manufactured law of divine retribution. Divine retribution is essentially an anthropocentric perspective, since its depiction of God's involvement in human affairs says more about human behavior than it does about divine. [25]

Regardless of our social or economic standing, Qohelet admonishes us to enjoy the God-given gift of life's simple pleasures as they come rather than neglect them in the hope of gaining some kind of profit from toil.[26]

Lifeform

What kind of life does adherence to Qohelet's brand of wisdom shape? It leads to four approaches to life that make up an integral whole. They would lend themselves beautifully to a four-part sermon series.

Week One: A Simple Life
Week Two: A Grateful, Joyful Life
Week Three: A Present Life
Week Four: A God-Fearing Life

Week One: A Simple Life.

Qohelet insists that we experience the joy inherent in constructive work, sufficient food, and fellowship. His advice is clear: do not take these simple pleasures that come from God for granted (2:24-25; 3:13; 5:18). God created human beings for straightforward simplicity in their dealings with one another, but they have become corrupt, preoccupied with self-serving schemes (7:29). Qohelet urges his readers to detach themselves from the anxieties of their uncertain situations (4:6), refrain from envying others (4:4), and from seeking wealth and hoarding it when they get it (5:10-12).

Qohelet urges people not to be too tightfisted with their money, but to take the risk to be generous, even though tragedies may happen in the future. He challenges his readers to take a chance and throw away a good deed: "Send out your bread upon the waters, for after many days you will get it back" (Ecclesiastes 11:1-2).[27]

The seventeenth-century poet-preacher John Donne installed his own coffin in his bedroom during his mature life and occasionally slept in it as a reminder of his mortality and of the life of sin he had renounced.[28] Such morbidity was not Qohelet's style, though he would have agreed with the point of Donne's object lesson. Qohelet's advice is clear: no matter how wealthy you are, you cannot take your wealth with you, and you still have to face death for yourself. While the wealthy occasionally bought the services of an underling to fulfill their military obligations, Qohelet reminds us that we cannot buy the services of a substitute to face death for us.[29]

"No one has power over the wind to restrain the wind, or power over the day of death; there is no discharge from the battle, nor does wickedness deliver those who practice it" (8:8).

Week Two: A Grateful, Joyful Life.

I don't picture Qohelet installing a coffin in his bedroom to remind him of his imminent death. I picture the movers hauling in the most comfortable mattress and box springs money can buy! Seven times Qohelet exhorts us to appreciate the simple pleasures of eating, drinking, and finding enjoyment in our work. (2:24-26; 3:12-13, 22; 5:18-20; 8:15; 9:7–10; 11:7-12:1*a*). These texts are arranged in such a way as to state their theme with steadily increasing emphasis and solemnity.

First comes the plain statement. "There is nothing better for mortals than to eat and drink and find enjoyment in their toil" (2:24*a*). Qohelet affixes an autobiographical phrase to the next two statements. "I know that there is nothing better" (3:12). "So I saw that there is nothing better . . ." (3:22*a*). He offers an even more solemn introduction to the fourth. "This is what I have seen to be good . . ." (5:17). The fifth is expressed in even more definitive terms. "So I commend enjoyment" (8:15*a*). The sixth and seventh, he expresses in the imperative, as he positively urges his young pupil to follow his advice. "Go, eat your bread with enjoyment, and drink your wine with a merry heart" (9:7*a*). "Enjoy life with the wife whom you love . . ." (9:9*a*). Rejoice, young man, while you are young, and let your heart cheer you in the days of your youth" (11:9). "Remember your Creator in the days of your youth . . ." (12:1*a*).[30]

Qohelet places a high value on work, but not as a means to an end. He views work, with all its rigor and repetition, as the source of inherent enjoyment and satisfaction in daily life. Interestingly, he severs the connection between toil and gain, but repeatedly points to the bridge between toil and joy. The wicked are rendered joyless by their obsessive pursuit of wealth and security. They may prosper, but they do not find joy in their work Despite their schemes they are a shadow (1:13*a*). A life well-lived is not measured by life-span or number of achievements, but by the grateful reception of joy into one's life.[31]

Week Three: A Life Focused on the Present

Qohelet is not one to sit around leafing through photo albums, yearning for a past that never was. "Do not say, 'Why were the former days better than these?' For it is not from wisdom that you ask this" (Ecclesiastes 7:10). He advises us to avoid nostalgia and to remember that death comes to wise and fool, rich and poor alike. There is no remembrance in death (2:16). Life, despite the fondest hopes of traditional wisdom, cannot be made secure from chaos and tragedy. In between the unrecoverable past and the unfathomable future lies the present, the only realm that warrants our attention. Qohelet urges us to exhaust each moment life offers as God's gift, fully open to receive its serendipitous joys (3:12, 22; 5:18-19; 8:15; 9:7-9; 11:9-10).[32] He would have been in full agreement with a contemporary piece of advice that goes like this: "The past is over and gone. The future is yet to be. Now is an invaluable gift waiting to be unwrapped. That's why it is called the present."

Week Four: A God-Fearing Life

References to fearing God occur in five passages in Ecclesiastes 3:14; 5:7; 7:18; 8:12; 12:13). Fearing God is the chief virtue for

Qohelet, but it means something very different than what is meant by "the fear of the Lord" in Proverbs. In Proverbs, the fear of the Lord is the beginning of wisdom. It is the recognition that all moral insights come from God. The emphasis is on God as a revealing God. When Qohelet enjoins us to "fear God," he is pointing to God as a concealing and mysterious God and to our human limitations by contrast.[33] In Proverbs, the fear of the Lord is a fountain of life, so that one may avoid the snares of death (14:27). In Qohelet the fear of the Lord is a response to the realization that death comes to wise person and fool alike.[34]

Self-determined destiny is an illusion before God whose work is clothed perpetually in mystery. There is a wall of impenetrable mystery between us and God. Fear of God is partly an awe before the mysterious, and partly reverence for God's permanency and sovereignty in contrast with our limitations (1:4, 11). Our actions and thoughts are fleeting and soon forgotten by those we leave behind (2:16). To fear God is to embrace one's creaturely status as well as to acknowledge the enduring work of God who freely extends the blessing of joy to us finite, ephemeral beings.[35]

To fear God is to acknowledge the chasm between a transcendent God and frail human beings. We show our deference by our reserve in matters pertaining to the divine. Qohelet places his injunction to fear God (5:7) in the context of comments about the advisability of brevity in our piety (5:1-6). Qohelet's ideal is the reserved, unassuming sage who enters into the realm of the divine presence quietly receptive to the Holy. In this realm human initiative is minimized.[36]

Barbara Brown Taylor puts it well. She speaks of people's varying reactions to disappointment. Some people retire "belief in God along with belief in Santa Claus, Lady Luck, and the Tooth Fairy." However:

> For those willing to keep heaving themselves toward the light, things can change. What has been lost gradually becomes less important than what is to be found. Curiosity pokes its green head up through the asphalt of grief, and fear of the unknown takes on an element of wonder as the disillusioned turn away from the God who was supposed to be in order to seek the God who is. Every letdown becomes a lesson and a lure. Did God fail to come when I called? Then perhaps God is not a minion. So who

is God? Did God fail to punish my adversary? Then perhaps God
is not a policeman. Then who is God? Did God fail to make everything turn out all right? Then perhaps God is not a fixer. Then
who is God?[37]

This is a question that ought to be fundamental in our preaching.
The wisdom virtues of simplicity, gratitude, and presence that
Qohelet recommends all flow from his answer to the question
"Who is God?" His God is distant and wants to stay that way. His
God is the giver of injustice as well as justice. Belief in his God
seems to lead Qohelet to a kind of social passivism. To his credit, he
sheds tears of empathy over the plight of those who have no one
on their side and are oppressed by society's powerful. Qohelet
laments that institutions are corrupt and perpetuate oppression,
but he seems to believe they are beyond human control. He does
not appear to think there is anything he can or should do about it
except lament it.

Qohelet's experience of his social setting has shaped his depiction of God as distant, wholly inscrutable, formidable and the
source of oppression as well as wisdom. His view of God in turn
shapes his resigned and melancholy social passivism.

Says Ecclesiastes scholar J.A. Loader, "Qohelet is no deist for
whom God has turned his back on the world. God is no problem
for him. But still God is distant and far-off. Therefore Qohelet has
a passive attitude towards God and therefore he just observes
God's acts without protesting. For who can resist the irresistible?
And how would Qohelet be able to speak of the near Yahweh when
he only knows of the remote and impenetrable *Elohim*-powers?"[38]

As is the case with every book in the Bible, Qohelet's answer to
the question "Who is God?" is a partial one. It calls for collaboration with other depictions of God in the Hebrew Scriptures, both
within and beyond the wisdom corpus. Qohelet's distant God
needs to be preached in the context of the God who is both invitational and informational in Woman Wisdom, and who is inti-
mately, if correctively, present in the divine address to Job.
Qohelet's God needs to be viewed in tandem with the God who
orchestrates seminal events in Israel's salvation history, and whose
outrage at injustice stirs and spurs the prophets.

The depiction of the divine stance toward the poor highlights the
need to preach Qohelet's depiction of God in the context of the

wider canon. Qohelet warns about the futility of pursuing wealth, yet he is in general agreement with the traditional notion that God helps the wise person avoid poverty. For the wise, poverty, like wealth, was accepted as one of the givens of existence with which the student must learn to cope. While a few texts root poverty in laziness, other texts insist that the wise respect the poor as beloved of God. Respect did not lead to action, however. The presumption was that the student, who comes from an elite background, would be able to avoid a lapse into poverty if he followed the advice of his teachers.

God is depicted far differently in the prophets. The prophets portray a God who calls the nation to anticipate a new order in which the poor will be vindicated (Isaiah 14:30, 26:6, 29:19; Zephaniah 3:12). The prophets experience a God who drives them to protest poverty. This God stirs the prophets to social critiques that consistently connect the poverty of the poor with the wealth of the rich. This God prods the prophets to be aware that the poor as a group are poor because they have been wronged by the ruling elite.[39]

"Who is God for you?" ought to be a key theological question we preachers pose in our exegesis of texts for preaching. When we do, we hear, echoing back to us from the text, "And who is God for you?" Exegesis becomes a dialogue when we allow the text to question our questions.

Contemporary self-help wisdom's arrogant assumption that our best intentions are just fine with God needs a dose of Qohelet's brand of God. "God is in me and God is me," says popular wisdom. But Qohelet says, "For God is in heaven and you upon earth" (5:2*a*). "The universe yearns to grant your heart's desire! Manifest your destiny! Follow my seventeen principles of personal success and prosperity!" say the self-help gurus. Qohelet says, "With many dreams come vanities and a multitude of words; but fear God" (5:7).

Distant, transcendent, demanding of respect, beyond our control, yet in control. Is this God warm and fuzzy? No. Is this God in need of theological complements from elsewhere in the canon? Most certainly. But if I had to choose between Qohelet's God and the God of self-help wisdom, God help me, but I would choose Qohelet's!

The fact is, I do have to choose. We all do. We can choose to spend our lives following somebody else's numbered and bulleted list of principles that will lead to the fulfillment of our heart's desire, though we will never quite be self-improved enough. We can spend our lives comparing our accomplishments and possessions with those of other middle-class people who are reading the same books. We can spend our days swilling *Chicken Soup for the Soul*, but never quite filling the chilly void. Or we can choose to come before God in this present moment, with reverent, grateful quietude, ready to receive the divine gifts of simplicity and joy.

CHAPTER EIGHT

The Wisdom Gospel: Matthew

"The rain fell, the floods came, and the winds blew and beat on that house, but it did not fall, because it had been founded on rock" (Matthew 7:25).

Understanding Wisdom in the New Testament

If we were studying weather patterns, we would look at a map and note by color-coding which geographical areas get the most rain every year. In studying wisdom in the New Testament, a color-coded map would reveal concentrations of wisdom in the Gospels of Matthew and John, the book of James, and selected Pauline passages.

We have seen how recent Old Testament scholarship has invited wisdom from the wings onto center stage. The same has been true in New Testament studies. Scholars of the past quarter-century have recognized that Jesus viewed himself as a sage and used wisdom forms in his teaching. Jesus was more than a prophet concerned with the end-times. He was also a sage whose radical wisdom teachings shaped a counter-cultural lifestyle in the here and now.[1]

Parables are a wisdom form best defined as "a short narrative fiction that references a symbol."[2] Used by the rabbis to offer explanations of scriptural passages, they became, on Jesus' lips, status-quo-challenging depictions of life in the inbreaking reign of God. With both proverbs and parables, Jesus borrowed wisdom forms and used them in a prophetic, tradition-subverting way.[3]

These wisdom forms are not just vivid and down-to-earth. They are demanding. They demand more from listeners than intellectual assent. They insist on concentration, and they evoke reflection. We can see why Jesus chose them, for they are tailor-made tools for a subversive sage to use to challenge the status quo.[4]

After Jesus' death and resurrection, his followers reflected on his identity. They harvested images and insights from existing Jewish reflection on God's self-expression as wisdom from Hebrew Scriptures (mainly Proverbs) and later Jewish writings (Wisdom of Solomon, Wisdom of Jesus Ben Sirach). John's Prologue attributes the qualities of Proverbs' Woman Wisdom to the Logos (Word). Matthew equates Jesus with Heavenly Wisdom (23:34). Paul, describing the cosmological role of Christ in 1 Corinthians 8:6, draws on the vivid picture of Wisdom as contributor to creation in the eighth chapter of Proverbs (Proverbs 8:22ff).

When we read the Prologue to the Gospel of John we hear the qualities and roles of Wisdom attributed to the Word (Logos). In this, John was influenced by the Hellenistic Jewish philosopher Philo, who, about a century earlier, identified the feminine-gendered Jewish Wisdom with the masculine-gendered Greek Logos. Most early church writers followed Philo's lead and identified Wisdom with the Logos, the divine in Jesus Christ. Others, like Irenaeus of Lyons, identified her with the third person of the Trinity. The affirmation of Sophia of Proverbs 8:22-31 as fully divine and consubstantial with the Father was crucial for Athanasius' claim that Jesus was begotten by God and not a creature who had a beginning in time.[5]

The upsurge of wisdom in New Testament studies is a great gift to us preachers. It clarifies for us Jesus' role as wisdom teacher and the sharpness of his teachings over against secular understandings. It points us toward fruitful imagery for envisioning Jesus' identity in a culture hungry for wisdom. Understanding our faith through the lens of New Testament wisdom offers us a theological corrective to our individualistic, self-sufficient mindset and the self-disappointment and isolation that are its bitter fruits. Wisdom holds out to preachers a Christological context within which we can preach Jesus' subversive teachings with persuasive grace. Jesus is present to us as a Living Wisdom abiding at the heart of the community.

The God-language and Christological reflection of biblical wisdom exposes the limits of the use of exclusively male language for God in preaching and worship. In the light of Wisdom, it becomes clear that such exclusivism is not faithful to the full range of metaphors, reflection, and imagery through which the biblical canon imagines God. There are profound pastoral, as well as theological, implications to this insight. In light of Wisdom, it also becomes clear that, throughout Scripture, women as well as men responded to God's initiatives by seeking and teaching Wisdom in their communities. To preach the Wisdom of God is to respect the needs and honor the contributions of women as well as men in contemporary congregations.

Our focus will be on the two Gospels most influenced by wisdom themes and purposes: Matthew and John. But before turning to them, I want to acknowledge two other concentrations of wisdom in the New Testament: Paul and James. My treatment of them in this context is suggestive rather than exhaustive.

Paul: Apostle of Wisdom

Paul knew what it was to live and suffer with congregations struggling to live by Jesus' subversive wisdom amid seductive alternatives. He knew about ecclesial division. He was acquainted with communities that allowed love of God and neighbor to be supplanted by rules of conduct subtly aimed at self-advancement (Galatians). He was no stranger to those who sought to enjoy spiritual benefits without thought of how their actions affected others (Corinthians). His letters, written roughly between 50 and 64 CE, place specific local problems in the context of the community's relationship to the risen Jesus. One of the key ways he imaged that presence was as the Wisdom of God.

As the Wisdom of God, Christ exists from eternity with God and is active in creation. The language used for Christ is drawn from language about Sophia in the Jewish tradition that in effect identifies Jesus with Wisdom. The preexistence of Christ is the preexistence of divine Sophia. For Paul, Jesus is the embodiment of Sophia.[6]

Several passages embody that vision, among them 1 Corinthians 1:5-9, 23-24, 30; Colossians 1:15-17; and Philippians 2:6-11.[7]

For Paul, Jesus' identity and teachings represent the wisdom of God over against the folly of so-called human wisdom. He encourages churches to accept the grace, forgiveness, and joy that come with the state of living "in Christ" and allow "their faith to rest, not on human wisdom but on the power of God" (1 Corinthians 2:5).[8]

Neither secular self-help wisdom nor the wisdom of Proverbs has room in their schema for the concept of forgiveness. Their version of forgiveness is a human-driven dynamic: redeem your mistakes by not repeating them. If you can learn from them, you've reaped their payoff. Both secular and biblical conventional wisdom recommend avoiding rather than embracing people whose unwise choices could complicate the tidy life of the wise.

In secular self-help wisdom, the self can achieve wisdom on its own steam, abiding by a set of rules that will assure material prosperity, social power, and personal fulfillment. The ability to meet these standards determined one's personal and social worth. This is the wisdom of the dominant culture from age to age. This is a version of what Paul meant by the "wisdom of this world." Paul's contrast between the "wisdom of this world" and the "wisdom of God" echoes the distinction Jesus made in his aphorisms and parables between a conventional worldview and an alternative, counter-cultural wisdom.[9]

James

The book of James contains no speculation on the identity of Jesus in relation to wisdom. It uses Jesus' proverbial sayings to stabilize a community tempted to waver because of persecution. It is a traditional use of Jesus' nontraditional wisdom. The book avoids Jesus' most subversive teachings on challenge of ritual convention and love of enemies.

The author of James does not cite the Jesus tradition directly, but weaves various ideas, themes, and phrases from that tradition into his own argument. He draws mainly on the teachings of Jesus in the Matthean version of the Sermon on the Mount. This material in James is not presented as sayings of Jesus, but rather as the teachings of James that have been influenced by the Jesus tradition.[10]

James' teachings lack a sense of the inbreaking dominion of God and its radical reordering of community and world. He uses Jesus' aphorisms to stabilize his community, in much the same way that Proverbs did for postexilic Israel and Ben Sirach and the Wisdom of Solomon did to help Judaism survive in a hostile environment. His goal to instill self-control in his listeners in their thoughts (1:14-16, 3:15-18), speech (3:1-12), and actions (2:1-26). Moral purity in behavior, emotions, and attitudes is paramount.[11]

Matthew and John: Different Sons of the Same Mother

My mother used to recite a delightful prayer to my children as part of their bedtime ritual. I would suspect it wore such a deep groove in their young minds that it still runs through their heads every night before they fall asleep.

Matthew, Mark, Luke, and John,

Watch the bed I lie upon:

Four corners to my bed.

Four angels there to spread,

One at head and one at feet,

Two to guard me to Heaven's gate:

One to sing and two to pray,

And one to fetch my soul away.[12]

While all four Gospels offer abundant blessings, the first and the last hold especially rich blessings in the area of wisdom. New Testament scholar Ben Witherington calls these two Gospels "different sons"... that .... "come from the same mother".[13]

All four Gospels bless us with their unique treatment of who Jesus is and what it means to follow him.[14] Matthew and John offer wisdom-shaped depictions of the origins and identity of Jesus in relation to God. Not only their Christologies, but also their understandings of discipleship has been shaped by wisdom. Both books present Jesus as a teacher with learners (disciples).[15] These two

Gospels present the most teaching material of all four Gospels. In Matthew, Jesus' public teaching takes the form of parables, aphorisms, and beatitudes. In John, it takes the form of wisdom discourses similar to those found in Proverbs 8 or Sirach 24. Forms differ, but the goal for both is instruction for faithful discipleship.

Both Gospels emphasize the importance of choice in the life of discipleship, defining it as a lifelong process that involves a gift from God as well as an ongoing human response. Two wisdom themes thread their way through both Gospels. One is that discipleship means hearing but also obeying. A second is that discipleship involves choice.[16]

Wisdom Themes

DISCIPLESHIP AS HEARING AND OBEYING

In both Gospels discipleship is defined as keeping Jesus' commands or words (Matthew 28:18-20; John 15:10). Discipleship means bearing fruit and loving one's neighbors (Matthew 12:50; 21:43; John 13:35; 15:2-8).[17]

Both Gospels stubbornly insist that would-be followers of Jesus need to make a choice. In Proverbs, Wisdom, a no-nonsense prophetess, challenges passersby to choose her path of life with its rich blessings or take the consequences (Proverbs 1:20-33f; 8:35-36). In John 3:16-17 God determines to save the world, but the response of the individual to God's sending of the Son leads either to life or death.[18]

The answer to the question, "Will people accept or reject Jesus' teaching?" serves as the watershed in both Matthew and John. In Matthew, the turning point comes in chapter 13 where Jesus, repeatedly rejected by his larger Jewish audience, turns his attention to his own disciples. In John the faithful fall away (John 6:66f) while enemy numbers escalate. And Jesus directs his words to his own disciples.[19]

Self-help wisdom offers the peppy reminder, "If it's going to be, it's up to me!" This is not the brand of choice our wisdom Gospels offer. They offer, not adherence to a set of rules, energized by one's own determination, but an urgent invitation to a relationship with Jesus-Wisdom that flows forth in a loving life. Why is it that when we preachers exhort listeners to make a decision, it is often a brand of decision that reflects self-help wisdom's version of decision: personal and boot-strappy? I am convinced that in most congregations there is an inaudible call-and-response going on when we preach for decision. "Will you or won't you?" we demand. They're saying back to us, "I already did, but it didn't take." "Why should I?" "How on earth can I?" or "If I do, then what?"

The substance of our sermons ought to answer these unspoken congregational questions. If it doesn't, who can blame them for turning elsewhere? We turn now to a deeper study of the wisdom teachings of our two sons of the same mother. First, let us look at Matthew.

Background Check

Controversy Shapes a Gospel's Contours

The author of the Gospel of Matthew was probably a Jewish Christian writing c. 85-90 CE. Some scholars feel that the Gospel was written in Antioch in Syria. Others argue for a Galilean origin. Wherever he was writing from, Matthew was probably writing to a Jewish-Christian congregation whose relations with Jewish synagogues had become strained. As a result, they were trying to appeal to Gentiles.

After the Romans destroyed the temple at Jerusalem (c. 70 CE), the revolutionary zealots faded into the hills and the Sadducees (the temple priests) struggled to find a reason for being. The Pharisees (the authoritative interpreters of the Law) set up a new center in Jamnia in northwestern Judah. They set to work settling the canon and text of Scriptures, and systematizing the interpretation of the Law and matters of belief and practice.[20]

Matthew agrees with some of the Pharisees' teaching (23:2-3) and is loyal to the Torah down to the smallest jot and tittle (5:17-19). However, he resents their opposition to Jesus' message and followers (23:29-37).[21] They charge that Christians oppose the law. Matthew counters that, on the contrary, Christians insist that love of God and neighbor, rather than desire for recognition or wealth, should govern its practice (23:23).

Matthew's Jesus expects his disciples to keep the Sabbath, to fast, to bring their offerings in accordance with Jewish tradition (6:16-18; 5:23-26), and to pay the Temple tax (17:24-25). At the same time, his aphorisms and parables challenge traditional observances of Sabbath, ritual purity and food laws that have become a substitute for obedience to God defined as radical mercy to our neighbor (15:10-20; 23:23-24).

Clearly this controversial context shaped the convictions that guide Matthew's Christology. To express the role of Christ as revealer, Matthew grounds his concrete historical coming in the eternal Wisdom of God. As Wisdom, Jesus was the God-authorized interpreter of Torah. His nontraditional teachings were true to the heart of Torah, but challenged its current observances.

I was once driving down an interstate so devoid of scenery that I was actually excited to see a billboard. It had a picture of Jesus with long auburn hair and blue eyes on it, with the question, "Where will you spend eternity?" writ large. Someone had spray-painted a line through that question and painted another over it: "How will you live today?"

The first question is the apocalyptic question. The second is the wisdom question. Matthew is interested in both questions. He has an apocalyptic, dualistic view of the human situation in the world. The world is the scene of activity of two hostile powers: God, working through the Son of Man, and the devil (Matthew 13:36-43). The evil power is temporarily effective. The followers of Christ await the final victory. Matthew's apocalyptic dualism is joined with a summons to obedience in the present, an obedience to Christ who brings a new interpretation or "realization" of the Law.[22]

Matthew's Wisdom Connections

The Hebrew Scriptures and late Jewish writings were filled with references to Wisdom as an expression of God's presence.[23] Wisdom reflection occurs in such writings as The Wisdom of Jesus ben Sirach, The Wisdom of Solomon, and Baruch. It is also found in 1 Enoch and 4 Esdras.[24]

From these writings we can arrive at a composite picture of Wisdom, though no single text brings all of them together. God created Wisdom in the beginning. She was hidden with God, dwelling in the heavens. Wisdom was present at Creation, in which she served as agent (or instrument). She came to earth, sent to call both

Israel and all humankind, some of whom listened to her, but most of whom did not. She was rejected by humanity and, finding no place of rest, she returned to dwell with God.

In the traditions about Jesus available to Matthew, there was one that was strongly shaped by this strain of Wisdom reflection. It consists of those sayings and parables and narratives common to Matthew and Luke. This material is called the Q document by many scholars (for *Quelle*, German for "source"). It presents Jesus' radical wisdom teachings and connects him with Heavenly Wisdom. About a quarter of the wisdom sayings attributed to Jesus in the Synoptic Gospels are found in the Q document. Q may have been the product of Galilean Christian communities and was compiled during the three decades after the crucifixion, reaching the form in which it was circulated sometime before 50 CE. Thus Q probably predates both Paul's letters and Mark. [25]

The Q source did not identify Jesus as Sophia herself, but saw him as a messenger and teacher of wisdom. Luke largely retains this notion, though with nuances of his own. Matthew, however, amends his source to identify Jesus with Sophia herself (Matthew 23:34=Luke 11:49). Words attributed to Sophia in both Q and Luke are found directly in the mouth of Jesus in Matthew. For Mark, Q, and Luke, Jesus is a messenger of Wisdom. For Matthew, Jesus is Wisdom.[26]

Q's sayings were probably grouped according to topics: blessedness, responding to reproach, judging, practical obedience, becoming a follower, working for the kingdom, confidence in God's care, anxiety, and personal goods.

It was these sayings that Matthew organized into the Sermon on the Mount and Luke into the Sermon on the Plain. Q also provided several parables not found in Mark that appear in both Matthew and Luke.[27]

Among the most familiar topics and sayings we encounter in Q as Matthew has placed them:

Enemies (5:43, 44)

Not Judging (7:1)

Blind leading the blind (15:14)

Trees and Fruit (7:18)

Asking, Seeking, Knocking (7:7, 8)

Light under bushel (5:15)

Anxiety (6:25)

Treasures in heaven versus on earth (6:19)

Narrow Gate (7:13)

Salt (5:13)

Loving father and mother (10:37)

Cross carrying (10:38)

Finding and losing (10:39)[28]

Along with short sayings, Q also contains narrative portions. Among the most familiar passages are

The Preaching of John the Baptist (3:1-12)

The Temptation of Jesus (4:1-11)

The Sermon on the Mount (chapters 5-7)

Jesus' words about John (11:2-19)

The Two Houses (7:24-27)

The healing of the Centurion's Servant (8:5-13)

Instructions for the Missionary movement (chapter 10)

The Lord's Prayer (6:9-13)

The Beatitudes (5:1-12)

Controversy over the source of Jesus' exorcizing powers (12:22-29)

Jesus' Thanksgiving to God (11:25-30)

The Empty House (12:43-45)

Woes against the Pharisees (chapter 23)

The Banquet (22:1-14)

The Lost Sheep (18:10-14)

The Talents (25:14-30)

Nutshell

What Is Most Important?

Matthew's goal is for readers to acknowledge Jesus as the God-authorized interpreter of tradition (the Wisdom of God) and to live by his teachings. Matthew presents the moral demand of Jesus' teachings more rigorously than any of the other three Gospels. For Matthew, the good news is that we can obey Jesus' rigorous teachings because of who Jesus is. In relation to Israel's hope, he is the Son of David. Like David's son Solomon, he is the very embodiment of Wisdom. In relation to the Father, he is the Son. He is savior (1:21). He is shepherd (2:6) come to lead Israel out of exile. He is healer whose healings are meant to spark faith that motivates observers to follow his teachings (4:23-25). Matthew's gift to us preachers is the insight that Jesus is both teacher of wisdom and Wisdom in Person. Jesus is both instructor and empowerer, both yoke-giver and yoke-bearer.

JESUS AS TEACHER

Matthew's Jesus is the teacher par excellence, and his teaching methods are indebted to Woman Wisdom from Proverbs. In Proverbs 1, she summons the simple to her teachings (1:20-33). Jesus' initial words "Repent, for the kingdom of heaven has come near" (Matthew 4:17) sound similar to hers: "Give heed to my reproof, I will pour out my thoughts to you; I will make my words known to you."

What immediately follows (Matthew 4:17) is the calling of the learners (disciples) like Wisdom's calling of the simple (Proverbs 1:22) and then the offering of teaching. The discourse ends in Matthew 7:24ff with the parable about the "wise man." The one who hears Jesus' instruction and follows it will become the wise person, rather than the fool.

Jesus partakes of Woman Wisdom's proverbial mode of address. His teachings are filled with images, themes, and metaphors from the book of Proverbs. Woman Wisdom in

Proverbs promises that Wisdom will be a tree of life to those who lay hold of her, more valuable than precious gems, the source of life and light to our way.[29] While Wisdom's path is pleasant and well lit, Jesus describes the path of following him as hard and narrow (Matthew 7:13-14). While Wisdom's message was primarily for young men, Jesus calls women as well as men. Both can be Wisdom's envoys.[30]

From Matthew 14 on into the passion narrative, Jesus is increasingly portrayed as a teacher at odds with the teaching authorities of his day, not primarily because of the miracles he performs, but because of his teachings, his subversive or counter-order wisdom.[31]

JESUS AS WISDOM

Matthew's understanding of Jesus' relation to Wisdom shines through in three key passages that he adopts and adapts from Q: 11:16-19, 11:25-30, and 23:34-39.[32]

The oracle of Wisdom in Matthew (23:34-39) is a key text in understanding Matthew's portrayal of Jesus in relation to Wisdom. Most scholars believe that Luke preserves the original character of the Q saying where it appears as a saying of Wisdom: "Therefore also the Wisdom of God said, 'I will send them prophets and apostles . . .'" (Luke 11:49). Matthew places the oracle on Jesus' lips. "Therefore, behold, I send you prophets, wise men and scribes . . ." (Matthew 23:34). Jesus is no longer one of many envoys of Wisdom, but is Wisdom-in-Person.[33]

Obstacles

Matthew's goal in writing his Gospel was to make disciples of his readers. A skilled narrative artist, he uses the example of the disciples in both positive and negative ways to invite our identification. Sometimes they are cautionary tales, and other times they model insight and progress. Following the narrative flow, experiencing the various teachings and encounters recounted in this Gospel, the reader experiences certain "don't's" and "do's" in the life of discipleship.[34]

Disobeying the following prohibitions impedes our ability to acknowledge Jesus as Wisdom and to follow him.[35]

Do not worry (6:25).

Do not judge (7:1).

Do not pile up for yourself treasures on earth (6:19).

Do not cry, "Lord, Lord," and not follow up by doing God's will (7:21-23).

Do not fear anything or anyone since God holds your life in his hands (10:28).

Do not send the needy away (14:15-16; 15:23; 19:13-15). Do not doubt Jesus' ability to provide that which he demands (15:33-38).[36]

Do not love family more than Jesus (10:37).

Do not try to save your life by seeking security and position as your goal in life (10:39; 16:25-26).

Do not cling to riches and so turn away from Jesus (19:16-24). Do not stand in the way of Jesus' redemptive ministry, bringing human wisdom to bear on divine dynamics (16:22-23).

Do not harbor ambition to be exalted over others in your heart. Such motives mirror secular hierarchical notions of authority and block entry into and ministry on behalf of God's kingdom (20:20-28).

Do not allow yourself to become indistinguishable from nonbelievers in your way of life and patterns of leadership in your community (6:32; 20:20-28).

Do not fall away through lack of love (24:9-13).

Do not stand in judgment of another's acts of devotion to Jesus (26:8-10).

Do not sleep while others suffer (26:36-46).

Do not desert Jesus once you have pledged to follow him (26:56).

Do not deny him when his cause needs you (26:69-75).

Do not exalt yourself (27:12).

Facilitators

What attitudes and behaviors permit us to acknowledge Jesus as Wisdom and follow him?

Love your enemies (5:39-44).

Ask and it will be given you (7:7).

Recognize and confess Jesus as Messiah and Son of God (14:33; 16:16).

Answer Jesus' call. Expect to experience hardship (8:20), leave your familiar comfort zone (10:37; 19:27-30), and deny yourself to take up your cross (10:38-39; 16:24-26).

Throng around Jesus. Try to be where he is (8:10; 9:2; 15:28).

Pay attention to Jesus' teachings, preaching, and healing (7:24; 13:23).

Love your neighbor, including your enemies (22:34-40; 7:12; 19:19; 5:43-46).

Accept the forgiveness of your sins Jesus offers and freely extend that gift to others (6:14-15; 18:21-35).

Respond to Jesus in faith[37].

Repent and bear fruit (3:2; 4:17; 3:8-9; 7:16, 21; 7:24-27; 12:33-36).

Grow in faith.[38]

Be steadfast under persecution (5:10-12; 10:16-36; 23:34-36; 24:9-14).

Actively seek righteousness if you want to enter the kingdom (5:6, 20).

Key Texts for Preaching

The Sermon on the Mount

The Sermon on the Mount is the first of five teaching segments in Matthew's Gospel. Matthew concludes each discourse with the formula, "And when Jesus finished these sayings, ..." (7:21; 11:1; 13:53; 19:1; 26:1). While Luke's Sermon on the Plain emphasizes Jesus as healer, Matthew's Sermon on the Mount is reminiscent of the giving of the law on Mount Sinai and calls attention to Jesus as Israel's God-authorized teacher. He wants his readers to view the Sermon on the Mount as an authoritative scribal teaching.[39] Here is the definitive interpretation of the Torah, the nucleus of which Moses received on Mount Sinai. Here the Sermon on the Mount is not a substitute legal code, but the proper interpretation for an existing one.

On first glance, the Sermon on the Mount appears to be a catalogue of impossible demands. The Sermon is not an impossible demand, however, but a gift from God analogous to the giving of the law on Mount Sinai that created a covenant people. This new commandment is, like the first, life-giving.

The Sermon has an eschatological orientation. It looks backwards from the consummation to the present. The Sermon proclaims the will of God as it should be lived in the kingdom, when God's will is done on earth as in heaven.

Says Matthew scholar Dale Allison, "This explains why it is seemingly heedless of all earthly contingencies, why it is so radical, why it always blasts complacency and shallow moralism, disturbs every good conscience and instills terror in those who take it seriously. The Sermon is not primarily concerned with what is practical or possible in the here and now but with the unobstructed, perfect will of God."[40]

The Sermon on the Mount is partly a poetic text. Unlike codes of law, it is dramatic and pictorial. The reader sees a man offering a sacrifice in Jerusalem (5:23), someone in prison (5:25-26), a body without eye and hand (5:29-30), someone being slapped (5:39), the sun rising (5:45), the rain falling (5:45), someone praying in a private (6:6), lilies in a field (6:28), a log in an eye (7:4), and wolves in sheeps' clothing (7:15). These images and the comments upon them do not add up to legislation! The Semitic habit of hyperbole (7:13-14; 5:40; 6:3) shows us that the Sermon is meant to be taken seriously but not literally. Many of its sayings are proverbial, partial generalizations the reader is meant to apply wisely to certain situations in his life, but not all. The Sermon in general (with the exception of the ruling on divorce) does not offer a set of rules. Rather, its purpose is to instill a moral vision. Literal (mis)interpretation leads to absurdities.[41] Jesus didn't mean for his disciples to go around naked, one-eyed, counting how many times they had forgiven their enemies!

The Sermon is not a book of proverbs by an anonymous and faceless author. It presupposes and teaches important things about its speaker, whose identity is crucial for the Sermon's interpretation.[42] When we read Matthew in its entirety, we find that Jesus is not just a moral authority but also a gracious presence whose demands are accompanied by a helping presence (28:20).

Unlike self-help wisdom, prayer resides at the midst of the Sermon on the Mount. God does not leave us at the mercy of our own efforts. God responds to our needs when we ask, seek, and knock (7:7-11). This God enables Jesus' followers to attain a righteousness that purifies the inward life and energizes the faithful to seek justice for the vulnerable. God is the unexpressed subject of the action in the second part of many beatitudes. "Blessed are those who____, for God will comfort, fill, and give mercy. " Blessedness does not come about by our passive resignation to present hardships. Rather, God gives blessedness to those who remain faithful despite present adversity.[43]

The Beatitudes

Beatitudes are common in the Old Testament (Isaiah 30:18; Jeremiah 17:7) and are also found in Greek literature where the blessings they promise are largely material.[44] Beatitudes are not only commands to be obeyed to enter the kingdom. Nor are they merely statements that those who trust God will be blessed. They are not entry requirements to the kingdom, but joyful responses God enables in those who actively accept God. Each one contains elements of eschatological grace and an implicit command.[45]

Some years ago Dr. Robert Schuller wrote a book entitled *The Be (Happy) Attitudes: 8 Positive Attitudes That Can Transform Your Life!* They are a personalized, therapeutic version of Jesus' beatitudes. Says Dr. Schuller,

> Blessed literally means "happy." So, whether you are winning or losing, succeeding or failing, enthusiastic or depressed, happy

or suffering, you can be happy if you will discover the eight positive attitudes given to us by Jesus in the Beatitudes. . . . Discover them! Apply them! Enjoy life with these "Be-Happy Attitudes."[46]

The Beatitudes (Matthew 5:3-10)	Schuller's "Be-Happy Attitudes"
Blessed are the poor in spirit, for theirs is the kingdom of heaven.	I need help—I can't do it alone!
Blessed are those who mourn, for they will be comforted!	I'm really hurting—but I'm going to bounce back!
Blessed are the meek, for they will inherit the earth.	I'm going to remain cool, calm, and corrected.
Blessed are those who hunger and thirst after righteousness, for they will be filled.	I really want to do the right thing!
Blessed are the merciful, for they will receive mercy.	I'm going to treat others the way I want others to treat me.
Blessed are the pure in heart, for they will see God.	I've got to let the faith flow free through me.
Blessed are the peacemakers, for they will be called children of God.	I'm going to be a bridge builder.
Blessed are those who are persecuted for righteousness' sake, for theirs is the kingdom of heaven.	I can choose to be happy anyway!

Schuller's analysis places an individualistic, therapeutic template over the Beatitudes, viewing them as aids to personal optimism. Matthew, by contrast, presents the Beatitudes as risky, counter-cultural, communal values for the creation and recreation of a people. They represent the wisdom of God, not of humankind.

In the Old Testament blessedness is made up of personal trust in God and of obedience to God's will. The Beatitudes of the Gospels (outside the Sermon they are found in Matthew 11:6; 13:16; 26:46) share four common characteristics. The first is that they are Christocentric: the blessedness they describe has its source in the presence and activity of Jesus. The second is that they do not consist merely in resignation, but in obedience to Christ despite present hardships. The third is that they have both an "already" and a "not yet" quality. While they begin and grow in this present life, their blessedness only fully blossoms in the time to come. The fourth is that the happiness they describe, while eschatological, also has a present focus. It is in the midst of life and within creation, a creation restored through Christ, that happiness is found.[47]

We have seen how self-help wisdom promises that following its principles will bring good results. The Beatitudes are stated as cause-effect clauses. But they are vastly different in means and ends from self-help wisdom. The means are the exact opposite of self-help wisdom. It encourages us to seek personal goals, likeability, and a good reputation. The Beatitudes encourage us to relinquish our hold on those goals so that we might be embraced by God and God's promises. In that embrace we are comforted, filled, forgiven, purified, and incorporated into God's family. They represent habits of character that are endorsed by God.[48]

Self-help wisdom's audience is the self-reliant, the emotionally resilient, the assertive, the ambitious, and the single-minded. Self-help wisdom's guidelines for time management and goal setting advise us to avoid the very people to whom the Beatitudes are directed!

Those the world views as pitiful, Jesus claims are genuinely joyful.[49] Although women are not directly mentioned as part of the audience, their situations are encompassed by Jesus' message and minstry.[50]

THE POOR IN SPIRIT (5:3)

"Poor in spirit" refers to those who, regardless of their economic or social status, manifest humble dependence on God. The New English Bible translation captures the verse's intention well. "How blest are those who know their need of God." Although the "poor in spirit" has a "spiritual" meaning in Matthew 5:3, "poor" has a more literal sense everywhere else in the Gospel (11:5; 19:21; 26:9, 11). Being "poor in spirit" will most likely require material sacrifice. The faithful hearers of the Sermon, those who risk becoming "poor in spirit," will suffer persecution (5:11-12), missionize and witness to God (5:13-16), pray for daily bread (6:11), refuse to serve mammon (6:24), and trust God for basic necessities (6:25-33).[51]

Israel's prophets repeatedly call the nation back to being "poor in spirit" (Isaiah 66:2; Habakuk 2:4). The Psalms reveal the prayers of those who, because of long economic and social distress, have confidence only in God (Psalm 69:28, 32, 33; 38:12-16; 40:18; Isaiah 61:1).[52] "But I am poor and needy; hasten to me, O God!" (Psalm 70:5). The quality of being "poor in spirit" has much in common with Proverbs' "fear of the Lord" (Proverbs 1:7).

This first Beatitude contains everything one must know to pass through this life into the next. All the Beatitudes and, indeed, the entire sermon that follow it, are a development of this one beatitude. It is the genesis for the interpretation of Torah (5:17-48 and 7:12), the reconstitution of the life of practical piety (6:1-18), and the conquest of everyday anxieties (6:19-7:12).[53]

The "kingdom of heaven" refers to the ideal, eschatological state when God's will "will be done on earth as it is in heaven." This phrase appears repeatedly in the Sermon on the Mount (5:10, 19, 20; 6:33; 7:21). In Matthew the kingdom is the focus of John the Baptist's public proclamation (3:2), as well as that of Jesus (4:17) and his disciples (10:7). Many of the expectations associated with the end were fulfilled in Jesus' ministry, death, and resurrection. Others remain to be fulfilled in the future.

The kingdom has in some sense already come (12:28). Yet the world remains full of evil. So the Sermon instructs disciples to pray "Your kingdom come."[54]

THE MOURNFUL (5:4)

This Beatitude is false as a statement about this life, for many sad people die without consolation. Jesus holds out an eschatological vision to encourage those who are mourning.[55] The background of this Beatitude is Isaiah 61:1-4. There God's Servant is anointed with the Spirit to bring good news to the poor and "to comfort all who mourn—to build up the ancient ruins." Isaiah is speaking to Israel's mourning after her devastation by the Babylonians.[56] Those who mourned in Jesus' day were the poor who were heavily taxed, prostitutes, and lepers. The Romans referred to them as "the expendables."

The Beatitude promises a blessing upon those who mourn over the injustices they suffer, as well as the whole nation, suffering in subjection to Roman rule. It challenges those who are materially comfortable with the message: act as agents of God's comfort now.

THE MEEK (5:5)

To be meek is not to be a doormat, but to evince the humility that flows from being poor in spirit. Moses is described as meek (some translations render this humble or devout) in Numbers 12:3, as is Jesus in Matthew 11:29 and 21:5. Meekness has been defined as "complete dependence on God."[57] The reason meekness is a blessed state is that, once we know our need for God and live in dependence on God, we are free from the need to get the better of others.

"Blessed are the meek" is not a praising of passivity, but rather a summons to active deeds that fulfill the new law of Christ: active dedication to the high goal of meekness, friendliness, and gentleness— deeds that are determined not by anger, brutality, or enmity, but entirely by goodness.[58]

THE SEEKERS OF RIGHTEOUSNESS (5:6)

Next to Luke's "Blessed are you who are hungry" (Luke 6:21), Matthew's wording, "Blessed are those who hunger and thirst for righteousness," seems domesticated. But Matthew's version is not a purely personalized one. The righteousness he talks about is God's righteousness as proclaimed by the prophets, God's vindication of the afflicted (Isaiah 51:1-5; 61:3).[59] A clearer rendition of this blessing would be, "Blessed are those who yearn for the manifestation of God's saving righteousness." The New English Bible aptly translates it "How blest are those who hunger and thirst to see right prevail; they shall be satisfied."

THE MERCIFUL (5:7)

At first glance, this beatitude sounds as if God's mercy toward us depends on our mercy toward others. Mercy is a response to a God who has first shown mercy (18:23-35). We show mercy out of loving gratitude toward and a willingness to be shaped in God's image, not to gain prestige (6:2).[60]

We have noted that each Beatitude involves a promise and a challenge. The promise here is the continuing reception of mercy and compassion from God. The challenge is for us to remember our dependence on those gifts. This remembrance keeps our own need for mercy constantly before us and motivates us to lavish it on other similarly flawed people.

This is in contrast to much self-help wisdom that emphasizes avoidance of difficult people rather than forgiveness.

Divine mercy is the theme of two parables unique to Matthew's Gospel. Parables in this Gospel largely underscore our need to make a choice to respond to Jesus and live by his risky teachings. They also highlight the reality of judgment if we make the wrong choice. Matthew has two parables unique to his Gospel that spark reflection on God's judgment, God's mercy (The Unmerciful Servant 18:23-34), and God's Grace (The Laborers in the Vineyard 20:1-16). Yes, God is gracious and merciful, these parables seem to agree, but if you begrudge that graciousness, judgment awaits. While Matthew is careful to demand moral rigor from his own community, his parables of judgment always blare their time-bound subtext: his controversy with the synagogues and the replacement of Israel with the church. In preaching his themes of judgment and grace, today's preachers need to be careful to preach grace and mercy to those beyond the church's walls, and judgment to all, not just those "outside" our faith borders.[61]

THE PURE IN HEART (5:8)

The Old Testament background to this verse is probably Psalm 24:4-5: "Those who have clean hands and pure hearts, who do not lift up their souls to what is false, and do not swear deceitfully. They will receive blessing from the Lord, and vindication from the God of their salvation." The reference is to spiritual purity rather than ritual or ceremonial cleanliness. The Greek adjective *katharos* (here translated "pure") connotes both the idea of cleanliness

(Matthew 27:59 refers to a clean linen shroud) and the idea of purity, in the sense of unalloyed, as in the pure gold of Revelation 21:21.[62]

Matthew is emphasizing the inward disposition of a person that leads to a change in behavior. Jesus knew well that the heart was a wellspring of evil intentions that can become evil deeds (15:19). He knew that it is possible to honor God in words while our hearts are far removed from him (15:8). Purity of heart cannot be achieved without God's help. The pure in heart are those who consistently and repeatedly allow God to cleanse them of corruption. They have a single-minded devotion to God, not attempting to serve both God and mammon (6:24). They are like trees that, out of their goodness, bear good fruit (12:33-37).[63]

To "see God" is a metaphor for the bliss of fellowship with and knowledge of God in the kingdom to come (Psalm 17:15; 1 Corinthians 13:12). Seeing God face-to-face is thematic in the Old Testament. The prophets urge the people to seek God's face (Hosea 5:15). The psalmists long for a vision of God's face as a positive blessing and express disappointment at its elusiveness (Psalms 44:24; 102:2). At the same time, it is a fearful thing to come face-to-face with God (Genesis 32:30; Is 6:5). Says God, "No one shall see me and live" (Exodus 33:20), except for Moses.

Humility is a key ingredient in purity of heart. Moses is unique in the intimacy of his experience of God (Deuteronomy 34:10) and in his humility (Numbers 12:3). In Jesus' day, humility was widely regarded as a mark of a true sage. Matthew emphasizes Jesus' humility (11:29), a quality Jesus instilled in his disciples.

The "poor in spirit" and the "pure in heart" are blessed in the Beatitudes. In his teachings, Jesus focuses our attention on the inward condition that leads to the act. Secret, evil thoughts are to be eradicated as they lead to public violence and infidelity.

Matthew is concerned, above all, with right motivation. What people do not see, that is, what is seen and known by God alone, is just as important, if not more so, than what people do see (23:1-12, esp. vv. 5-7).[64]

The substance of that inward focus is not creative visualization of a personal goal, but the love commandment (5:43-8, 19:19, 22:34-40, 43:8). Inwardly focusing on the love commandment results in a life of forgiveness and reconciliation. This theme is emphasized in the Beatitudes, the Lord's Prayer, and the instructions to Peter to forgive a brother "seventy times seven" (5:21-26; 6:14-15; 18:21-35).[65]

THE PEACEMAKERS (5:9)

The Hebrew word *shalom* (peace) connotes not just the absence of conflict but the presence of harmony and justice in the community. The Roman legions who established the Peace of Rome (*Pax Romana*) could bring an end to armed conflict but could not establish *shalom*. Peacemaking was highly valued by the rabbinical literature and the writings of Judaism between the Old and New Testaments. "Blessed is he who brings peace and love" (2 Enoch 52:11).[66] Peacemakers build bridges rather than walls. They work at loving their enemies and returning good for evil. God bestows on peacemakers the title "children of God," Israel's destiny and title (Deuteronomy 14:1; Hosea 1:10). The peacemakers are the true Israel.

THOSE PERSECUTED FOR RIGHTEOUSNESS (5:10-12)

By righteousness Matthew means faithfulness and obedience to the law of God as interpreted by Jesus. To live by the teachings of Jesus meant to embrace voluntary poverty (6:19-21), love of enemies (5:43-48), non-retaliation (5:38-42), a cutting loose of home and family ties (8:22; 10:34-39; 12:46-50), and a fearless, carefree attitude toward life based on confidence in God's care (6:25-34).

This final Beatitude may well reflect the opposition Jewish Christian missionaries of Matthew's day encountered in their attempts to live by and to spread the good news of such a radical commitment. Such opposition from outside may well have helped to crystallize the group's identity. The term for "be glad" in 5:12 is often a technical term for joy in persecution and martyrdom used in the New Testament (1 Peter 1:6, 8, 4:134; Revelation 19:7).[67] Scripture is filled with the theme of the persecution of true prophets from God through the ages (2 Chronicles 36:15-16; Nehemiah 9:26; Acts 7:52; Matthew 23:34). A good reputation in the community was important in the Jewish tradition. Being publicly reviled was dreaded. This Beatitude assures Jesus' followers that, regardless of peer opinion, God's approval will grant them glory in the kingdom that is to come.

God's call is to faithfulness, not popularity. The Bible witnesses to those who listen to the voice of God rather than the voice of the people. Witness Moses, David, Samuel, Elisha, Jeremiah, Vashti, Esther, Joseph, Mary, Jesus' disciples, and the women who stood by the cross and spread the post-resurrection good news to both Jesus' enemies and his disciples.[68]

Lifeform

The following attitudes and actions mark those who are obedient to Jesus and his radical wisdom.

> *Voluntary poverty and critique of riches* "Is not life more than food, and the body more than clothing?" (Matthew 6:25). "Where your treasure is, there your heart will be also" (Matthew 6:21).
>
> *Critique of hypocrisy* "Why do you see the speck in your neighbor's eye, but do not notice the log in your own eye? How can you look for the splinter in your neighbor's eye when you have a log in your own?" (Matthew 7:3).
>
> *Non-retaliation* "If anyone strikes you on the right cheek, turn the other also" (Matthew 5:39). "With the judgment you make you will be judged" (Matthew 7:2).
>
> *Rejoicing in the face of reproach* "Blessed are you when people revile you and persecute you and utter all kinds of evil against you falsely on my account" (Matthew 5:11).
>
> *Subordination of family ties to discipleship* "Follow me, and let the dead bury their own dead" (Matthew 8:22).
>
> *Fearless and carefree attitude that elevates faith over foresight* "Those who find their life will lose it, and those who lose their life for my sake will find it" (Matthew 10:39).
>
> *Confidence in God's Care* "For everyone who asks receives, and everyone who searches finds, and for everyone who knocks, the door will be opened" (Matthew 7:8).
>
> *Discipleship without pretensions* "Can the blind lead the blind?" (15:14). "A disciple is not above the teacher, nor a

slave above the master" (Matthew 10:24). "All who exalt themselves will be humbled, and all who humble themselves will be exalted" (Matthew 23:12).

Single-mindedness in the pursuit of God's kingdom "Strive first for the kingdom of God and his righteousness, and all these things will be given to you as well" (Matthew 6:34).

Together We Stand

When we gather, Christ is in our midst (18:20) and shapes us individually and as a community. We become those who fish for people (4:19; chapter 10). We become those who act in such a way that others, observing our lives, will give the glory to God (5:13-16). We become the true family of Jesus (12:46-50). We are blessed by special revelation (11:25-27; 13:11-17). We achieve understanding (13:51; 16:12). We build the church (16:17-20). We tell others the good news (17:9) and we proclaim the gospel to the world (24:14).

The life formed by wisdom according to Matthew is a life in community. We derive our identity as a community from Jesus' life and teachings and his death and resurrection. This new wisdom community is drawn from all nations and is bound to him through baptism and adherence to his commands (28:19-20). This gathering is to be a visible, counter-cultural community of salt and light, within itself and in relation to the wider world (5:13-16).

It is also a community of grace. Self-help wisdom's way of life lacks the quality of grace. It lacks the realities of forgiveness and forbearance.

Even in Matthew's morally rigorous Gospel, grace abounds. Jesus multiplies the loaves, stills the storm, heals the sick, and forgives sins. While many reject Jesus' wisdom because it threatens their authority or security, we are told that with God all things are possible (19:26), even the salvation of one with many possessions. Matthew's Gospel includes the parable of the treasure and the pearl, two joyful similes about the kingdom of heaven (13:44-45). The community is continually reminded that judgment belongs to God and final determination awaits the last days. Until then the weeds and the wheat grow together in the field. The church is a mixed body until the final judgment (13:24-30, 36-43; 22:11-14). Love forbids premature attempts to uproot weeds from the field.

Matthew's Gospel is home to Jesus' poignant words from the cross "My God, My God why hast thou forsaken me?" (27:46). Luke has the more serene "Father, into thy hands I commit my spirit" (Luke 23:46). Matthew's anguished version of Jesus' last words invites us to identify with Jesus in his suffering, just as it inspires us to invite the resurrected Lord to enter into our present pain. The Matthean Jesus portrays God as one who demands all but also gives all. We are assured that Jesus shares the wisdom and nature of God and offers a life of partnership with him as together we bear the yoke his grace makes easy (11:28-30). We are assured that God will care for our needs, that we have no need for anxiety, that our success does not depend on others' acceptance of us, and that Jesus will be with us always (28:20). To embrace these assurances is to be wise. To hold fast to both teachings and Teacher is to be freed from fear and hypocrisy to participate in the power of divine wisdom in daily life.

CHAPTER NINE

The Wisdom Gospel: John

"Lord, to whom shall we go? You have the words of eternal life."
(John 6:68-69)

In talking with preachers over the years, I have noticed that the Gospel of John is not everyone's favorite. One irreverent soul went so far as to say "I have never cared for the Gospel of John. Jesus hovers six feet above the ground and delivers one longwinded monologue after another!" Some preachers mistakenly regard the Gospel as too mystical and abstract to touch the everyday lives of their parishioners. On a closer look, however, we find that the exalted cosmological affirmations about Jesus' identity as Word of God, the stately I AM speeches, are precisely the tools the author used to speak in a pointed way to his congregation to counter competing versions of wisdom and to encourage them in paths of faith and perseverance.

John writes his Gospel to counter two forms of "wisdom" current in his milieu. One said Jesus was not the Messiah and Son of God but merely a human teacher. The other said that Jesus was the Messiah and the Son of God but that he was not fully human; i.e., the Divine came into Jesus at his baptism and left before the crucifixion (the thinking being the Divine cannot suffer). We face similar false teachings in the self-help philosophies that surround us. They all imply that the will and determination of the individual is all we need to achieve a happy, successful life. Who needs Jesus to help us do anything? They also imply that the lion's share of suffering and bad luck are due to wrong thinking. A Messiah who is humiliated and killed is not a good advertisement for "you create your own reality" thinking! It is no less a stumbling block now than it was at the end of the first century when the fourth Gospel was written. John can help us address it in our sermons.

Background Check

Exploring the context of John's Gospel reminds me of the process of doing tomb rubbings. One takes paper and a piece of charcoal shaped like a piece of chalk and lays the paper over the stone and rubs over it with broad strokes. Gradually an image appears that depends on what lies beneath, perhaps the letters of an inscription, perhaps the features of a face.

In John's case, what appears is a face, that of Wisdom-in-person, Jesus Christ. It is a face that is serene, yet searching and determined. John painted this portrait to set it up on an easel in the center of his community. The challenges they faced had a role in shaping its contours.

John's Gospel was probably written around 90 CE in a community that faced conflict with the followers of John the Baptist, the Jewish authorities, and other groups in society.[1] Their affirmation that Jesus is the Messiah caused conflict so sharp that their members were being put out of the synagogues. The consensus among scholars is that the author of this Gospel was not an eyewitness reporting events of Jesus' life. The author, writing in the final two decades of the first century, drew on a variety of traditions filtered through several decades of his community's experience and reflection.

Those traditions included a fairly complete narrative of the passion and death of Jesus, much of the material presented as the farewell discourse of chapters 13-17, and collections of stories of Jesus' public ministry on the order of what has been called the "signs source." [2]

The community of John may well have been a small community living in the Jewish sector of a Diaspora city in the final quarter of the first century. It appears to have included a core of Samaritans and Gentiles who needed to be brought on board by the explanation of various Jewish festivals. The community was experiencing a tension that related to some sort of split between the Johannine community and the parent synagogue (9:22; 12:42; 16:2).

This event seems to be the lens through which the story of Jesus is refracted. It explains the Gospel's focus on the community's internal life and survival rather than on mission and evangelism. It accounts for Jesus' depiction as one who provides comfort, healing, and support.[3]

The Johannine letters were written at a later period in the history of the Johannine community and addressed specific concerns of that time. While maintaining the central theological tenets of the Gospel, they are addressed, not to the synagogue, but to former members of the community who have broken away. There is a polemical tone, designed to counter those who denied the significance of Jesus' coming in the flesh and rejected the saving power of his death.[4]

John's depiction of Jesus is shaped by two factors: his community's relationship with the synagogue, and, to a lesser degree, by a desire to refute those who denied the full humanity of Jesus.

Relationship with Synagogue

John presents Jesus as incarnate revelation, Wisdom descended from on high to offer humankind light and truth. In his famous "I AM" discourses he proclaims his divine and celestial origins. He treats plots against him and attempts to arrest him with majestic disdain. While some scholars have sought the origins for this portrait in Gnostic, Mandean, or Hermetic passages, it is more likely that the evangelist draws primarily from an identification of Jesus with personified divine Wisdom as described in the Old Testament and intertestamental writings.[5]

Jesus' credibility and authority flow from his identity as Wisdom. Because he is Wisdom, he emanates from God, preexists creation, and is an active agent in creation and in Israel's salvation history. The Johannine community has accepted him and is being persecuted as a result. Jesus' identity as Wisdom offers them the succor they need to endure their trials. His benefits include life, peace, joy, and glory. As Wisdom, he comes to bring light to the whole world, but at the same time he demands decision and will mete out judgment. John's focus on Jesus as Wisdom suggests a mode of preaching that is urgent, invitational, and personal.

There may well have been three periods in the history of this community: early, middle, and late. During the early period a community within the synagogue coheres around its members belief that Jesus is the awaited Messiah. In the middle period the group is born as a separate community by experiencing two major traumas: excommunication from the synagogue and martyrdom (16:2). During the late period the group develops a distinct social and theological identity that functions as an alternative to society at large. It is shaped by Jesus, Wisdom-in-Person, who came down from heaven and is "not of this world" just as they are now "born from above" and therefore not of this world (6:38; 17:14-16; 8:23).[6]

A series of allegories (door, shepherd, vine) developed that testify to the community's concern for its own survival and confidence in Jesus' sustenance.

Now the Johannine community felt cut off from both synagogue and world, as evidenced by texts that emphasize the rejection of Jesus' message by "his own people" (1:10-13; 3:17-21) and the mixed feelings the community has toward "the world."

At times "the world" refers to those who reject Jesus (chapter 17). At other times, however, "the world" refers to the whole of humanity (3:16). Universalism and isolationism coexist. Sometimes the community shields itself from a world it perceives as hostile. This is the same world, however, that God loves and wishes to save (3:16-17).[7]

Wisdom was a particularly effective resource to draw on in the Johannine community's struggle with the synagogue. The rabbis had already focused on the identification of Wisdom and the Law by the time of the writing of the Gospel. At the same time that the rabbis identified Wisdom with the Law, the Johannine community identified Wisdom with Jesus.

John's Prologue offers a lens on the Gospel, a conceptual key to all that follows. The Gospel has strong elements of Wisdom Christology, but no word from the *sophia/sophos* family appears in the text. The presence and activity of Wisdom is implied in the use of the word *logos* in the Prologue. There were precedents for this connection in the Hebrew Scriptures, intertestamental Jewish thought, and in Greek philosophical thought. The use of the word *logos* is suggested by the Old Testament tradition that God's word, when spoken, has an effect on the world.

The precedents to the Prologue to John's Gospel lie in the intertestamental period in several works that refer to Wisdom. These include The Wisdom of Jesus Ben Sirach, The Wisdom of Solomon, and Baruch. Sirach, a document dated in the early second century BCE, closely relates Wisdom to the Law. The Law is the concrete form of a transcendent, hidden Wisdom.

The Wisdom of Solomon found the word logos to be another way to speak of God's immanent involvement in human affairs, but in male terminology. The Jewish philosopher Philo ascribed to the Logos the functions previously ascribed to Sophia in the world in the Wisdom tradition. For him, while Sophia represents the embodiment of unlimited knowledge of God, the Logos is the guide to that goal. By the end of the first century of the Christian era, *sophia* and *logos* were used interchangeably in many circles.[8]

Refutation of Docetism

While a polemic against Docetism is far more pronounced in the Johannine letters, the Fourth Gospel may include themes that combated this perspective. Docetism was not so much a heresy by itself as it was an attitude found in a number of heresies. The word Docetism or Docetist comes from the Greek verb *(dokeo)* which means "to seem." The central contention was that Jesus Christ did not truly come in the flesh, for his flesh was only an appearance—he only seemed to be a human being. The insistence that "The Word became flesh" (1:14) may be directed against the docetists. Likewise the eucharistic realism of John (6:51-58) may have been a message to the docetists who neglected the Eucharist and denied that it was the flesh of Jesus. The realism of blood and water pouring from the side of the wounded Jesus works against a theory that he was a phantasm. Wisdom Incarnate, the one who worked miracles and walked on water, is the same one who hangs, bleeding and suffering, on the cross.

A Christ who only seemed human is much less threatening than one who really is. He demands so much less of us. Aren't many of us content to seem to be Christians? We are courteous to others, we strive for excellence, we care about our children, and we do not engage in conspicuous consumption. If discomfort or inconvenience is a stepping stone to future personal reward, we will endure it. Going to bed hungry is necessary to drop those five pounds. Taking that night class is necessary to earn the degree that will increase one's salary.

Christ and church membership is appealing to us because it offers a community to support us when we are ill, a place for our children to learn good values, a place to meet friends when we are new to a town, or a place to network in ways that will ultimately benefit our careers. Beyond that, our aim is to factor discomfort and inconvenience out of our lives. Many of us, preachers as well as people, are content to seem to be Christian and pray that we are never put to the test when other people are looking. That's why docetic preachers thrive today. "Name it and claim it. Jesus wants you to be prosperous." A shallow, miracle-based faith is a commodity that lots of people are willing to sell us.

There are still crowds of us ready to make Jesus our king, but not to accept that he will be exalted by death and enthroned on a cross (6:2, 15, 26; 12:9-18).

Nutshell

What Is Most Important?

JESUS, THE WISDOM OF GOD

As preachers, we often preach about the teachings of Jesus when we preach from the Gospels. But we don't adequately connect them with an answer to the question "Who is the teacher?" How often do we proclaim that Jesus is the Risen, Ever-Present Wisdom of God? This is the strong implication of Matthew's Gospel. It is the strong theme of the Christological hymns of the Pauline letters. And it is the explicit message of the entire Gospel of John, stated most pointedly in the Prologue. With all the competing versions of the wise life all around us, we owe it to our people to preach Jesus the Wisdom of God with all the urgency and vividness John can help us muster.

John states the purpose for writing his Gospel clearly: "These things are written so that you may come to believe that Jesus is the Messiah, the Son of God, and that through believing you may have life in his name" (John 20:31). At the heart of the Gospel is the revelation of God in Christ: Jesus is God incarnate. Distinctive to this

Gospel is the exploration of the relationship of the Father to the Son. The relationship is one of mutual indwelling (14:10-11). It is a relationship of love (14:31; 15:9; 17:23-24). It is one of identity of wills (15:10), and it finds expression in the willing obedience of the Son to the Father (14:28).

The story of Jesus' life follows the Wisdom trajectory of one who pre-exists and comes to earth, teaches but is rejected, and must go back up into heaven again. This theme pervades intertestamental wisdom writings and is most clearly expressed in 1 Enoch 42. This plot is expressed in John 1:11-14: "He came to what was his own, and his own people did not accept him. But to all who received him, who believed in his name, he gave power to become children of God, who were born, not of blood or of the will of the flesh or of the will of man, but of God. And the Word became flesh and lived among us, and we have seen his glory, the glory as of a father's only son, full of grace and truth."

JESUS AS SON OF MAN

Jesus' identity as Wisdom is closely tied to his identity as the Son of Man.

In 3:13 the evangelist tells readers: "No one has ascended into heaven except the one who descended from heaven, the Son of Man. And just as Moses lifted up the serpent in the wilderness, so must the Son of Man be lifted up, that whoever believes in him may have eternal life."[9]

The background of the term Son of Man can be found partly in the Hebrew Scriptures. Son of Man is used there for humankind in general, for a prophet (Ezekiel 2:1f), for a corporate or representative figure of humankind (Psalm 8:4), or of the people of God (Daniel 7:13).[10]

Another source of background for the Son of Man title may well be a mysterious figure in late Jewish writings. In Daniel 7 he is a representative human-like figure chosen by God to ascend to heaven to receive instruction and to return to earth to exercise a just rule. In 1 Enoch, 4 Ezra, and 2 Baruch, the Son of Man is identified more and more closely with the Messiah and the Messiah's role as judge rubs off on the Son of Man. In the synoptics the Son of Man is sometimes used as a present reference, but more often as a future heavenly judge coming on the clouds of heaven. In the Synoptics Jesus never definitively identifies himself with that figure.[11]

In John, Jesus clearly is the Son of Man. For John the title embodies the theme of Jesus' heavenly origin and destiny, adding to the themes of Messiahship and Sonship the notion of preexistence. The theme of preexistence is difficult to trace. It is most likely a confluence of ancient Jewish angelology, the depiction of Wisdom in Proverbs 8, and the account of Wisdom's descent to earth in 1 Enoch 42. The result is John's portrait of a mysterious figure who is already here, empowered with the authority to judge, already engaged in a ministry of teaching and healing that demands a choice. The Son of Man's triumph is no longer reserved for an indeterminate future as it is in the Synoptics. It is the immediate, inevitable sequel to his imminent death.[12]

The title Son of Man bears the imprint of Wisdom influences in its current shape in John's Gospel. It almost could be said to be a synonym for "Wisdom made flesh." The parallels between his identity and that of Personified Wisdom familiar to us from Hebrew Scriptures and later Jewish writings are numerous and obvious. The Son of Man is the only one who has seen the Father (6:46). This equips him to speak for the Father and to give the teaching which is from God (7:16-17; 8:28). He has the authority to execute judgment (5:27). The Son of Man gives the food that endures to eternal life (6:27). Therefore believers are nourished by his flesh and blood (6:53). When in the presence of the Son of Man, we are in the presence of the divine (9:38). The Son of Man will return to where he was before (6:62). The Son must be lifted up in order that salvation may come (3:14).

John's Wisdom Christology

A Wisdom Christology underlies John's depiction of Jesus the Word of God. Jesus is the one who came into the world to reveal the way to eternal life. (1:9; 3:19; 9:39; 11:27; 12:46; 16:28; 18:37). He brings salvation, and he brings judgment. He provokes decision. Conflict and controversy surround him. Some accept him and some reject him. His coming and the responses to him are the focus of the first twelve chapters.

In the second half of the story (chapters 13-21), Jesus is the one who departs. He departs by laying down his life in death. In departing he returns to the Father through death and resurrection. Thereby he glorifies the Father, shows that the world has been overcome, prepares a place for those who come after, and makes possible the coming of the Holy Spirit and life under the guidance of the Holy Spirit.

Because of his relationship with the Father, Jesus functions as the divine agent sent from above to reveal God's glory in the world (17:1ff). Some aspects of this relationship are unique. Jesus is the Son. Jesus is the way. Jesus goes ahead to prepare a place for those the Father has given him. Some aspects of the relationship are meant to provide the pattern for our human interactions in community. Jesus' followers are to partake of the relationship of mutual indwelling in love among Father, Son, and believer (15:9-10).[13]

Key to this Gospel is the underlying insight that the life of faith is a response to revelation, a response to grace. That theme was present in Matthew's Gospel, but is sounded even more loudly here. It is true of the pattern of biblical spirituality as a whole. As we have seen, secular wisdom relies on the self or sometimes, at best, a rather vague connection to a universal will. The life of faith according to John's Gospel is specific and personal: it is a response to Jesus as divine.

JESUS' SYMBOLIC ACTIONS

John conveys Jesus' divinity through a series of symbolic actions. The most important are the seven miracles or "signs" that he performed during his public ministry. They are: changing water into wine, the healing of the Galilean official's son and the invalid at Bethzada, the feeding the 5,000, walking on the sea, the healing of a blind beggar, and raising Lazarus from the dead. The signs are not meant to be ends in themselves, but are to point to the identity of Jesus in relation to God and to inspire belief in him.[14]

Several nonmiraculous actions also contribute to the Gospel's symbolism. They include the cleansing of the temple, the anointing at Bethany, the footwashing, and the great catch of fish. Both types of actions reveal facets of Jesus' identity in a way that is perceptible to the sense.[15] Each of these actions has a Christological focus. It reveals aspects of Jesus' identity as Messiah, prophet, and divine Son of Man. Allusions to Jesus' crucifixion and resurrection appear in connection with each of the symbolic actions in the Gospel.[16]

JESUS' I AM SAYINGS

John also depicts Jesus as uttering several self-revelatory discourses, the "I AM" sayings. Jesus is the life-giving bread, the water of life, the light, the door and the way, the good shepherd, the vine. As the good shepherd who knows his sheep, so Jesus summons disciples to follow him. As the source of abundant life, Jesus turns water into wine at the wedding feast (2:1-12), offers living water to the woman at the well (4:1-15), makes the lame man walk (5:1-9), heals the official's son (4:46-54), and raises Lazarus from the dead (11:1-44). As the true light, Jesus gives sight to the man born blind (chapter 9). As the lamb of God, he dies for the sins of the world (1:29-34). The "I AM" sayings make it clear that the life of faith is a response to Jesus exclusively and to none other.

These sayings depict the life of faith as a response to Jesus exclusively and to none other. In four instances, Jesus uses the "I AM" in the form of an absolute statement with no predicate (8:24, 28, 58; 13:19). For example, in 8:58 Jesus says "Before Abraham was, I am." This construction is reminiscent of the self-revelation of God in the Hebrew Scriptures (Exodus 3:14).[17]

In seven instances John's Gospel includes the "I AM" with a predicate nominative, as Jesus speaks of himself figuratively.

I am the bread of life (living bread) (6:35, 51).

I am the light of the world (8:12; 9:5).

I am the sheepgate (10: 7,9).

I am the good shepherd (10:11,14).

I am the resurrection and the life (11:25).

I am the way, the truth, and the life (14:6).

I am the true vine (15:1, 5).

These metaphors draw motifs and imagery from across the Hebrew Scriptures and apply them to Jesus. This is a theological process of reflection, which draws upon the familiar to express the new. "The way" is a symbol applied previously to Torah (Deuteronomy 5:32-3). The shepherd is a symbol used of God and the leaders of the nation in the Psalms and the prophets (Psalms 23;

78:70-72; 80; Isaiah 40:11; Jeremiah 31:10; Ezekiel 34; 37:24). The shepherd is also the term used of the Teacher of Righteousness at Qumran, the seat of the separatist Jewish group known as the Essenes. Jesus is the *good* shepherd in contrast to the leaders of Israel who are false shepherds (Ezekiel 34). He is good because he is willing to lay down his life for the sheep (10:11f).

The "I AM" sayings show a strong reliance on Israel's wisdom tradition. They characterize Jesus as living bread; the light of the world; the door; the way; the life; and the authentic vine. All of these realities are said at one point or another to characterize or to come from personified Wisdom.[18] In Proverbs 8:35 Wisdom says, "For whoever finds me finds life and obtains favor from the Lord." In The Wisdom of Solomon 7:26 she is said to be a "reflection of eternal light." In John's Gospel repeated statements identify Jesus as "the light of the world" (1:9; 3:19; 8:12; 9:5; 12:46). The image of light serves a Christological function in the Gospel. The Messiah was expected to be the "light of the nations" (Isaiah 42:6; 49:6), a term that was also interpreted to refer to the Law brought by Moses.[19] In calling himself "the light of the world," Jesus is claiming that he is indeed the Messiah and the prophet like Moses, but one whose saving power extends to the whole world. As the light of the world Jesus is also claiming to be the Divine Son of Man. People throughout the ancient world recognized the divine character of light. Readers would not need a familiarity with the Old Testament and Jewish traditions to grasp what Jesus was claiming when he said "I am the light of the world."

This claim also makes a statement about discipleship. "Whoever follows me will never walk in darkness but will have the light of life" (8:12*b*). In Proverbs something very similar is said of those who follow Wisdom: "the path of the righteous is like the light of dawn... but the way of the wicked is like deep darkness" (Proverbs 4:18-19).[20] Following Jesus we become "children of the light" (12:36).

The characterization of Jesus as vine can be compared to the description of Wisdom in Sirach 24:17ff. "Like the vine I bud forth delights, and my blossoms become glorious and abundant fruit. Come to me you who desire me, and eat your fill of my fruits...those who eat of me will hunger for more and those who drink of me will thirst for more."

In John 6:35 Jesus says, "I am the bread of life. Whoever comes to me will never be hungry, and whoever believes in me will never be thirsty." Woman Wisdom beckons us to "Come eat of my bread, and drink of the wine I have mixed. Lay aside immaturity, and live, and walk in the way of insight" (Proverbs 9:5, 6). Wisdom is said to be a tree of life in Proverbs 3:18. Like the Gospel of John, the Wisdom literature uses food and drink metaphors to indicate deeper spiritual nourishment.

John 6 has clear echoes of Wisdom as hostess and nourisher. The very topic of bread reminds us that women sowed, reaped, ground, kneaded, baked, and served bread. Jesus, like Wisdom and like nearly all mothers in antiquity, prepares and distributes the meal of bread and fish.[21]

Behind this passage and the discourse that explains it, lie images of Wisdom as a nourishing mother, nourishing with spiritual food, seen especially in Sirach 14:20-15:10.

> She will come to meet him like a mother,
> and like a young bride she will welcome him.
> She will feed him with the bread of learning,
> and give him the water of wisdom to drink. (Sirach 15:2-3).[22]

The bread of Wisdom implicitly refers to the manna in the wilderness (Exodus 16:32; Deuteronomy 8:16). In rabbinic sources, the manna signifies the Law.[23] Again, as in Proverbs, Wisdom acts as a nourisher, even as Yahweh did in the Exodus salvation history. Both Wisdom and Jesus are nourishers; both are the bread of life and living water. So Jesus, identifying himself as the provider of the bread of life, presents himself as Woman Wisdom.

John uses Wisdom theology as his model in the bread of life discourse. Jesus descends from heaven by the will of the Father; he comes to save; he gives life; he is both nourisher and nourishment.

There are important differences between Jesus and Wisdom. Wisdom's return to heaven is not part of her saving mission. It is her retreat. She is not incarnate. Wisdom theology does not have a full eucharistic doctrine. Wisdom does not explicitly identify herself with the bread of life. Sirach 24:20 says, "Those who eat me will still hunger and those who drink me will still thirst." John 6:35

says, "I am the bread of life. Whoever comes to me will never be hungry, and the one who believes in me will never be thirsty."

In John's view, there are three kinds of bread that cannot give eternal life: the bread given to the 5,000 (and the 4,000), the manna, and the law. The nourishment Jesus offers is different from that offered by Moses. The disciples of Jesus, unlike those of Wisdom, are not unsatisfied; Jesus gives himself in his teaching and in the Eucharist.[24]

In John's Gospel, Jesus affirms that "I am the way, and the truth, and the life" (John 14:6). In Proverbs, wisdom is repeatedly referred to as the way or the path. Following wisdom is a way that leads to life and peace. "...the path of the righteous is like the light of dawn, which shines brighter and brighter until full day" (Proverbs 4:18). In the wisdom corpus the message is that all one truly longs for and needs can be found in Wisdom. The Fourth Evangelist is trying to make the same point about Jesus. [25]

Preaching on these vivid metaphors requires the preacher to ask herself: Where in everyday life are images and experiences of entry (door), connectedness (vine), illumination (light), nourishment (bread and water), and life? All kinds of visions come to mind. There is the anguish someone fresh out of prison feels when walking into his first job interview. There is the slight shock we feel when, in a prayer circle on a camping trip, we take one another's hands and join in prayer. There are beautiful, warm arms of the volunteer who holds the babies in the hospital nursery for an hour a day. There is the sensation of lights coming on in a darkened room. There is an elderly person lying connected to tubes for monitoring and nourishment. When we are caught in a riptide, fearing for our life, there is the wave that comes along behind us and gently pushes us toward shore. Our yearning for fresh starts, entry points, acceptance and connection, direction, and spiritual nourishment are all supplied in Jesus the Wisdom of God. God is here to help us in every way.

Facilitators

The way of life commended by John's Gospel means to believe in Jesus, and to bear the fruit that comes from knowing him, and abiding in him and in his love. It means being called his friends. It means to follow him, to obey his commandment to love one another, and to serve the community out of that love. By contrast, to reject Jesus is to cut oneself off from life.[26]

Lifeform

The life formed by Johannine wisdom is a life that has at its center a relationship with Jesus Christ the Word and Wisdom of God out of which flow all other relationships. It is a life based on a decision to believe in Christ and a life lived in expectation of continually fresh, one-on-one encounters with Christ. It is eternal life (3:36).

A Relational Life

The life of discipleship is relational. Images of shepherd and sheep and vine and branches emphasize the intimate connection between Jesus and his followers. It is also emphasized in Jesus calling his followers "friends" (15:14).[27]

This relational life is summed up in the concept of being "friends" with Jesus. The vocabulary of friendship, the noun (*philos*) or the verb (*phileo*) pervade the Gospel. John 15:12-17 epitomizes the Gospel's treatment of the theme of friendship. This passage comes in the middle of the Farewell Discourse (John 13–17), which John places at the final meal shared by Jesus and the disciples. It follows the precedent of other speeches of dying leaders in exhorting followers to care for one another.

The figure of the beloved disciple, a key figure in the Gospel, epitomizes one who does not just listen to Jesus' teachings, but enters into deep friendship with Jesus. Some scholars have suggested that he is a composite figure. Others have argued that he is John of Zebedee, Lazarus, or Thomas.[28] Sharon Ringe has raised the possibility that the beloved disciple could have been a woman.[29]

The beloved disciple appears throughout the last half of the Gospel (13:23; 19:26; 20:2; 21:7, 20). This disciple is present at the Last Supper, the trial, the foot of the cross, the empty tomb, and the resurrection appearances. In each case, this disciple is portrayed favorably. He has intimate knowledge of Jesus' intentions and sufferings at the supper; he remains loyal in adversity at Caiphas' house; he receives a commission to care for Jesus' mother at the cross; he believes in Jesus at the empty tomb; and he is singled out for honor by Jesus in the resurrection appearance that concludes the Gospel.

The beloved disciple serves as a model for the kind of faith the Gospel seeks to inspire and strengthen in readers. As Judas is a type of the kind of follower who falls away, and Thomas of one whose faith is immature, the beloved disciple is for John's Gospel the epitome of the true believer. John repeatedly reminds us of the closeness of his relationship with Jesus (13:23, 25; 21:20). He stands at the foot of the cross and becomes Jesus' mother's new son. He "sees and believes" at the empty tomb (20:8). He recognizes the risen Jesus by the Sea of Tiberias (21:7).

John describes this relationship of intimacy with Jesus as analogous to that of Jesus with the Father (14:20-21). He indicates that it is available to all followers who become sensitive to Jesus through love. Raymond Brown points out, "Faith is possible for the beloved disciple because he has become very sensitive to Jesus through love...The lesson for the reader is that love for Jesus gives one the insight to detect his presence".[30]

A Life of Abiding Love

To be a disciple of Jesus means not only to believe in Jesus but to abide in his love. Sharon Ringe calls *meno* (abide) a "verb with staying power!" She points out that it is "like a red thread running through the Fourth Gospel from beginning to end, but its presence is masked by translators who render it by a variety of words, such as "live," "dwell," "remain," or "abide." The word (*meno*) is used in John 1 where the question is where Jesus is "staying" (1:38, 39). The Samaritans who have come to believe ask Jesus to "stay" with them (4:40). It is used in various notes about Jesus' travel plans (2:12; 7:9; 10:40; 11:6, 54). Wherever it occurs, it signifies that Jesus is present with those who receive him. In 14:25, it reminds them that he will not always be with them. This stretches the word's meaning deeper than the level of itinerary to signify Jesus' divine presence. In this light the question of 1:38 "Where are you staying?" becomes the question of discipleship. For Jesus abides with those who will receive him.

In John the verb (*meno*) is used to convey the mutual indwelling of God, Jesus, and those united to them (see 6:56; 14:10-11, 17; 15:4-7, 9-10). That unity depends on a constant flow of energy that has its origin in God. The disciples' ability to live out of that unity is rooted, not in their own moral excellence (obeying the commandment to love one another), but in the mutual love of God and Jesus (15:9-12). The relationship of mutual indwelling conveyed by the verb (*meno*) emphasizes the permanence of that relationship and the blessings it conveys (12:26; 15:16).

Abiding in Jesus is the diametrical opposite of self-improvement, for the energy that sustains it, while we must offer it a human home, is ultimately a divine gift. God's gift is to initiate the love for Jesus that he passes on to the others. God's gift is to be the source of all that Jesus makes known to us.

It is God who empowers Jesus' followers to abide or remain in Jesus. The activity of abiding describes a relationship that is essential to life. The disciples must abide or remain in Jesus as the branches abide in the vine (14:4, 5, 6, 7). The disciples must abide in Jesus' love, just as he abides in God's love (14:9, 10). The call to abide is both a commission and a gift. The friendship to which the Gospel calls us is contingent, not on the disciples' obedience, but on God's prior love.[31]

A Life in Community

While secular self-help wisdom is radically individualistic, John's version of discipleship emphasizes unity in community. Jesus prays to the Father in chapter 17, "The glory that you have given me I have given them, so that they may be one, as we are one, I in them and you in me, that they may become completely one, so that the world may know that you have sent me and have loved them even as you have loved me" (John 17:22, 23). Adherence to Jesus' wisdom results in a communal life in which members love one another because they live and dwell and find their being in God. The result is unity. The closing line of Jesus' famous unity prayer asks God that "the love with which you have loved me may be in them, and I in them" (17:26).

The revelation of God's love the Gospel proclaims for the world (3:16) displaces boundaries of race and gender. The Pharisees,

Jews, Caiphas, and Pilate try to maintain these boundaries. But Jesus himself repeatedly teaches and demonstrates how membership among Jesus' followers is no longer restricted to the descendants of Abraham (8:31-59). Women are prominent in this Gospel: the mother of Jesus, the Samaritan woman, Martha and Mary, and Mary Magdalene. Racial and gender differences no longer determine spiritual status. Jesus proclaims a society in which those who choose him become children of God (1:12; 11:52; 1 John 3:1, 2, 10; 5:2). "The direct, personal, unmediated access to the Father which the divine Son makes possible, brings into being a new, reconstituted people of God."[32]

John uses corporate metaphors for Jesus in relation to his followers. Examples are the good shepherd who lays down his life for the sheep (10:11, 15) and the vine that gives life to the branches (chapter 14). The story itself presents several group portraits with which we are to identify. They include the disciples, the family of Martha, Mary, and Lazarus (chapter 11), and the mother of Jesus and the beloved disciple at the foot of the cross (19:25-27).[33]

A Costly Life

For Jesus, the divine Word, the cost of his mission means "his own" not receiving him (1:11), and having "no honor in his own country" (4:44). It means not being believed, even by his own brothers (7:5), and attracting the enmity of religious and political leaders.[34]

John's Gospel is that the Word (Wisdom) *became flesh* and dwelt among us. The same Jesus who uttered the I AM speeches, multiplied the loaves and fishes, and walked on water, washed feet and went on trial. Wisdom-in-person was belittled, abused, and put to death on a cross.

Without a doubt, John's Gospel lacks the pathos of the synoptics. Jesus strides serenely across the earthly stage, knowing the future and staring suffering in the face without blinking. Yet at the same time, John's Jesus is truly human. He experiences hunger, thirst, and weariness. Blood and water pour from his side when he is pierced on the cross. He is Wisdom-in-person. He knows where he came from and where he is going. He knows that dying on the cross is the first stage of being lifted up to return to the Father (8:28).

A Truth-ful Life

The revelation of the Father by the Son is not a secret wisdom, like the kind the gnostic sects of the first few centuries after Jesus' birth advocated. Rather, it is available to anyone who believes in Jesus, whether they have seen him in the flesh or not (20:8). The verb *to know (gineo)* is used about 100 times in this Gospel. Its meaning for this Gospel is close to that of the verb *to believe.* The content of knowing Jesus is to know he has been sent by the Father, that he is the Messiah, the Son of Man, and that all this is related to eternal life. "This is eternal life, that they may know you, the only true God, and Jesus Christ whom you have sent" (17:3).[35]

The central content of this knowledge is truth. "You will know the truth and the truth will make you free" (8:32). The fourth evangelist's use of the word truth (*alatheia*) is not the Greek notion of knowledge of eternal realities. It is not the gnostic sense of secret truths that guarantee ascent to the realm of light and truth. Truth here is the essential principle of the moral life.[36] In fact, truth sounds a lot like wisdom! For John, truth is the word of the Father addressed to humankind incarnate in Christ and illuminated through the action of the Spirit. Salvation consists in communion with the Father. Such communion is communicated by the gift of eternal life, which is nothing other than "the truth."

The truth, then, has similarities to the concept of Wisdom in Proverbs. It is knowledge of how to live and it is personified in Jesus. As Jesus says, "I am the way and the truth and the life."[37]

The Holy Spirit is defined as the "Spirit of truth," or "the Spirit who communicates truth."[38] The Holy Spirit is the guarantor of continuity between Jesus and the disciples. The Holy Spirit guarantees the continuity of the Christian tradition, for the Spirit continues the work of revelation in the community (14:16). The Holy Spirit glorifies Jesus by continuing the work of revelation (16:14) and continually calling for a response from the world (16:8-11).[39]

A Life of Perseverance

We have seen how the historical context in which the Gospel was written affected its thematic focus. Believers were facing persecution, excommunication from the synagogues, and martyrdom

(9:22, 34; 12:42; 16:1-4). They were prone to disunity, faction, and falling away. In such a context they were to remember the perseverance of Jesus. The second half of the Gospel begins, "having loved his own who were in the world, he loved them to the end" (*eis telos*) (13:1). And on the cross his final words were "It is finished" (19:30). Jesus does not "fall away." In this he is a model for his followers.

Key Texts for Preaching

Encounters with Jesus

The Prologue reveals to us Jesus' identity as Wisdom-in-Person and the potential effects Wisdom's Presence can have on human lives. The narrative invites us into a series of encounters between Jesus and representative figures. In them, those who encounter Wisdom-in-Person are faced with a challenge, a chance for transformation and a choice.

Alan Culpepper points out that "One of John's distinguishing features is the depiction of Jesus as the Revealer and the various responses to him in a narrative that draws the reader to affirm Jesus' idenitity through a series of episodes that describe attempted, failed, and occasionally successful *anagnorises* (recognition scenes)."[40] There are many such encounter scenes in the Gospel. Jesus has interchanges with the royal official; the invalid at Bethzada; the crowds; the disciples, both individually and as a group; the woman caught in adultery; Mary, Martha, and Lazarus; the High Priest; and Pilate.

In the discussion that follows I have chosen three people: Nicodemus (chapter 3:1-21; 7:45-52; 19:38-42), the Samaritan woman (chapter 4), and the man born blind (chapter 9). All three are people who were not among Jesus' initial disciples. One is a respected member of society who, judging by appearances, has his life in order. Two are people who, because of nationality, life circumstances, and physical limitations, are at the margins of Israelite society. All three are people who are struggling with emotions, conditions, and situations from which they have not been able to extricate themselves. They are just three of many encounters Jesus has with people in the Gospel of John. I encourage preachers to ask of the others the same question we are about to ask of these three: What happens when they encounter Wisdom-in-person?

NICODEMUS

Nicodemus, a public figure with impressive credentials that would be known to all in the community, comes to Jesus "by night." The public figure takes pains to keep this visit private. This detail is so important to the fourth evangelist that he reminds us of it when Nicodemus reappears (19:39). The negative symbolism of darkness is prominent in this narrative. Nicodemus may be representative of those who "loved darkness rather than light" (3:19). Still, it cannot be denied that he came to the light, he came "to Jesus" (3:2).[41]

Why did this man wish to hide himself? In Proverbs there are frequent connections between folly and darkness. Is there a tension between him and his community? Is his self-assurance a front? With these mixed signals, we are not sure what to expect from him.

The encounter with Nicodemus is preceded by this account:

> When he was in Jerusalem during the Passover festival, many believed in his name because they saw the signs that he was doing. But Jesus on his part would not entrust himself to them, because he knew all people and needed no one to testify about anyone; for he himself knew what was in everyone (John 2:23-25).

His first words indicate that his profession of trust in Jesus is based on the evidence of signs. Nicodemus comes to him as one of the many who were impressed by the signs Jesus performed. We, too, are drawn to gurus who promise results, benefits. Who doesn't want more money, better health, a better position, more satisfying relationships? We are drawn to Jesus in the hopes that following him will bring us visible benefits. We have no room to look down on the crowds or Nicodemus.

Jesus responds with a teaching that puts the burden of interpretation onto Nicodemus and the reader. It is as if Jesus were saying "If I am a teacher as you say, then be taught."[42]

Jesus' twice-repeated teaching is "You must be born *anothen*" (3:3,7). The Greek has a double meaning: "again" and "from above." Either way, Jesus is referring to the necessity for transformed human existence. When Nicodemus admits that Jesus is a teacher who comes from God, he has said more than he realizes. Jesus is not merely a teacher. He is also the subject matter with whom we must interact—the Word that comes from God. The birth that comes through Jesus is a birth from above. He is the only one who has both descended from and ascended into heaven as Son of Man (3:13).[43]

Transformed human existence can only come from the activity of the Holy Spirit. "The wind blows where it chooses and you hear the sound of it, but you do not know where it comes from or where it goes. So it is with everyone who is born of the Spirit" (3:8).

The ensuing dialogue, however, demonstrates that he is not yet able to grasp who Jesus is. The scene is a failed recognition scene. Nicodemus' inability to understand Jesus is characteristic of the Jewish authorities and the Pharisees throughout John's Gospel (8:13, 19, 22).[44]

In reading this dialogue we as readers experience a befuddlement similar to Nicodemus'. We will either reject Jesus and his puzzling words or stick with them until, moving through the narrative, we reach a degree of clarity.[45]

Nicodemus is so sure of what is possible, based on his human expectations and experiences (3:4, 9). The challenge for him and for us lies in this question: Do we have the courage to allow what we consider to be possible to be shaped and reshaped by Jesus?

New Testament scholar Jouette Bassler, examining the three appearances of Nicodemus in this Gospel, comments that Nicodemus appears in the narrative often enough to evoke curiosity, but not often enough to satisfy it.[46] Nicodemus is mentioned as one from the ranks of the Pharisees who rises to Jesus' defense. But it is an example of cautious and guarded speech and falls far short of the bold, candid profession of faith this Gospel demands.[47]

In chapter 19 Nicodemus appears a third and final time, and we hope for some resolution to the ambiguity. He brings a boatload of spices for Jesus' burial and helps to wrap Jesus' body. We are not sure why he brings such a lavish gift. Is it a sign of faith or of a desire to preserve the body at all costs, not realizing the significance of the resurrection?

Asking for Jesus' body might be seen as an act of faith, and yet there is a clandestine tone to the scene. Nicodemus helps Joseph of

Arimathea, described as a disciple, but as a secret one, "out of fear of the Jews." Though both Joseph and Nicodemus are, technically, Jews themselves, their allegiance to Jesus has apparently distanced them from their own community of origin.

As a reader, I would like a clear progression from the doubt of the initial nocturnal visit to bold, outspoken faith at the tomb. At the very least I would appreciate a final, definitive encounter between Jesus and Nicodemus so that I could clearly categorize him as an example of true faith or one who remains mired in a sign-based faith.[48] But no such encounter occurs. It is like a sermon whose ending the listener must provide. Nicodemus' persistent ambivalence invites us to identify with him yet frustrates us at the same time. We wonder, "What will become of him?" We are left with the pinprick of a realization that the answer is up to us.

THE SAMARITAN WOMAN

The Samaritan woman is the mirror opposite of Nicodemus. Nicodemus was a man, a Jew, and a respected member of society who came to Jesus by night. She was a woman, a Samaritan, and a marginal member of society who encountered Jesus in broad daylight. She is there to draw water that will slake her thirst only temporarily. She encounters the water of life. She is representative of the Samaritans, held in contempt by the Jews. In contemporary terms she is someone who has been edged too far to the margins to be elevated in the slightest by self-help philosophies. Jesus is her only hope. Her opening question "How is it that you a Jew…" points to the fact that the Jew who asks the woman for water is not just any Jew, bound by national and gender restrictions. He is the king of the Jews (19:19).[49]

The setting beside the ancestral well and the references to Jacob seem to launch us into a type scene: the meeting of a young woman and her future groom at a well. In the Old Testament several of the woman's ancestors, including Jacob and Rachel, first met beside a well. The pattern of these stories is that a man traveling in a foreign country meets a young unmarried female relative beside a well. She gives him water and he reveals his identity to her. She hurries home to tell her family about the visitor. The man is invited to stay and a betrothal is arranged.

Here the woman is neither young nor unmarried. Her personal history appears to be as troubled as that of the relationship between the Jews and the Samaritans. She and Jesus engage, not in a courtship, but in a verbal interchange in which he tries to reveal his identity to her, as living water (4:14) and as the one through whom her people and the Jews may worship God "in spirit and truth" (4:24). She runs home to tell her townspeople, and they grasp the truth that, in Jesus, differences between Jews and Samaritans are transcended. The Samaritans associated worship with Gerizim, while the Jews connected it with Jerusalem. Jesus points the woman at the well toward a worship not tied to a human city. Worshiping God " in spirit and in truth," meant focusing on the Living Water, Jesus his Son.

The episode begins like the betrothal stories of Israel's ancestors but ends with the kind of civic reception that cities throughout the empire granted to the Roman generals who became emperors. People streamed out to the roadside to greet him, then escorted him into their town, calling him "savior and benefactor." By giving this treatment to Jesus, the people of Sychar witness to the universal scope of his power.[50]

Jesus' encounter with the Samaritan woman (4:1-42) is a successful recognition scene, in which the woman comes by stages to suspect who Jesus is: "You, a Jew" (4:9); "Sir, I see that you are a prophet" (4:19). Then, after Jesus says "I am he" (the Messiah who will proclaim all things), the woman returns to the city, saying, "Come and see a man who told me everything I have ever done! He cannot be the Messiah, can he?" (4:29). The result is that many believe in Jesus because of her and say, "We know that this is truly the Savior of the world" (4:42).

Judith McKinlay suggests that one intriguing interpretation of this passage is to view it as an encounter between Wisdom and a pupil reminiscent of Proverbs 1:20-33. There Wisdom places herself where she will encounter people in their daily round. Here Jesus rests by a well. Wisdom herself is described as a fountain of life in Proverbs 16:22. Here Jesus is the living water.

At first Jesus is the supplicant, asking for water (4:7), and the woman is the teacher, instructing him on the inappropriateness of his request (4:9). The roles reverse and Jesus becomes the teacher, and the woman the pupil. In Proverbs, Woman Wisdom offers wisdom to recalcitrant young men. Here Jesus acts as Wisdom, offering the water of life whose ultimate giver is God to a female student. In response to the woman's question, "Where do you get that living water?" (4:11), Jesus, in effect, answers, "I am he. I am Wisdom." To receive the living water is to discover the identity of Jesus. This is the living worship that is not bound by place (4:22-24f). The gift quality of the water is a major theme of the passage. The water brings life (see Proverbs 8:35; 9:6; Sirach 24:21).[51]

The woman continues to interpret the water literally, still not clued in to what it represents and who offers it. Still, she goes back to her townspeople and shares her astonishment at the knowledge Jesus had of her inward and outward life. Her faith was piqued by the strange phenomenon of having been fully known, but still offered a gift (4:29).

Self-help wisdom is preoccupied with helping us make a good impression on others by eliminating our weaknesses and sources of embarrassment. By our concerted efforts we earn our place in life. Jesus, in his Wisdom, knows all about us and still invites us onto the path of Wisdom, still offers us the gift of living water "gushing up to eternal life" (4:14). The Wisdom that he offers is a gift—it is a relationship with him that is from God and leads to God. We see in the scene between the Samaritan woman and her townspeople that even imperfect, not fully-formed faith, when shared, can lead others to Wisdom.

THE MAN BORN BLIND

The story of the man born blind is bracketed by verses that point to the full significance of the miracle. Jesus opened the man's eyes to show that he is the light of the world (9:5) and came into the world that "those who do not see may see" (9:39*a*). The coming of the light could mean that "those who see may become blind" (9:39*b*). Those who stare into the light without responding can become blind to Jesus and the God who sent him.[52]

The story operates on three levels. On one level it relates what happened to one man during Jesus' ministry in the early part of the first century. On another level it is the story of Jesus' followers and their conflicts with the Jewish authorities toward the end of the first century. On yet another level it is the story of the world encountering God in the person of Jesus, some coming into the light of faith and others becoming blind in their unbelief, which is at the heart of sin.[53]

His disciples ask the question that makes the same assumption as Job's friends: "Who sinned, the man or his parents?" A believer in karma would ask, "What former life experiences is this person working through by spending this lifetime blind?"

The notion that disability is caused by the sins of the parents has its roots in Exodus 20:5 and 34:7 which are quoted and reiterated in Numbers 14:18 and Deuteronomy 5:9. Some Jews believed in the preexistence of the souls and in the ability of these souls to sin in the womb.[54] Despite the book of Job, the theory that there was a direct, causal relationship between sin and sickness was still operative in Jesus' time. If an adult got sick, the blame could lie in his own behavior. A baby born with an illness was more difficult, but there was always Exodus 20:5 to fall back on. "I, the Lord your God am a jealous God, punishing children for the iniquity of parents, to the third and fourth generation…"[55]

Jesus generally refutes the notion that adversity, physical limitations, and illness are the result of sin.[56] They are, rather, avenues through which God's works can be revealed (John 9:3). Verse 3 clearly states that this man was born blind so that God's works might be revealed in him. This requires careful reflection when preaching to people with chronic health conditions. The rabbis spoke of God giving people "punishments of love," chastisements which, if a person suffered them generously, would bring him long life and rewards. This may be Jesus' thought here. Or he may be referring to God's manipulation of history to glorify his name. For example, in Exodus 9:16 (cited in Romans 9:17) God tells Pharaoh, "this is why I have let you live: to show you my power, and to make my name resound through all the earth."[57]

There are several traditional theories of suffering that may well be part of the mindset of our people.

Afflictions are God's will. Attributing misfortunes and disabilities to God's will is rooted in a belief that things are the way they are because God wills it. God is in control of this universe at every step of the way. In our affirmation of God's omnipotence, we neglect to factor in God's love and compassion. Attribution of physical adversity to God ends up portraying a God who is distant, erratic, and manipulative. What about God as loving, nurturing, and comforting?[58]

Suffering/Trials are a punishment for your sins. The need to trace every negative event that occurs in the human sphere either to God's doing or to human sin pervades the Hebrew Scriptures. It is at work in Proverbs and in Deuteronomy in the assumption that wise living leads to health, wealth, and longevity and that foolish living leads to death. The prophets repeatedly trace Israel's misfortunes to her sin. The New Testament attributes Jesus' crucifixion to the foreordained plan of God. I would allow my preaching of this text to be informed by the wisdom of Job. For he reminds us that human suffering is a mystery beyond human understanding, and that it is not the result of sin.

Kathy Black offers an invaluable caution with respect to a wide range of disabilities: we need to avoid the traditional equation of physical blindness, deafness, and paralysis with spiritual sin. She tells of a friend who has been blind from birth who, when the congregation sings "Amazing Grace," stands proudly and sings, "I once was blind, and I still can't see!"[59]

Suffering/Trials are a test of your faith. God wants you to be healed, but you just can't muster the faith. This text's assertion that disability is not caused by sin goes against the implied theology of some of the other healing narratives. Here, in contrast to many of the healing narratives in the synoptics, faith is not needed before healing can place.[60] We may preach to people who believe at some level that their illness or disability is their own fault but who do not yet believe in Jesus. This is a tall order!

Suffering/Trials are for the purpose of strengthening your character. God doesn't want you to be healed yet, because your character still needs work. This calls to mind Mother Teresa's whimsical statement: "I know God never gives us more than we can handle. I just wish God didn't have such a high opinion of me!" Scripture, particularly the books of Proverbs and Hebrews, speaks of the Lord disciplining those he loves. "My child, do not despise the Lord's discipline or be weary of his reproof, for the Lord reproves the one the loves, as a father the son in whom he delights" (Proverbs 3:11, 12). "For the Lord disciplines those whom he loves; and chastises every child whom he accepts. . . . Endure trials for the sake of discipline. . . . he disciplines us for our good, in order that we may share his holiness. . . . Now, discipline always seems painful rather than pleasant at the time, but later it yields the peaceful fruit of righteousness to those who have been trained by it" (Hebrews 12:6-11). The focus in these passages seems to be discomfort resulting from foolish behavior rather than debilitating physical conditions. The message is that God sees to it that we face the painful consequences of our actions so that we may grow in wisdom.

Suffering/Trials are your cross. Jesus suffered on the cross for our sins. We must suffer to be redeemed. This neglects to mention that suffering in and of itself is not redemptive. God's love was able to transform the crucifixion into a resurrection, but that is not the same as saying that God caused the crucifixion in order for there to be a resurrection.

Kathy Black, in her book *A Healing Homiletic: Preaching and Disability*, says, "devastations, sufferings, frustrations, and disabilities happen in this world. God does not cause them, but God is present in their midst to uphold us and transform us. Resurrection can happen in our lives without God causing the suffering and death *in order for* the resurrection to occur. God's grace is all-powerful and can turn pain into healing."[61]

One of the ways God works is through us. We experience God's presence through the nurture of others in difficult times. Paul reminds us that, "If one member suffers, all suffer together with it" (1 Corinthians 12:26). We need to preach against the American cultural deification of independence a theology of interdependence. Our Christian tradition is based on community and on our interdependence on God and one another.[62]

God sent you adversity so that, when you are healed, God's power can be manifested.[63] We are all born for the purpose of showing forth the glory of God. We each have limitations and obstacles that impede that task. Physical blindness is not the point here. It is in no way being equated with spiritual error. There should be an intentional effort on the preacher's part to make that clear. We cannot remove those obstacles without the grace of Christ.

Says Kathy Black, "Many in the disability community interpret this verse to mean that the man was born (like all of us) to show God's love to the world."[64]

The man blind from birth is minding his own business as a beggar. Jesus does not ask him if he wants to be healed. He spits on the ground, makes mud and spreads it on the man's eyes, telling him to go wash in the pool of Siloam (9:6, 7). The word Siloam means "sent," John tells us, in an attempt to connect this event with Jesus' identity as the one who is sent. He does so without any questioning of Jesus.

His neighbors refuse to believe he is the same person who used to be blind. He keeps saying, "I am the man" (9:9). That is a powerful word of testimony for contemporary preachers.

There is a school of preaching influenced by Karl Barth that believes recounting personal experience is inappropriate in the pulpit. After years of teaching preaching, preaching, and sitting in the pews, I could not disagree more! Our people have plenty of places to go to get advice on how to improve themselves. They come to church to be invited to experience the power of God in Christ. That was the ex-blind man's testimony when he cried out repeatedly, "I am the man!"

Our people need to hear from us that we are the ones who have been healed, corrected, directed, and blessed by Christ. They need to hear how, where, and when. This is a message that can be preached without using blindness as a metaphor or symbol of sin.[65] People need to hear where we have been in our walk of life and where, guided by the Wisdom of God, we are going and leading them. They do not need to be told what to do as much as they need to be invited into the presence of Wisdom in person, their guide to life. He is the source of power, motivation, and moral direction for a life of living by the great commandment. If we would preach in the spirit of Johannine wisdom, we would be less concerned with making three points than we would with making introductions between our congregation and Wisdom in person.

The formerly blind man tells his story in a terse and straightforward way. "Just the facts." Its brevity and matter-of-factness carries great authority. Can we recount the story of where we have been and where we are with like conviction? Our people need to hear sermons that are not ashamed to admit "I am the man!" and "I am the woman!" in a way that connects our story with their stories, and both stories with God's story in Christ.

If I were this man, I would be so ecstatic at my new gift of sight, shape, color, and brightness in the world around me that I would be walking around with upturned face and a big smile. I would be irritated beyond measure by the pestering questions of the Pharisees.

They were incensed that Jesus healed on the Sabbath and convinced that this proved he was a sinner. They question the ex-blind man twice, asking him, "How can a man who is a sinner perform such signs?" (9:16) and objecting that, "We do not know where he comes from" (9:29). They even haul his parents in to verify that he really had been blind!

The blind man continues to stubbornly point them to the facts: "Though I was blind, now I see" (9:25). "He opened my eyes" (9:30). Because the power that healed the man is beyond their control, does not fit their categories of how God reveals Godself, the religious authorities not only reject Jesus, but deride the man he has healed (9:34). They reiterate the fallacy Jesus refuted in verse 1, that he had been born blind because of sin, his parents and/or his own, "You were born entirely in sins, and are you trying to teach us?"

Contemporary society tends to discredit people with disabilities, assuming they are objects of pity, not vital persons with something to teach the rest of community. We can easily repeat their error today, for we, too, know the kind of people God chooses to work through—educated, self-supporting people like ourselves, not blind beggars. In place of Nicodemus' question, "How can this be?" the Jewish authorities of that day insist, "This cannot be!"

Opposition seems to only strengthen the ex-blind man's faith and resolve. When his neighbors first question him, he refers to Jesus as "the man called Jesus" (9:11). By the time he is interrogated for the first time by the Pharisees, he says of Jesus, "He is a prophet."

As the authorities incessantly pressed their questions, the man became impatient and asked, "Why do you want to hear it again? Do you also want to become his disciples?" (9:27). His question implies that he now considers himself one of Jesus' disciples.[66] He makes a trenchant observation.

"Here is an astonishing thing! You do not know where he comes from, and yet he opened my eyes…if this man were not from God he could do nothing" (9:30, 33).

After they drive him out of the synagogue, Jesus finds him and asks him directly "Do you believe in the Son of Man?" He answered, "And who is he, sir? Tell me, so that I may believe in him."

Jesus said to him, "You have seen him, and the one speaking with you is he" (9:37).

He said, "'Lord, I believe,' and he worshiped him" (9:38).

The unspoken question that brings people to church is "Who is Jesus?" Preaching the wisdom of the Gospel of John equips us to introduce them to who he is and who he waits to be in our lives together and alone. Wisdom in person takes the initiative from beginning to end, but in this man Wisdom finds a ready pupil.

The former blind beggar comes to faith in Jesus by stages. First, Jesus finds him. Second, he accepts Jesus' instructions for healing without question. Finally, he experiences the healing power of Jesus in his life.

Afterward, he fends off Jesus' detractors with a no-nonsense panache. This encounter with the opposition sharpens his faith.

Finally he meets Jesus halfway in a close encounter that challenges him to answer the question, "Do you believe?"

Jesus seeks him out yet again in the Temple. He asks Jesus the question our people are asking us as preachers: "Who is Jesus? Tell me so that I may believe in him" (9:36).

The Power of Testimony

The disciples in John's Gospel came to faith by hearing about Jesus from someone they knew. This pattern is repeated throughout the Gospel. Those who come to genuine faith do so on the basis of hearing the testimony about Jesus or from Jesus. Examples are numerous. The Samaritan townspeople heard about Jesus from the woman at the well (4:39, 41). The royal official had heard about Jesus and so came to him, and his faith was confirmed by the healing of his son, but not based upon it (4:47, 50, 53). Before he was healed, the blind beggar responded in trusting obedience to Jesus' command to go and wash. He came by stages from initial trust to tenacious faith . Before Jesus called Lazarus out, Martha responded to Jesus' words with a confession of faith (11:27, 40).

By contrast, those whose response to Jesus was dependent on the miraculous did not grow and persevere in faith. Examples are Nicodemus, the invalid at Bethzada, and the crowds that followed

Jesus because he filled their stomachs, not because they sought his Wisdom.[67]

Faith comes by hearing. And the wisdom by which the Christian lives must be taken on faith, because it looks like folly to the naked eye. It needs to be taken on faith that, while everything will not go my way, in everything God works together for good with those who trust in God.

There is a lot of hollow advice and half-truth out there that passes for wisdom. It is like chaff which the winds of adversity blow away (Psalm 1:4). "Do it yourself! Be your own best friend! Jesus will bring you prosperity! Create your own reality! The universe yearns to bring you self-fulfillment." Then there is the Christian message, with its roots deep in the nourishing soil of biblical wisdom, absorbing the living water that flows beneath the surface of our lives. Living by it we become like trees planted by streams of water, which yield our fruit in its season (Psalm 1:3). Our role as Christian preachers is to call people, who are casting about for self-help wisdom anywhere they can find it, to the biblical wisdom in which they live and move and have their being.

African-American educator Booker T. Washington was fond of telling a story about how a vessel in the south Atlantic Ocean signaled for help from another vessel not far off: "Help! Save us, or we perish for lack of water!" The captain of the other vessel's reply was, "Cast down your buckets where you are." Supposing that the second captain had not gotten the message accurately, the troubled ship signalled yet again. "Help! Save us, or we perish for lack of water!" Again the nearby ship signalled back, "Cast down your buckets where you are!" This exchange went on until the first ship, in desperation, decided it had nothing to lose by following this outlandish advice. When crew members cast down their buckets, they drew them up filled with clear, cool, sparkling water from the mouth of the Amazon. They had not realized that the powerful current of the Amazon River carried fresh water from the South American rain forests many miles out into the South Atlantic.[68]

There is self-help wisdom and there is Wisdom that is available for those times when we just can't help ourselves. There is wisdom that teaches us how to be our own best friend, and there is Wisdom that points us to an infinitely more reliable, relentlessly faithful friend waiting in the wings. There is wisdom that spurs us to exceed our limitations, and there is Wisdom that whispers when we encounter God precisely in those moments that we have reached the end of our rope. There is wisdom that promises good fortune in exchange for good deeds. And there is Wisdom that proclaims that God is a powerful force whose comfort must be reckoned with, even in the throes of unendurable pain. There is wisdom that can only survive by ignoring situations that contradict its glib guarantees. And there is Wisdom unafraid to see life for what it is, embracing each passing moment, with its precarious joys, as a gift from God. There is wisdom that promises to minimize our risks and give us material payoffs, and there is Wisdom that prods us to exit our comfort zone to walk out into the sunshine, following One whose way leads to life. There is wisdom that promises future gains for present pains. And there is Wisdom that dwells among us, full of grace and truth, nourishing, consoling, correcting, and guiding us toward a life that lasts forever.

Now, as in John's day, people still come to faith by hearing about Jesus from the witness of a believer. Now, as in John's day, God still uses frail, flawed human preachers to communicate the gospel with power and grace. Now more than ever, people need Wisdom for the living of these days. And how will they hear without a preacher?

But how are they to call on one in whom they have not believed? And how are they to believe in one of whom they have never heard? And how are they to hear without someone to proclaim him? (Romans 10:14).

Notes

Introduction

1. I begin with a time-honored wisdom form, the reflection, in which an author narrates autobiographical vignettes and makes wisdom inferences. This is one of the wisdom genres we find in Qohelet and the book of Proverbs. Contemporary manifestations are editorials, memoirs, and topical self-help manuals.

Chapter One

1. Two apocryphal books known as the *Wisdom of Sirach* (or *Ecclesiasticus*) and the *Wisdom of Solomon* also belong to this same genre. Wisdom influences have also been discerned in The Song of Solomon, Deuteronomy, the Joseph story, the Succession Narrative (2 Samuel 9-20; 1 Kings 1-2) and several psalms (1, 32, 34, 37, 49, 112, 128). Roland E. Murphy, *The Tree of Life: An Exploration of Biblical Wisdom Literature The Anchor Bible Reference Library* (New York: Doubleday, 1990), Chapter 7 "Wisdom's Echoes," 97-110.

2. Kathleen A. Farmer, "The Wisdom Books," Chapter 5 in *The Hebrew Bible Today: An Introduction to Critical Issues*, eds. Steven L. McKenzie and M. Patrick Graham (Louisville, Kentucky: Westminster John Knox Press, 1998) 130-131.

3. Dianne Bergant, *Israel's Wisdom Literature: A Liberation-Critical Reading* (Philadelphia: Fortress Press 1997), 81-82.

4. The Hebrew word for wisdom is *hokmah*, which has implications surrounding the notion of order. The Greek word for wisdom is *sophia*.

5. For an elaboration of these concepts, see my *Preaching Proverbs: Wisdom for the Pulpit* (Louisville, Kentucky: Westminster John Knox Press, 1996), 31.

6. Karlyn Kohrs Campbell and Kathleen Hall Jamieson, *Form and Genre: Shaping Rhetorical Action* (Falls Church, Virginia: Speech and Communication Association, Fall, 1993), 20.

7. Alan Dundes, "Text, Texture, and Context," *Essays in Folkloristics* (New Delhi: Folklore Institute, 1978), 22-37.

8. The word proverb comes from the Hebrew word *mashal*. A *mashal* is a term used in the Hebrew Scriptures to refer to a number of literary forms: similitudes, popular sayings, aphorisms, riddles, allegories, and taunt songs. *Old Testament Form Criticism*, ed. John H. Hayes (San Antonio: Trinity University Press, 1974), 230.

9. Murphy, *The Tree of Life*, 8.

10. Hayes, 231.

11. Roland Murphy, *Wisdom Literature: Job, Proverbs, Ruth, Canticles, Ecclesiastes, and Esther, Volume XIII The Forms of the Old Testament Literature* (Grand Rapids, Michigan: William B. Eerdmans Publishing Company, 1981), 4-6.

12. They include Pascal, Lichtenberg, Kafka, Oscar Wilde, Friedrich Nietzsche, Jean Paul Sartre, Karl Kraus, Paul Valery, Stanislaw Lec, Abraham Heschel, and Norman O. Brown. James G. Williams, *Those Who Ponder Proverbs: Aphoristic Thinking and Biblical Literature* (Sheffield, England: The Almond Press, 1981), 13-14.

13. Peter McWilliams, *The Portable Life 101*, (Los Angeles: Prelude Press, 1995), 72.

14. *The Best of Women's Quotations*, edited by Helen Exley (Waterford, UK: Exley Publications, Ltd.), p. 49.

Women as well as men have coined aphorisms in this century. Artists, actresses, authors, and comediennes have been the source of biting wisdom for contemporary living. Many aphorisms by women from the first two-thirds of this century debunk traditional standards for women's worth: beauty, the approval of men, and motherhood. "Don't compromise yourself, you're all you've got." Janis Joplin (1943-1970). "The only thing that seems eternal and natural in motherhood is ambivalence." Jane Lazarre, American Writer (b. 1943). "Creative Minds have always been known to survive any kind of bad training." Anna Freud, Austrian psychoanalyst (1895-1982). "Plain women know more about men than beautiful ones do." Katherine Hepburn, American actress (b. 1909). *Quotable Women* (London: Running Press, 1994), no page numbers.

15. These wisdom poems appear in Proverbs 1-9, in the speeches of Job, and also throughout The Wisdom of Jesus Ben Sirach and The Wisdom of Solomon. Murphy, *The Tree of Life*, 10.

16. Murphy, *Wisdom Literature*, 10.

The third chapter of James on "the taming of the tongue," is an example of the reflection genre in the New Testament.

17. Roland R. Murphy, *The Tree of Life*, 10.

18. Ibid.

19. Allegories are another wisdom genre (see Proverbs 5:15-23 and Ecclesiastes 12:1-6). Hymns in praise of Wisdom are still another genre. (Proverbs 1:20-33; 822-36; Job 28; Sirach 24:1-22; The Wisdom of Solomon 6:12-20; 7:22-8:21.) *Ibid.* 246-8. Other wisdom genres include the riddle (Proverbs 30:4), the fable, the wisdom psalm (1, 32, 34, 37, 49, 112, 128), and, in the teachings of Jesus, the parable. Hayes, *Old Testament Form Criticism*, 246-8, 256.

20. Tim Wyatt, "Daze of our lives," *The Dallas Morning News*, Entertainment Section, July 27, 2000.

21. The Hebrew word for wisdom is *hokmah*, which has implications surrounding the notion of order. The Greek word for wisdom is *sophia*.

22. Randy L. Maddox, *Responsible Grace: John Wesley's Practical Theology* (Nashville, Tennessee, Kingswood Books, 1994), 147.

23. Marianne Meyer Thompson, "Thinking About God: Wisdom and Theology in John 6," *Critical Readings of John 6*, edited by R. Alan Culpepper (New York: Brill, 1997), 231.

24. Kathleen O'Connor, *The Wisdom Literature* (Wilmington, Delaware: Michael Glazier, 1988), 34.

25. These are sometimes known as "conservative" and "skeptical" forms of wisdom. They have parallels in other Ancient Near Eastern cultures. *The Instruction of Amenemope* is an Egyptian collection of advice from a royal official to his youngest son that is similar to Proverbs 22:17-24:22. Skeptical parallels include the Babylonian text known as the "Counsels of a Pessimist," reminiscent of Ecclesiastes, and the "Babylonian Theodicy," a debate between a sufferer and a traditionalist similar to Job. Kathleen A. Farmer, "The Wisdom Books," Chapter 5 in *The Hebrew Bible Today: An Introduction to Critical Issues*, eds. Steven L. McKenzie and M. Patrick Graham (Louisville, Kentucky: Westminster John Knox Press, 1998), 134-35.

26. Farmer, 132.

27. Marcus J. Borg, *Meeting Jesus Again for the First Time: The Historical Jesus and the Heart of Contemporary Faith* (New York: HarperCollins Publishers, 1994), 70.

28. David Bland, "The Formation of Character in the Book of Proverbs," *Restoration Quarterly* vol. 40 No. 10 (1998), 221.

29. William P. Brown, *Character in Crisis: A Fresh Approach to the Wisdom Literature of the Old Testament* (Grand Rapids, Michigan: William B. Eerdmans Publishing Company, 1996), 1.

30. Gerhard von Rad's *Old Testament Theology* (1960) gave his readers an inkling of a stronger focus on wisdom, one that eventually appeared in *Wisdom in Israel* (1970). In the late 1970s and early 1980s Samuel Terrien called for an understanding of biblical theology that honored the distinctive voice of wisdom. He insisted that observations based on experience can witness the divine presence in human life just as surely as can visionary experiences. "The Play of Wisdom: Turning Point in Biblical Theology," *Horizons in Biblical Theology* (1981): 125-153. *The Elusive Presence: Toward a New Biblical Theology* (New York: Harper and Row), 1978. Israel's wisdom has become an inviting area of research for biblical scholars.

31. Dianne Bergant, *Israel's Wisdom Literature: A Liberation-Critical Reading* (Philadelphia: Fortress Press, 1997), 4.

32. Ernest Gellner, *Postmodernism, Reason, and Religion* (London: Routledge, 1991), 22.

33. I deal with this interpretation at greater length in my article "Different Strokes for Different Folks: America's Quintessential Postmodern Proverb," *Theology Today*, July 1996.

34. In its radical, deconstructionist forms, of which literary critic Stanley Fish is a representative, postmodern hermeneutics asserts that the only meaning texts have are those interpretive communities ascribe to them. Edgar V. McKnight's *The Post-Modern Use of the Bible*, (Nashville: Abingdon, 1988) offers an overview and guide to postmodern reader-response strategies of biblical interpretation. Elizabeth Schussler Fiorenza in her work on feminist biblical interpretation affirms the importance of context in traditional male-oriented biblical criticism and in newer methods of feminist criticism. Building on her *Bread Not Stone: The Challenge of Feminist Biblical Interpretation* (Boston: Beacon Press, 1984), her more

recent *But She Said: Feminist Practices of Biblical Interpretation* (Boston: Beacon Press, 1992) examines the social locations and political contexts of biblical interpretation in the United States, showing how a feminist practice of biblical interpretation can empower women of all colors and classes to rethink the Bible's meanings.

35. See Craig Kennet Miller, *PostModerns: The Beliefs, Hopes and Fears of Young Americans (1965-1981)* (Nashville: Discipleship Resources, 1996), 8-9.

36. Nora Tubbs Tisdale's groundbreaking book *Preaching as Local Theology and Folk Art* (Minneapolis: Fortress Press, 1997) is an extremely helpful treatment of congregational exegesis for preaching. John McClure's *The Four Codes of Preaching* (Minneapolis: Fortress Press, 1991) examines culture as one of the "codes" of the sermon that influences both how the preacher hears and how she preaches.

37. The field of genre-sensitive preaching over the past two decades has flourished, yielding a rich harvest for preachers. Representative authors include Thomas G. Long, Mike Graves, Eugene L. Lowry, John C. Holbert, and Alyce M. McKenzie.

38. Authority through authenticity and a more egalitarian understanding of the relationship between preacher and hearer is a theme of much contemporary homiletical literature. Examples include the following: Lucy Atkinson Rose, *Sharing the Word: Preaching in the Round Table Church* (Louisville, Kentucky: Westminster John Knox Press, 1997), Christine Smith, *Weaving the Sermon: Preaching in a Feminist Perspective* (Louisville, Kentucky: Westminster John Knox Press, 1989), John S. McClure, *The Roundtable Pulpit: Where Leadership and Preaching Meet* (Nashville: Abingdon Press, 1995).

39. See Lee MeGee with Tom Troeger, *Wrestling with the Patriarchs: Retrieving Women's Voices in Preaching* (Nashville: Abingdon, 1996), and Mary Donovan Turner and Mary Lin Hudson, *Saved from Silence: Finding Womens' Voice in Preaching* (St. Louis, Missouri: Chalice Press, 1999).

40. They include Thomas G. Long, Fred Craddock, Nora Tubbs Tisdale, Charles Rice, Christine Smith, John McClure, Lucy Rose, David Buttrick, and Richard Lischer.

41. Richard Lischer, "Preaching as the Church's Language," *Listening to the Word: Studies in Honor of Fred B. Craddock*, eds. Gail R. O'Day and Thomas G. Long (Nashville: Abingdon Press, 1993), 120.

42. Charles F. Melchert, *Wise Teaching: Biblical Wisdom and Educational Ministry* (Harrisburg, Pennsylvania: Trinity Press International, 1998) is a thorough and insightful treatment of educational ministry through the lens of biblical wisdom.

43. For treatments of the relationship of preaching and teaching, see the following: Maria Harris, *Fashion Me A People: Curriculum in the Church* (Louisville, Kentucky: Westminster John Knox Press, 1989), chapters 5 and 6; Clark M. Williamson and Ronald J. Allen, *The Teaching Minister* (Louisville, Kentucky: Westminster John Knox Press, 1991), chapters 3 and 5; and Ronald J. Allen, *The Teaching Sermon* (Nashville, Tennessee: Abingdon Press, 1995).

44. Richard Robert Osmer, *A Teachable Spirit: Rediscovering the Teaching Office in the Church* (Louisville, Kentucky: Westminster John Knox Press, 1990), 14-15.

Chapter Two

1. Gallup Poll Website, Religion from A-Z.

2. Wade Clark Roof, *A Generation of Seekers: The Spiritual Journeys of the Baby Boom Generation* (HarperSanFrancisco, 1993), 5.

3. Lauren Winter, "Gen X revisited," *The Christian Century*, November 8, 2000.

4. Robert N. Bellah, Richard Madsen, William M. Sullivan, Ann Swidler and Steven M. Tipton, "Individualism and the Crisis of Civic Membership," *The Christian Century*, May 8, 1996. This article is an excerpt from the Introduction to a ten-year anniversary edition of *Habits of the Heart* (Los Angeles and Berkeley: University of California Press, 1996).

5. *Journal of Democracy*, January 1995.

6. Robert Wuthnow, *After Heaven: Spirituality in America Since the 1950s* (Berkeley and Los Angeles: University of California Press, 1998), 2.

7. Robert Wuthnow, quoted in *US News and World Report*, "Spiritual American" April 4,1994, p. 50.

8. "The Ways of Wisdom," *The Philadelphia Inquirer*, Murray Dubin, Sunday, March 23, 1997.

9. *The Virtues: Contemporary Essays on Moral Character.* Robert B. Kruschwitz and Robert C. Roberts, editors (Belmont, California: Wadsworth Publishing Company, 1987), 10-11.

10. Dale Carnegie, quoted on p. 41 of *The Portable LIFE 101: 179 Essential Lessons from LIFE 101* by Peter McWilliams (Los Angeles, CA: Prelude Press, 1995).

11. This is the understanding of their relationship most interpreters took from Freidrich Schleiermacher's *Brief Outline of Theological Study* (1811), one that became normative for American Theological Education in the twentieth century. Edward Farley, *Theologia: The Fragmentation and Unity of Theological Education* (Philadelphia: Fortress Press, 1983), 84.

12. Charles M. Wood, *Vision and Discernment: An Orientation in Theological Study* (Atlanta: Scholars Press, 1985), 51ff.

13. Don S. Browning, *A Fundamental Practical Theology: Descriptive and Strategic Proposals* (Minneapolis: Fortress Press, 1991), 47-54

14. Ibid, 47.

15. "The analysis of the human situation employs materials made available by man's creative self-interpretation in all realms of culture. Philosophy contributes, but so do poetry, drama, the novel, therapeutic psychology, and sociology." Paul Tillich, *Systematic Theology:Volume One* (Chicago: The University of Chicago Press, 1951), 63.

16. This process follows the flow of practical theology, which includes four sub-movements. They are descriptive theology, historic theology, systematic theology, and strategic practical theology. Don S. Browning, *A Fundamental Practical Theology*, 8.

17. Feminist theologian Rebecca Chopp voices a criticism of this method, charging that it tends to become a comparison-contrast of abstractions distant from concrete situations and that the conversation tends to be dominated by a bourgeois, individualistic, privatized view of religion. My use of Browning's

method, it is hoped, avoids these pitfalls by its concrete focus on specific biblical traditions and specific contemporary construals of wisdom. My intention in employing the method is to allow the worldviews of concrete textual traditions and contemporary wisdoms in congregations to emerge, rather than to impose a rational grid upon them. Rebecca Chopp, "Practical Theology and Liberation,". *Formation and Reflection: The Promise of Practical Theology,* eds. Lewis S. Mudge and James N. Poling (Philadelphia: Fortress Press, 1987), 120-138.

18. Kruschwitz and Roberts, 11.

19. John Kekes, *Moral Wisdom and Good Lives* (Ithaca and London: Cornell University Press, 1995), 17. Aristotle's discussions of philosophical and practical wisdom are found in his *Metaphysics* 993b26-28 and *Nicomachean Ethics* 1140a26-29 respectively.

20. Ibid.

21. Stephen R. Covey, *First Things First* (New York: Simon and Schuster: 1994), 12-13.

22. Browning, 11.

23. Marjorie J. Thompson, *Soul Feast: An Invitation to the Christian Spiritual Life* (Louisville, Kentucky: Westminster John Knox Press, 1995), 138-139.

24. Alexander Greimas' narrative theory offers a story-shaped version of Browning's "Five Alive" questions. For elaborations of Greimas' scheme see A.J. Greimas, *Semantique structurale* (Paris: Larousse, 1966). For a helpful discussion of Greimas' contribution, see Robert Scholes, *Structuralism in Literature: An Introduction* (New Haven: Yale University Press, 1978), 105-6. See also John S. McClure's homiletical application of Greimas' narrative theory in *The Four Codes of Preaching Rhetorical Strategies* (Minneapolis: Fortress Press, 1991), 95-101.

25. Stephen Crites, "The Narrative Quality of Experience," *Journal of the American Academy of Religion*, XXXIX, 3 (September 1971), 291-311.

Chapter Three

1. Stephen R. Covey, *The 7 Habits of Highly Effective People: Restoring the Character Ethic* (New York: Simon and Schuster, 1989), 18-19.

2. William P. Brown, *Character in Crisis: A Fresh Approach to the Wisdom Literature of the Old Testament* (Grand Rapids, Michigan: William B. Eerdmans Publishing Co, 1996), 9.

3. *The Virtues: Contemporary Essays on Moral Character, eds.* Robert B. Kruschwitz and Robert C. Roberts (Belmont, California: Wadsworth Publishing Company, 1987), 2. A prominent name in recent moral philosophy is Alasdair MacIntyre, who employs the insights of Aristotle to ground our definitions of the good person and the good life. His book *After Virtue* was the most widely read American book of moral philosophy of the 1980s. He and other philosophers have become less concerned with theoretical questions about the foundation of moral rules and language and more focused on the nature and traits of the moral person. Other contributors to this field of reflection are James Q. Wilson, Martha Nussbaum, Charles Taylor and Bernard Williams.

For a perceptive discussion and evaluation of Aristotle's ethics in light of current work in feminist ethics, see Marcia Homiak, "Feminism and Aristotle's

Rational Ideal," in *A Mind of One's Own: Feminist Essays on Reason and Objectivity* (Boulder, Colorado: Westview Press, 1993), 1-18.

Joel Kupperman's *Character* (New York: Oxford University Press, 1991) presents a character-based ethical theory that places the discussion of particular virtues and vices within the context of the individual's character.

4. Robert Wuthnow points out that the need to restrict our economic appetites is as important as the need to curb permissive sexuality. He cites the "ill effects of material promiscuity" that are all around us: in the greed that plagues brokerage houses and that costs taxpayers billions in bailing out gutted savings and loan companies, in the career stress that results in alcoholism and broken families, in the incessant consumerism that has itself become the consumer of our nation's youth, and in the daily stress and strain that stems from overwork. *Poor Richard's Principle: Recovering the American Dream Through the Moral Dimension of Work, Business and Money* (Princeton, New Jersey: Princeton University Press, 1996), 12.

5. *Nicomachean Ethics* 6.3-7. Aristotle distinguishes the four moral virtues from the intellectual virtues by the manner in which they are appropriated: we acquire intellectual virtues through pedagogical instruction, whereas we acquire virtues of character primarily from habitual exercise. According to Aristotle, neither class of virtue is implanted by nature. We become just by the practice of just actions, self-controlled by exercising self-control, and courageous by performing acts of courage. *Nicomachean Ethics* 2.1. See discussion in William P. Brown's *Character in Crisis*, 11.

6. While Proverbs admonishes readers to avoid the easy path and persist in the way of wisdom, it does not talk much about courage. Courage is implied, for it is often necessary in acting wisely. It is not the lone individual "standing tall." In Proverbs, courage is relational. It begins, as we hear repeatedly in the opening chapters of Proverbs, with the trust of a child in parents and teachers and reaches out to trust in Woman Wisdom and Yahweh (3:5). Charles F. Melchert, *Wise Teaching: Biblical Wisdom and Educational Ministry* (Harrisburg, Pennsylvania: Trinity Press International, 1998), 67.

7. Kruschwitz and Roberts, 15.

8. Stanley Hauerwas and Charles Pinches, *Christians Among the Virtues: Theological Conversations with Ancient and Modern Ethics* (Notre Dame, Indiana: University of Notre Dame Press, 1997), 34,78.

9. Brown, 10.

10. "Virtuecrats," *Newsweek*, June 13, 1994, p. 30. For an insightful analysis of historical views of virtue, see Richard White's, "Historical Perspectives on the Morality of Virtue," *The Journal of Value Inquiry*, Vol. 25 (1991), 217-31.

11. Stephen Covey uses this term to refer to the proliferation of time management books and tools over the past several decades. *First Things First* (New York: Simon and Schuster, 1994), 21.

12. Christina Hoff Sommer, "What College Students Don't Know," *The Power of Character*, edited by Wes Hanson and Michael Josephson (Jossey-Bass, 1998)

13. See *www.josephsoninstitute.org* or *www.charactercounts.org* The nationwide survey of 8,600 high school students revealed alarming rates of cheating, lying, stealing, drunkenness, and a propensity toward violence. The grim highlights

include that, in the past 12 months, 71% of high students surveyed admit they cheated on an exam; over a third had shoplifted; 68% said they had hit someone because they were angry; and almost half said that if they wanted to, they could get a gun.

14. Wade Clark Roof, *A Generation of Seekers: The Spiritual Journeys of the Baby Boom Generation* (HarperSanFrancisco: 1993), 6.

15. *The Book of Virtues: A Treasury of Great Moral Stories*, edited, with commentary by William J. Bennett (New York: Simon and Schuster, 1993), Introduction. A PBS cartoon series based on this book has been produced and aired to teach character to young children. Bennett's *Moral Compass: Stories for a Life Journey* (New York: Simon and Schuster, 1995) is a second helping of stories, this time from a wider cultural spectrum. In addition to stories from Western literature, history, and mythology, Bennett adds entries from Asia, Africa, and Latin America.

16. Bernard T. Adeney, *Strange Virtues: Ethics in a Multicultural World* (Downers Grove, Illinois: InterVarsity Press, 1995), 173-4.

17. Hauerwas and Pinches, 63.

18. Ibid, 69.

19. A best-selling self-help manual of the 1990s was Stephen R. Covey's *The Seven Habits of Highly Effective People.* Covey's implied ultimate for offering his seven prescriptions is this: they will lead to the contentment that comes from fulfilling one's potential and helping others to fulfill theirs amid the competing demands of life.

Be Proactive (personal vision)

Begin with the End in Mind (personal leadership)

Put First Things First (personal management)

Think Win/Win (interpersonal leadership)

Seek First to Understand, Then to Be Understood (empathic communication)

Synergize (creative cooperation)

Sharpen the Saw (balanced self-renewal)

Covey's son Sean has recently written a book entitled *The Seven Habits of Highly Effective Teens: The Ultimate Teenage Success Guide* (Simon and Schuster, 1998).

20. Collections of such vignettes are the stock in trade of the *Chicken Soup for the Soul* series that now has volumes specializing in the souls of pet owners, college students, preteens, teens, and mothers.

21. Nathan McCall, *Makes Me Wanna Holler: A Young Black Man in America* (New York: Random House, Inc., 1994), 205.

22. Norris is the author of *Dakota: A Spiritual Geography* (New York: Houghton Mifflin Company, 1993), *Cloister Walk* (New York: Riverhead Books, 1996), and *Amazing Grace: A Vocabulary of Faith* (New York: Riverhead Books, 1998). Anna Quindlen's collected columns are entitled *Thinking Out Loud: On the Personal, The Political, The Public, and the Private* (New York: Ballantine Books, 1993).

23. Norris, *Amazing Grace: A Vocabulary of Faith*, 165-166.

24. Anna Quindlen, *Thinking Out Loud*, "No More Waiting," July 22, 1992 (New York: Ballantine Books, 1993), 252.

25. Anne Lamott, *Bird by Bird: Some Instructions on Writing and Life* (New York: Doubleday, 1994), 18-19.

26. Mitch Albom, *Tuesdays with Morrie: An Old Man, a Young Man, and Life's Greatest Lesson* (New York: Doubleday, 1997), 192.

27. A helpful bibliography of historical and contemporary memoirs can be found in Tristine Rainer's *Your Life as Story: Discovering the "New Autobiography" and Writing Memoir as Literature* (New York: Penguin Putnam, Inc., 1998). Roberta Bondi and Alan Jones are contemporary Christian memoirists.

28. Richard Carlson, Ph.D. *Don't Sweat the Small Stuff: and Its's All Small Stuff: Simple Ways to Keep the Little Things From Taking Over Your Life* (New York: Hyperion, 1997), 1, 2. Carlson has followed up his initial book with *Don't Sweat the Small Stuff at Work* and *Don't Sweat the Small Stuff in Love.*

29. Stephen R. Covey, with A. Roger Merrill and Rebecca R. Merrill, *First Things First: To Live, to Love, to Learn, to Leave a Legacy* (New York: Simon & Schuster, 1994), 49.

30. Ibid., 72.

31. Ibid., 54-56.

32. Ibid., 73.

33. Randy L. Maddox, *Responsible Grace: John Wesley's Practical Theology* (Nashville, Tennessee: Kingswood Books, 1994), 147.

34. John Calvin, *Institutes of the Christian Religion 1536 Edition* (London: Collins Liturgical Publications, 1986), Chapter I "The Law: Containing an Explanation of the Decalogue," Section I " Justification," Number 38, p. 41.

35. Ibid., Section H, "Uses of the Law," p. 36.

Chapter Four

1. Russell Chandler, *Understanding the New Age* (Grand Rapids, Michigan: Zondervan Publishing House, 1993), 23.

2. Mark B. Woodhouse, *Paradigm Wars: Worldviews for a New Age* (Berkeley, California: Frog Ltd., Books, 1996), 52.

3. Rachel Storm, *In Search of Heaven on Earth* (London: Bloomsbury Publishing Ltd., 1991), 2.

4. Storm's book *In Search of Heaven on Earth* traces the Western as well as the Eastern roots of New Age.

5. John Drane, *What is the New Age Still Saying to the Church?* (London: Marshall Pickering, 1999), 13.

6. M. D. Faber, *New Age Thinking: A Psychoanalytic Critique* (Canada:The University of Ottawa Press, 1996), p. 14.

7. Chandler, 29-30.

8. For a history and background on the phenomenon of channeling, see Paul Roland's *New Age Living: A Guide to Principles, Practices and Beliefs* (London: The Octopus Publishing Group, 2000), 52-55.

9. Woodhouse, 473-474. More outlandish claims concern the extraterrestrial origins of Adam and Eve and the galactic role of Christ.

10. Roland, *New Age Living*, 140.

11. Spiritualism stresses the survival of one's personal identity at death and the existence of a spiritual dimension with which human beings can be in constant

contact. Wicca, not to be confused with satanism, is a folk religion that looks on the earth as a manifestation of the divine. Finding God in nature is central, along with the belief that there is a unity to existence and that every living being has a sacred power that can be called upon for various purposes. The Mother Goddess is revered. Roland, *New Age Living*, 36-37.

12. LordRolfing is a form of intensive body massage. Reiki and Seichem are complementary forms of psychic healing that involve the release of energy and reprogramming of the body's energy centers. Roland, *New Age Living*, 158.

Tai Chi is a system of free-flowing movements designed to improve physical and spiritual health. Ibid., 142.

13. John A. Saliba, *Christian Responses to the New Age Movement: A Critical Assessment* (London: Geoffrey Chapman, 1999), 7-17.

14. Such a survey is provided in Roland's *New Age Living*.

15. Shakti Gawain, *The Path of Transformation: How Healing Ourselves Can Change the World* (Mill Valley, California: Nataraj Publishing, 1993). Dan Millman, *The Laws of Spirit: Simple, Powerful Truths for Making Life Work* (Tiburon, California: H J Kramer, 1995).

16. www.acim.org

17. L. David Moore, *Christianity and the New Age Religion: A Bridge Toward Mutual Understanding* (Atlanta, Georgia: Pendulum Plus Press, 1992), 115-117. Recent polls show that as much as 25% of the American public is sympathetic to reincarnation. (Woodhouse, 136). Half the world's population believes in the doctrine of Samsara: the eternal bondage of rebirth, the cycle of life and death. Buddhists, Hindus, and their offshoots, as well as Western Esoteric teaching, all agree on this. John Mumford, *Karma Manual* (St. Paul, Minnesota: Llewellyn Publications, 1999), 24.

18. Psychic Sylvia Browne expresses a commonly held New Age belief when she states that we compose a blueprint on The Other Side before we are born and choose the life themes we want to work on this time around, *The Other Side and Back: A Psychic's Guide to Our World and Beyond* (New York: New American Library, Signet Books, 1999), 121ff.

19. Woodhouse, 139. Westerners tend to assume that reincarnation and karma are exclusively Eastern notions from Buddhism and Hinduism. While they are prevalent there, these ideas were also taught in the early Gnostic Christian Church, in sects of Judaism related to Kabbalistic thought, in Taoism, in Egyptian and Persian religions, in classical Greek schools, and even in the Sufi sect of Islam. It was such a powerful notion in early Christian thought that the Emperor Constantine the Great had references to it deleted from Christian writings in AD 325 and the Second Council of Constantinople condemned the teachings of Origen on the preexistence of the soul (Woodhouse, Paradigm Wars, 136).

20. Huston Smith, *The World's Religions: A Guide to Our Wisdom Traditions* (New York: HarperCollins Publishers, 1995), 49.

21. Roland, *New Age Living*, 26.

22. Huston Smith, *The Illustrated World's Religions: A Guide to Our Wisdom Traditions* (HarperSanFrancisco, 1994), 49.

23. Mediums through the last several decades and channelers of entities today agree on several principles:

All is One in the synergy of Deity.

We are divine beings but have chosen to exist as physical humans.

In this life there are no victims, only opportunities.

We can control reality through the powers of Universal Mind.

Messages from outer space impart somewhat similar insights.

We are not alone in the universe. Highly cultured beings who are light years ahead of us both spiritually and scientifically inhabit other planets.

All things are interconnected. What affects one, affects all.

We are poised for a quantum leap forward on both the biological and spiritual levels (This is the principle of Harmonic Convergence).

This shifting of energy fields will entail pain, stress, and change as we enter the "Age of the Apocalypse."

Cosmic intelligences have come via UFOs to guide us into the New Age, teaching us to rise to higher levels of consciousness.

Death is an illusion, merely a doorway to another existence.

Chandler, 80, 88.

24. Ibid., 28.

25. The New Age movement has adopted and adapted Theosophy's evolutionary-eschatological view of history. Saliba, 21.

26. Michael York, "The New Age and neo-Pagan movements," *Religion Today* 6.2 (1991): 1-2.

27. Chandler, 30.

28. New Age self-help authors include Gerald Jampolsky, Jackie Woods, Jean Houston, George Leonard, John Bradshaw, Wayne Dyer, Ken Keyes, Wallace Black Elk, Starhawk, and Deepak Chopra.

29. While New Age insights have been shaped by Eastern religions, they do not always reflect their nuances. To take an example from Hinduism, bhakti yoga emphasizes the otherness of God and the goal, not of identifying with God but of adoring God with every element of one's being. One is to love God for no ulterior reason but for love's sake alone. Smith, 29.

30. Woodhouse, 331-348.

31. Chandler, 31-32.

32. James Redfield, *The Celestine Prophecy: An Adventure* (New York: Warner Books, 1993). Its sequel is *The Tenth Insight: Holding the Vision, Further Adventures of the Celestine Prophecy* (New York: Warner Books, 1996).

33. Ibid., "Author's Note."

34. Ibid., 141.

35. Ibid., 164.

36. Ibid., 200-201.

37. Ibid., 207-208.

38. Ibid., 222-223.

39. Ibid., 241-242.

40. A similar approach is outlined in Shakti Gawain's *Creative Visualization: Use the Power of Your Imagination to Create Whatever You Want in Your Life* (San Rafael, California: New World Library, 1991), 13.

41. Wayne W. Dyer, *Manifest Your Destiny: The Nine Spiritual Principles for Getting Everything You Want* (New York: HarperCollins Publishers, 1997), 15.

42. Ibid., 30.

43. Ibid., 31.

44. Ibid., 33.

45. Ibid., 46.

46. Ibid., 72.

47. Ibid., 74.

48. Ibid., 91.

49. Ibid., 92.

50. Ibid., 97.

51. Ibid., 100, 102.

52. Ibid., 118, 120.

53. Ibid., 139.

54. Ibid., 166.

55. Ibid., 169.

56. Ibid., 188-189.

57. Matthew 15:10-11; 5:27-28.

58. Saliba, 89.

59. Ibid., 91.

60. For a full discussion, see chapters 3 and 4 of Saliba.

Two balanced discussions of the strengths and weaknesses of the New Age are Ted Peters' *The Cosmic Self: A Penetrating Look at Today's New Age Movements* (New York: HarperSanFrancisco, 1991) and Glenn A. Olds' "The New Age" historical and metaphysical foundations" in *New Age Spirituality: An Assessment,* ed. Duncan S. Ferguson, pp. 59-76. Peters is Lutheran and Olds is United Methodist.

61. What follows are two classic statements about Divine Providence.

The Westminster Confession, (1646) Chapter III "Of God's Eternal Decree" www.reformed.org/documents/index.html

I. God from all eternity, did, by the most wise and holy counsel of His own will, freely, and unchangeably ordain whatsoever comes to pass;

The Heidelberg Catechism, (1563) question 27

(http://logosresourcepages.org/heidelbe.html)

What do you mean by Providence? The almighty and everywhere present power of God....whereby He still upholds, as it were by His own hand, heaven and earth together with all creatures, and rules in such a way....(that everything comes to us) "not by chance but by His fatherly hand."

62. Woodhouse, 51. One of Matthew Fox's criticism of the New Age is that its belief in reincarnation fosters insensitivity toward social injustice. This is not entirely accurate. There is nothing in the doctrine itself which necessarily leads to this effect.

63. Ibid., 450-452.

64. Gawain, *The Path of Transformation,* 143. See pp. 163-176 "Making a Difference in the World."

65. Jan Milic Lochman, *The Faith We Confess: An Ecumenical Dogmatics,* translated by David Lewis (Philadelphia: Fortress Press, 1984), chapter 16, "The Communion of Saints," 209-217.

66. Saliba, 176.

67. See *The Rule of Benedict: Insights for the Ages* (New York: Cross Road, 1995) by Joan D. Chittister, O.S.B. See also Margaret Silf's *Inner Compass: An Invitation to Ignatian Spirituality* (Chicago, Illinois: Loyola Press, 1999). Kathleen Norris' *The Cloister Walk* (New York: Riverhead Books, 1996), is a poet's account of her experience of immersion in Benedictine spirituality filled with rich homiletical insights.

68. For a helpful bibliography of works on these disciplines, see Marjorie J. Thompson's *Soul Feast: An Invitation to the Christian Spiritual Life* (Louisville, Kentucky: Westminster John Knox Press, 1995).

69. Saliba, 231.

Chapter Five

1. Roland E. Murphy, O. Carm., *The Tree of Life: An Exploration of Biblical Wisdom Literature* (New York: Doubleday, 1990), 7.

2. Bernard Brandon Scott, *Hear Then the Parable: A Commentary on the Parables of Jesus* (Minneapolis: Fortress Press, 1989), 7-17.

3. "Wisdom," in *Old Testament Form Criticism*, ed. John H. Hayes, Trinity University Monograph Series in Religion,2, ed. John H. Hayes (San Antonio: Trinity University Press, 1974), 230.

4. Alan Dundes, "Folk Ideas as Units of Worldview," *Essays in Folkloristics* (Kailash Puri Meerut: Ved Prakash Vatuk. Folklore Institute, 1978), 109-10.

5. Ronald E. Osborn, *Folly of God: The Rise of Christian Preaching* (St. Louis, MO: Chalice Press, 1999), 169. Chapter 6, "The Homiletic of Judaism" offers an overview of themes and forms used by the teachers of Judaism.

6. See Alyce M. McKenzie, *Preaching Proverbs: Wisdom for the Pulpit* (Louisville, Kentucky: Westminster John Knox Press, 1996), Chapter 9, p. 127, where the "Dueling Proverbs" model is described.

7. Kathleen M. O'Connor, *The Wisdom Literature* (Wilmington, Delaware: Michael Glazier, 1988), 35. Scholarly consensus supports O'Connor's postexilic dating for this material. Representative authors are Hartmut Gese, Patrick Skehan, Dave Bland, Raymond Van Leeuwen, and Ronald E. Clements. Claudia V. Camp argued persuasively for a postexilic origin of this material in her *Wisdom and the Feminine in the Book of Proverbs* (Sheffield, England: The Almond Press, 1985). Interestingly, she has amended her dating of the first nine chapters from the late sixth or early fifth century to a later, Hellenistic one. "What's So Strange About the Strange Woman?" in *The Bible and the Politics of Exegesis: Essays in Honor of Norman K. Gottwald*, ed. David Jobling, Peggy L. Day, and Gerald T. Sheppard. Cleveland: Pilgrim Press, 1991), 17-31.

8. Harold C. Washington, "Wealth and Poverty in the Instruction of Amenemope and the Hebrew Proverbs: Two Test Cases in the Social Location and Function of Ancient Near Eastern Wisdom Literature," Ph.D. dissertation, Princeton Theological Seminary, 1992, 239ff.

9. Murphy, *Tree of Life*, 25.

10. O'Connor, 35.

11. Murphy, *The Tree of Life*, 22-23.

12. Scholars have long debated the origins of the female depiction of Wisdom in Proverbs 1-9. Some believe she is rooted in ancient Near Eastern worship of a goddess of wisdom. Others assert that she is a hypostasis, the transformation of a personal trait into a person with its own existence, who exists independently of Yahweh. Still others affirm that she is a personification of a quality and ongoing action of Yahweh toward humankind: moral guidance and instruction. The final interpretation seems most likely in light of several features of Wisdom's presentation in Proverbs. Wisdom is always in Yahweh's control: she is the medium whereby God created the earth and a divine gift to human beings that enables us to obey. She is the 'principle of operation of protection, salvation and life,' 'a representation of Yahweh, his will and his offer of salvation.' Wisdom is not, like the Egyptian goddess *Ma'at*, the divine, eternally-valid order of creation itself. Rather, she represents the effort to learn that order by observation and to respect it in the execution of life. Christa Bauer-Kayatz, *Studien zu Proverbien 1-9, Wissenscaftliche Monographien zum alten und neuen Testament 22.* (Neukirchen-Viuyn: Neukirchener, 1966), 139. For a discussion of hypostasis and personfication, see Claudia Camp, *Wisdom and the Feminine in the Book of Proverbs*, (Sheffield: Almond Press, 1985), chapters 1 and 7. Camp concludes that Woman Wisdom is a personification in literary terms and a religious symbol in theological terms.

13. Camp, *Wisdom and the Feminine in the Book of Proverbs*. See Chapter 6, "Proverbs 1-9 and 31: The Literary Re-Contextualization of the Proverb Collection" and Chapter 7, "Personification as a Stylistic Device. "

14. Leo G. Perdue, "Wisdom Theology and Social History in Proverbs 1-9," *Wisdom, You Are My Sister: Studies in Honor of Roland E. Murphy, O. Carm., on the Occasion of His Eightieth Birthday*, edited by Michael L. Barré, S.S. (Washington, D.C.: The Catholic Biblical Association of America, 1997), 79.

15. O'Connor, *The Wisdom Literature*, 36.

16. R.B.Y. Scott, *The Anchor Bible: Proverbs and Ecclesiastes*, Volume 16 (New York: Doubleday, 1985), xviii.

17. In the last two centuries of the modern era much of the literature of Israel's neighbors has been recovered in excavations and by chance finds. Hundreds of thousands of clay tablets have been dug up in Mesopotamia and Syria. Monuments have been excavated in Palestine, and papyri in Egypt. These shed light on the common genres of Israel and her neighbors: chronicles, hymns, laments, stories about ancient heroes, laws, liturgical regulations, collections of laws, prophecies, love songs, proverbs, instructions, theological disputes, and skeptical literature. Richard Clifford, *The Wisdom Literature* (Nashville: Abingdon, 1998) 24.

18. For a discussion of the role of court sages, see James L. Crenshaw, *Old Testament Wisdom* (Atlanta: John Knox Press, 1981), 28-39. This school view is held by Gerhard von Rad and his student H.J. Hermisson, as well as H.D. Preuss, all of whom reject any connection between proverbs and oral folk wisdom.

19. This is the view of Claus Westermann, Carole R. Fontaine, J. G. Williams, H. W. Wolff, E. Gerstenberger, and J. M. Thompson.

20. For a synopsis of arguments for an early postexilic dating, see Leo G.

Perdue, "Wisdom Theology and Social History in Proverbs 1-9," *Wisdom, You Are My Sister* edited by Michael L. Barre, S.S. (Washington, D.C.: The Catholic Biblical Association of America, 1997), 79-80. Most wisdom scholars from the end of the nineteenth century until the present have agreed that the present form of Proverbs dates from the early postexilic period, while acknowledging that individual sayings and collections within the book may be much older. Bernard Lang, however, in his book *Wisdom and the Book of Proverbs: An Israelite Goddess Redefined* (New York: Pilgrim Press, 1986) is convinced that chapters 1-9 are of a preexilic origin. He insists that Wisdom is a deity in her own right, modeled on other ancient Near Eastern goddesses.

21. Dave Bland, "The Formation of Character in the Book of Proverbs," *Restoration Quarterly* Volume 40 No 4, 1998, 222. Bland draws on Ronald E. Clements' assessment of the postexilic milieu. See Clements' *Wisdom in Theology* (Grand Rapids: Eerdmans, 1992) and his "Wisdom and Old Testament Theology," in *Wisdom in Ancient Israel*, eds. John Day, Robert Gordon, and H. G. M. Williamson (Cambridge: Cambridge University Press, 1995).

22. See Carol A. Newsom's "Woman and the Discourse of Patriarchal Wisdom: A Study of Proverbs 1-9," in *Gender and Difference*, edited by Peggy L. Day (Philadelphia: Fortress Press, 1989).

23. There are four women in the book of Proverbs. Most conspicuous is Woman Wisdom. Her opposite number is Woman Folly (9:13-18). Further, there is the woman who is one's marriage partner (5:15-19); and finally, the "Stranger" (2:16-19; 5:1-14, 20; 6:24-32 [35]; 7:25-27). See Roland Murphy's Excursus on Woman Wisdom and Woman Folly, in *The World Biblical Commentary on Proverbs* (Nashville: Thomas Nelson Publishers, 1998), 279ff. See also Claudia Camp's "What's So Strange About the Strange Woman?" in *The Bible and the Politics of Exegesis: Essays in Honor of Norman K. Gottwald*, ed. David Jobling, Peggy L. Day, and Gerald T. Sheppard. (Cleveland: Pilgrim, 1991), 17-31.

24. William P. Brown, *Character in Crisis: A Fresh Approach to the Wisdom Literature of the Old Testament* (Grand Rapids, Michigan: William B. Eerdmans Publishing Company, 1996), 22. Character formation has been the focus of recent scholarship on the book of Proverbs. Scholars like William Brown and Dave Bland have identified character formation as the central function of the book. The theological contexts become the character of God as personified by Wisdom, the character of the community and the sage, and the character of their pupils.

25. Dianne Bergant, *Israel's Wisdom Literature: A Liberation-Critical Reading* (Minneapolis: Fortress Press, 1997), 105.

26. Lennart Boström, *The God of the Sages: The Portrayal of God in the Book of Proverbs* (Stockholm: Almqvist and Wiksell International, 1990), 239.

27. In later chapters, we will examine the wisdom genre in the teachings of Jesus, and the reflections on his significance of the four Gospels, Paul, and James. In my view, not every sermon on an Old Testament text has to explicitly mention the New. Still the New Testament's wisdom reflection constitutes part of the setting of silver in which we preach Old Testament wisdom texts and themes. This rich canonical context suggests intriguing textual pairings for preachers. Lectionary preachers can relate proverbial themes and texts to lectionary texts

from all corners of the canon. Non-lectionary preachers can preach creative series on proverbs in the context of canonical wisdom.

28. Alan W. Jenks identifies the three theological pillars of Proverbs as order, knowability, and justice. "Theological Presuppositions of Israel's Wisdom Literature" *Horizons in Biblical Theology* Vol. 7, No. 1, June, 1985.

29. "Fear of the LORD" had many meanings in the Hebrew Bible. In Isaiah 6 it referred to the awareness of the gulf between the human and divine realms. In the Psalms it is a sort of cultic piety. In Deuteronomy it refers to covenant loyalty. Roland E. Murphy, "The Faith of Qohelet," *Word and World* 7 (1987): 256.

30. Roland Murphy, "Wisdom Theses," in *Wisdom and Knowledge*, ed. J. Armenti (Villanova, Pennsylvania: Villanova University Press, 1976), 198. Proverbs 16:1, 2, 9; 19:21; 20:24; 21:30-31.

31. McKenzie, *Preaching Proverbs*, 31. *Hayim* is used to refer to life in 3:22; 8:35; 10:27; 13:14; 21:21; 22:4. *Nephesh* is the term of choice in 13:3; 16:17; 19:16; 29:10.

32. 1 Kings 3:9. The young King Solomon asked for a "listening heart," or an "understanding mind" so that he could discern the difference between good and evil, and rule God's people faithfully. The Hebrew understanding of heart does not know our modern dichotomy between head and heart, rational thought and emotions. The heart for the Hebrews was the seat of the will and the imagination, not only the emotions.

33. Ronald J. Williams "The Sage in Egyptian Literature," *The Sage in Israel and the Ancient Near East* edited by John G. Gammie and Leo G. Perdue (Winona Lake: Eisenbrauns, 1990), 29-30.

34. Verses that advocate corporal punishment are 10:13, 13:24; 22:15; 23:13; 23:14; 26:3; 29:15.

35. Ellen F. Davis, *Proverbs, Ecclesiastes and the Song of Songs* (Louisville, Kentucky: Westminster John Knox Press, 2000), 25-26.

36. Ibid., 26.

37. Richard J. Clifford, *The Wisdom Literature* (Nashville: Abingdon Press, 1998), 45-46.

38. Leo G. Perdue, *Proverbs, Interpretation: A Bible Commentary for Teaching and Preaching* (Louisville, Kentucky: John Knox Press, 2000), 69.

39. Ibid., 70.

40. I am indebted for this understanding of "beginning" to a conversation with my colleague Dr. Roy Heller, Assistant Professor of Old Testament, Perkins School of Theology, Southern Methodist University.

41. Roland E. Murphy, "The Faith of Qohelet," *Word and World* 7 (1987): 256.

42. Davis, 28-29.

43. Dan Millman, *Living on Purpose: Straight Answers to Life's Tough Questions* (Novato, California: New World Library, 2000), 52.

44. Wisdom could not find a place in which she could dwell; but a place was found for her in the heavens. Then Wisdom went out to dwell with the children of the people, but she found no dwelling place. So Wisdom returned to her place and she became settled among the angels (1 Enoch 42:1-2). Ben Witherington III, *Jesus the Sage: The Pilgrimage of Wisdom* (Minneapolis: Fortress Press, 1994) p. 115. Witherington is quoting this passage from the *OT Pseudepigrapha* I, p. 33.

45. Kathleen O'Connor, *The Wisdom Literature*, 72.

46. Perdue, *Proverbs*, 142.

47. Murphy, *The Tree of Life*, 135-36.

48. Clifford, 60-61.

49. Murphy, *World Biblical Commentary on Proverbs*, 52-53.

50. Roland E. Murphy, "Wisdom and Creation," *Journal of Biblical Literature* 104 (1985), 9-10.

51. Carole L. Fontaine, "Wisdom in Proverbs," *In Search of Wisdom: Essays in Memory of John G. Gammie*, edited by Leo G. Perdue, Bernard Brandon Scott, and William Johnston Wiseman (Lousiville, Kentucky: Westminster John Knox Press, 1993), 114.

52. Roland E. Murphy, *The Tree of Life*, 83. For an overview of the historical, sociological, theological and literary features of the Wisdom of Solomon, see Anthony R. Ceresko, O.S.F.S., *Introduction to Old Testament Wisdom: A Spirituality for Liberation*, (Maryknoll, New York: Orbis Books, 1999), chapter 15 and 16.

53. Clifford, 62.

54. Ralph L. Lewis with Gregg Lewis, *Inductive Preaching: Helping People Listen* (Wheaton, Illinois: Crossway Books, 1983), 24.

55. The instruction by a royal mother in Proverbs 31:1-9 may reflect Mesopotamian culture's tradition of royal daughters destined for diplomatic marriages being given a degree of education to enable them to serve as liasons and information-gatherers for their fathers. They may have been trained by older women, royal mothers, nurses, or low-level palace administrators. Carole R. Fontaine, "The Sage in Family and Tribe," *The Sage in Israel and the Ancient Near East*, 156ff.

56. Recent scholarship asserts that "A Poem to a Woman of Worth," (*eset hayil*) literally a woman of strength, depicts, not a role model for women's daily accomplishments, but Woman Wisdom herself. Thomas P. McCreesh, O.P. "Wisdom as Wife: Proverbs 31:10-31," *Revue Biblique*, 1985, 25-46. See Judith E. McKinlay *Gendering Wisdom the Host: Biblical Invitations to Eat and Drink, Journal for the Study of the Old Testament Supplement Series* 216 (Sheffield: Sheffield Academic Press, 1996), Chapter 5, "Women in Proverbs."

57. O'Connor, 78-79.

Chapter Six

1. Elie Wiesel, *Messengers of God: Biblical Portraits and Legends*, (New York: Summit Books, 1976), 21.

2. Among them are the Egyptian work *A Dispute over Suicide*, written around 2000 BCE and the poetic essay from Mesopotamia, *A Man and His God*. During the sixth century BCE in northern India, the young prince Siddartha developed a philosophy and way of living to deal with this common experience of suffering. He came to be known by his followers as the "Buddha" or "enlightened one." Anthony R. Ceresko, O.S.F.S. *Introduction to Old Testament Wisdom: A Spirituality for Liberation* (Maryknoll, New York: Orbis Books, 1999), 66.

3. Gustavo Gutiérrez *On Job: God-Talk and the Suffering of the Innocent*, translated from the Spanish by Matthew J. O'Connell (Maryknoll, New York: Orbis Books, 1987), 1.

4. Ceresko, 88.

5. Gutiérrez, 3.

6. Roland E. Murphy, *The Tree of Life: An Exploration of Biblical Wisdom Literature*, *The Anchor Bible Reference Library* (New York: Doubleday, 1990), 34.

7. Roland E. Murphy, O. Carm, *Wisdom Literature: Job, Proverbs, Ruth, Canticles, Ecclesiastes, and Esther, Volume XII, The Forms of the Old Testament Literature* (Grand Rapids, Michigan: William B. Eerdmans Publishing Company, 1981), 16-18.

8. Ibid., 17.

9. Georg Fohrer, *Das Buch Hiob* (Gutersloh: Gerd Mohn, 1963), 50-53.

10. Murphy, *The Tree of Life*, 33-34.

11. *The Tree of Life*, 34.

12. Eli Wiesel, *Messengers of God*, 226.

13. This theory of older patient sufferer corrected by the insertion of impatient Job is marred by the fact that Job is not uniformly impatient. Job is left saying things we don't expect, like defending the moral order (24:18-25; 27:7-13) and eloquently speaking of the limits of human wisdom (chapter 28). Explanations for the text's present "disordered" shape are legion. Christopher Seitz, *Interpretation*, January 1989. "Job: Full-Structure, Movement, and Interpretation," 9.

14. Kathleen M. O'Connor, *The Wisdom Literature* (Wilmington, Delaware: Glazier Press, 1988), 88.

15. Edwin M. Good, *In Turns of Tempest: A Reading of Job* (Stanford, California: Stanford University Press, 1990), 22.

16. Ibid.

17. William P. Brown, *Character in Crisis: A Fresh Approach to the Wisdom Literature of the Old Testament* (Grand Rapids, Michigan: William B. Eerdmans, 1996), 52

18. Ibid., 56-57.

19. O'Connor, 93.

20. Ibid., 94.

21. Wolfers, *Deep Things*, 49.

22. Carol A. Newsom, "Job," in *The Women's Bible Commentary*, ed. Carol. A. Newsom and Sharon H. Ringe. (Louisville, Kentucky: Westminster John Knox Press, 1992), 131.

23. Ellen F. Davis, "Job and Jacob: The Integrity of Faith," in *Reading Between Texts: Intertextuality and the Hebrew Bible*, ed. Danna Nolan Fewell (Louisville, Kentucky: Westminster John Knox Press, 1992), 205.

24. See the helpful article by Lindsay Wilson, "The Book of Job and the Fear of God," *Tyndale Bulletin* 46 (May 1995), 59-79.

25. Ceresko, *Introduction to Old Testament Wisdom*, 86-87.

26. Dianne Bergant, *Israel's Wisdom Literature: A Liberation-Critical Reading* (Minneapolis: Fortress Press, 1997), 44-45.

27. Wilson, "The Book of Job and the Fear of God," 67.

28. John E. Hartley, *The Book of Job The New International Commentary on the Old Testament* (Grand Rapids, Michigan: William B. Eerdmans Publishing Company, 1988), 491.

29. Holbert, *Preaching Job* (St. Louis, Missouri: Chalice Press, 1999), 125.

30. Bergant, *Israel's Wisdom Literature*, 44-45.

31. Holbert, 129.

32. Robert L. Wise, *When There is no Miracle* (Ventura, California: Regal Books, 1977), 119-120, quoted in an unpublished sermon entitled "Why Do Bad Things Happen to Good People?" by Charlotte A. Coates, August 6, 2001.

33. Holbert, 133-134.

34. Ibid., 134.

35. Dianne Bergant, C.S.A *Job, Ecclesiastes; Old Testament Message: A Biblical Theological Commentary* (Wilmington, Delaware: Michael Glazier, Inc., 1982), 196.

36. Holbert, 136.

37. Bergant, *Job Ecclesiastes*, 196.

38. Holbert, 135-137.

39. Bergant, *Job Ecclesiastes*, 198.

40. Holbert, 137.

41. Ibid., 146-147.

42. Leo G. Perdue, "Wisdom in the Book of Job," *In Search of Wisdom : Essays in Memory of John G. Gammie*, edited by Leo G. Perdue, Bernard Brandon Scott, and William Johnston Wiseman (Louisville, Kentucky: Westminster John Knox Press, 1993), 96.

43. Laurence Hull Stookey, *Baptism: Christ's Act in the Church* (Nashville: Abingdon, 1982), 36.

44. *Summa Theologiae*, I, 9, 3, quoted in the introduction to Gustavo Gutierrez' *On Job: God-Talk and the Suffering of the Innocent*.(Maryknoll, New York: Orbis Books, 1987), xi.

45. Mayer I. Gruber, "Three Failed Dialogues from the Biblical World ," *Journal of Psychology and Judaism*, Vol. 22, No. 1, Spring 1998, p. 58.

46. Ibid., 58.

47. Gruber, 60.

48. Gustavo Gutiérrez, 16. Diane Bergant points out that liberation theologians have in common with the book of Job a desire to "free themselves of false identities and perceptions that have been forced on them by the prevailing worldview. They set out then to devise methods of understanding and approaches to life that are more compatible with their own experience." The experience of those who wield economic and social power in a society determines what is considered conventional. Bergant, 46-47.

49. Gutiérrez, 12-13.

50. Gutiérrez, 17.

51. Kubler-Ross, *On Children and Death* (New York: Macmillan Publishing Company, 1983),149-152, quoted in an unpublished sermon by Charlotte A. Coates entitled "Why Do Bad Things Happen to Good People?" August 6, 2001.

52. John C. Holbert, " 'Troubling Physicians are You All': On Becoming a Joban Preacher," Paper published in the Papers of the Annual Meeting of the Academy of Homiletics, December, 1998, p. 4.

53. Bergant, *Israel's Wisdom Literature*, 45.
54. Ibid., 48.
55. This story is recounted by Joseph R. Jeter, Jr. in his book *Crisis Preaching: Personal and Public* (Nashville: Abingdon, 1998), 23-24.
56. Holbert, *Preaching Job*, 144.
57. Holbert, "Troubling Physicians," 8. Holbert is quoting Normal Habel's commentary *The Book of Job* (Philadelphia: Westminster Press, 1985), 583.

Chapter Seven

1. Choon-Leong Seow, *Ecclesiastes, The Anchor Bible Commentary* Volume 18C (New York: Doubleday, 1997), 3,4.
2. Ellen E. Davis, *Proverbs, Ecclesiastes, and the Song of Songs. Westminster Bible Companion* (Louisville, Kentucky: Westminster John Knox Press, 2000), 160.
3. Seow, 97.
4. Richard J. Clifford, *The Wisdom Literature* (Nashville: Abingdon Press, 1998), 99. Qohelet is the participle of the Hebrew verb *qahal*, "to assemble, to gather." The feminine participle seems to designate a functionary, someone who gathers or collects wisdom writings. Ecclesiastes is the Latinized form of the Greek translation of the Hebrew word.
5. Clifford, 98. See James G. Williams, *Those Who Ponder Proverbs: Aphoristic Thinking and Biblical Literature* (Sheffield, England: The Almond Press, 1981), Chapter III.
6. For a discussion of linguistic and epigraphic evidence that places Ecclesiastes in the Persian period, see Clifford, 100-101 and Seow, 16-21.
7. Leo Perdue, "Wisdom Theology and Social History in Proverbs 1-9," in *Wisdom, You Are My Sister: Studies in Honor of Roland E. Murphy, O. Carm., on the Occasion of His Eightieth Birthday* (Washington, D.C.: The Catholic Biblical Association of America, 1997), 87.
8. Seow, 21.
9. Ibid., 23. See Ecclesiastes 5:10-12; 7:12.
10. Ibid.
11. Ibid., 24.
12. Ibid., 24-25.
13. Seow, 27-28.
14. Ibid., 35-36.
15. Ibid. 54-55. While the book has 40 explicit references to God (*Elohim*), it has even more (48) for humanity (*adam*).
16. Qohelet is profoundly disappointed in the traditional wisdom in which he was schooled. He yearns for it to be adequate, but his observations and experience of life show its shortcomings. This is the dynamic behind his perplexing habit of juxtaposing sayings that affirm traditional wisdom with sayings that undercut it. Chapter seven is a litany of such apparent contradictions. For a full discussion of this dynamic see Michael V. Fox, *Qohelet and His Contradictions* (Sheffield: The Almond Press, 1989).

17. Michael V. Fox, "Wisdom in Qoheleth," in *In Search of Wisdom: Essays in Memory of John G. Gammie* (Louisville, Kentucky: Westminster John Knox Press, 1993), 118-119.

18. Ibid., 126.

19. Michael V. Fox, *Qohelet and His Contradictions*, 29-30. See also Michael V. Fox, "The Meaning of *Hebel* for Qohelet" *JBL (Journal of Biblical Literature)*105/3 (1986) 409-427.

20. James Loader argues that Qohelet's notion of *hebel* is shaped by his experience that God is remote. Qohelet has a passive attitude towards God, merely observing his acts without protesting. He does not attempt to fill the vacuum he senses between humanity and God with intermediaries or explanations, but describes it as *hebel*, the "vacuum of senselessness." I am convinced that Fox's understanding of *hebel* as absurdity more adequately encompasses Qohelet's use of *hebel* to describe injustice, the futility of toil, the pursuit of wealth, and the inevitability of death that awaits both wise and fool. J.A. Loader, *Polar Structures in the Book of Qohelet* (Berlin: Walter de Gruyter, 1979), 129-130.

21. Fox, *Qohelet and His Contradictions*, 31-32.

22. Ibid., 32.

23. James G. Williams, "What Does It Profit A Man?: The Wisdom of Koheleth," *SAIW (Studies in Ancient Israelite Wisdom)* The Library of Biblical Studies, ed. Harry M. Orlinsky (New York: Ktav Publishing House, 1976), 375.

24. Ralph Marston, *Daily Motivator Email Edition,* Monday, March 5, 2001; Copyright © 2001 Ralph S. Marston, Jr. All rights reserved. The Daily Motivator web site at *http://greatday.com* is a helpful site that features an archive of more than 1,000 daily motivational messages.

25. Dianne Bergant, *Israel's Wisdom Literature*, 116.

26. Ibid., 117.

27. Seow, *Ecclesiastes*, 33.

28. Paul Scott Wilson, *A Concise History of Preaching* (Nashville: Abingdon Press, 1992), 113 .

29. Seow, 29.

30. R.N. Whybray, "Qoheleth, Preacher of Joy," *Journal for the Study of the Old Testament* 23 (1982) 87.

31. William P. Brown, *Character in Crisis: A Fresh Approach to the Wisdom Literature of the Old Testament* (Grand Rapids, Michigan: William B. Eerdmans Publishing Company, 1996), 146.

32. Ibid., 147.

33. Qohelet consistently uses the generic name *Elohim* instead of Yaweh, the name for the God of the covenant with Israel. Yaweh emphasizes God's direct dealings with indidivuals and nations. *Elohim* is the universal term for the deity, the God of the universe. Roland E. Murphy, "The Faith of Qohelet," *Word and World* 7 (1987), 255.

34. Roland E. Murphy, "Qohelet's Quarrel with the Fathers," *From Faith to Faith* (Pittsburg, PA: Pickwick Press, 1979), 256.

35. Brown, 144-45.

36. Ibid., 146.

37. Barbara Brown Taylor, *The Preaching Life* (Boston, Massachusetts: Cowley Publications, 1993), 9.

38. J. A. Loader, *Polar Structures in the Book of Qohelet*, 129.

39. J. David Pleins, "Poverty in the Social World of the Wise," *JSOT (Journal for the Study of the Old Testament)* 37 (1987), 67-68.

Chapter Eight

1. Proverbial sayings and a related wisdom form, the parable, pervade the Synoptic Gospels. Their prevalence supports the claim that Jesus, prophet and healer, was also a sage. Charles E. Carlston discerns 102 wisdom sayings in the Synoptic Gospels. About a quarter of them are clustered in what many scholars call the Q document, a sayings source many scholars believe was used by both Matthew and Luke. "Proverbs, Maxims, and the Historical Jesus," *Journal of Biblical Literature*, Volume 99. March 1980 87-105. Leo G. Perdue's article "The Wisdom Sayings of Jesus," *Forum* (1986) Volume 2:3-35 offers a detailed form-critical breakdown of Jesus' wisdom sayings.

2. Bernard Brandon Scott, *Hear Then the Parable: A Commentary on the Parables of Jesus* (Minneapolis: Fortress Press, 1989), 8.

3. For a full treatment of Jesus' subversive use of parables, see William R. Herzog II, *Parables as Subversive Speech: Jesus as Pedagogue of the Oppressed* (Louisville, Kentucky: Westminster John Knox Press, 1994).

4. Ben Witherington III, *Jesus the Sage: The Pilgrimage of Wisdom* (Minneapolis: Fortress Press, 1994), 159.

5. Leo D. Lefebure, "Sophia: Wisdom and Christian Theology," *Christian Century*, Oct. 19, 1994, 953.

6. Marcus J. Borg, *Meeting Jesus Again for the First Time: The Historical Jesus and the Heart of Contemporary Faith* (New York: HarperCollins, 1995), 107.

7. A number of scholars believe that Colossians, along with Ephesians and 2 Thessalonians were not written by Paul himself. Whether or not Colossians was written by Paul, it shows strong similarities with Paul's thought.

8. Elisabeth Schussler Fiorenza, "Wisdom Mythology and the Christological Hymns of the New Testament," *Aspects of Wisdom in Judaism and Early Christianity*, ed Robert L. Wilken (Notre Dame: University of Notre Dame Press, 1975), 17-41.

9. Borg, 106.

10. Witherington, *Jesus the Sage*, 241.

11. Ibid, 246.

12. This prayer can be found in novel *The Wrong Plantagenet*, by Marian Palmer, (New York: Popular Library, 1972), p. 35.

13. Witherington, 336

14. The gospel genre has similarities and differences from Greco-Roman biographies. They were most often written to showcase the achievements of a prominent individual and to encourage imitation of their achievements. The kind of values they encouraged were usually traditional, status quo, stabilizing values. The same is true of many contemporary autobiographies. Matthew's Gospel, however, was written to inspire faith in Jesus and his teachings are far from tradi-

tional. See David E. Aune's *The New Testament in Its Literary Environment* for a full discussion of the gospel genre as contrasted with Greco-Roman and Jewish biography. (Philadelphia: The Westminster Press, 1987), chapter 2.

15. The term disciple ("learner") occurs much more frequently in Matthew and John than in Mark or Luke (Matthew, 73 times; John 78; Mark 46; Luke-Acts 65 combined; and in Luke, 37). R. A. Culpepper, *The Johannine School* (Missoula: Scholars Press, 1975), 270-271, cited by Witherington, 337.

16. Wisdom influences are not, of course, entirely lacking in Mark and Luke. See Hugh M. Humphrey's "Jesus as Wisdom in Mark" *Biblical Theology Bulletin* Vol. 19, April, 1989, No. 2.

17. Witherington, *Jesus the Sage*, 338.

18. Marian Meyer Thompson, "Thinking About God: Wisdom and Theology in John 6," in *Critical Readings of John 6*, edited by R. Alan Culpepper (New York: Brill, 1997), 239.

19. Witherington, 340-41.

20. Norman Perrin, *The New Testament: An Introduction* (Chicago: Harcourt Brace Jovanovich, Inc. 1974), 170-71. See the Introduction to Anthony J. Saldarini's *Matthew's Christian-Jewish Community* (Chicago: The University of Chicago Press, 1994).

21. Many scholars are convinced that the diatribe against "the scribes and Pharisees" in Matthew 23 reflects the conflict between Matthew and the rabbis of his day more than it does a contest between Jesus and the scribes and Pharisees of his day (Perrin, 171).

22. William A. Beardslee, "The Wisdom Tradition and the Synoptic Gospels," *Journal of the American Academy of Religion* 35 (1967), 234.

23. Relevant writings from the Hebrew Scriptures include Proverbs, Job, Ecclesiastes, and Deuteronomy. Later Jewish writings that address wisdom themes include The Wisdom of Solomon (mid-first century BCE), the Wisdom of Jesus Ben Sirach (also called Ecclesiasticus), and 4 Ezra.

24. These are called deutero-canonical writings and are found in Roman Catholic and Eastern Orthodox Bibles. Protestants call them apocryphal, and Jews call them extra-canonical. Neither Protestants nor Jews consider these writings a part of the Biblical canon. 1 Enoch and 4 Esdras are considered extra-biblical. These works are relatively late Jewish writings in comparison with other Old Testament works. They probaby predated the Q document, which shows evidence of having been shaped by their Wisdom reflection. Ivan Havener, *Q: The Sayings of Jesus* (Collegeville, Minnesota: The Liturgical Press, 1987), 78, note 63.

25. David Buttrick, *Speaking Parables: A Homiletic Guide* (Louisville, Kentucky: Westminster John Knox Press, 2000), 132.

26. Martin Scott, *Sophia and the Johannine Jesus* Journal for the Study of the New Testament Supplement Series 71 (Sheffield, England: Sheffield Academic Press, 1992), 86-87.

27. Two houses (Matthew 7:24-27; Luke 6:47-49); Children in the Marketplace (Matthew 11:16-19; Luke 7:31-35), Empty House (Matthew 12:43-45; Luke 11:24-26); Leaven (Matthew 13:33; Luke 13:20); Weather Report (Matthew 16:1-4; Luke 12:54-56); Lost Sheep (Matthew 18:12-13; Luke 15:4-6); Feast (Matthew 22:1-14;

Luke 14:16-24); Closed Door (Matthew 25:1-12; Luke 13:25); Entrusted Money (Matthew 25:14-28; Luke 19:12-24).

28. Ivan Havener's *Q: The Sayings of Jesus* features a complete text of Q with references to where its sayings occur in both Matthew and Luke.

29. Citations for these images include tree (3:18), light (4:18;15:4), treasure (3:13; 8:10; 8:18-21), bread (9:1-16), life (4:23; 5:22; 10:11), and way (3:18; 4:18; 16:17).

30. Elisabeth Schlussler Fiorenza, *Jesus: Miriam's Child, Sophia's Prophet: Critical Issues in Feminist Christology* (New York: Continuum, 1995), 152.

31. Jesus' miracles in this Gospel are in service to his teachings. They are intended to spark faith in Jesus the teacher and inspire obedience to his instruction. They may also connect him more tightly to Solomon. There is a tradition in late Jewish Wisdom of Solomon's healing powers. Between the birth narratives and the entry into Jerusalem, whenever the phrase Son of David arises, it is in the context of someone's request for healing (9:27; 12:23; 15:22; 20:30-31), Witherington, 357.

32. For a discussion of the passages in chapter 11, see Celia M. Deutsch, *Lady Wisdom, Jesus, and the Sages: Metaphor and Social Context in Matthew's Gospel* (Valley Forge, Pennsylvania: Trinity Press International, 1996), 117-118. See also Ben Witherington, *Jesus the Sage*, 359-360. Celia Deutsch's *Hidden Wisdom and the Easy Yoke: Wisdom, Torah, and Discipleship in Matthew 11:25-30* (Sheffield: JSOT Press, 1987) is a book-length treatment of this key text.

33. Schlussler Fiorenza, *Jesus, Miriam's Child, Sophia's Prophet*, 151. James M. Robinson, "Jesus as Sophos and Sophia," *Aspects of Wisdom in Judaism and Early Christianity*, ed. Robert L. Wilken, (Notre Dame: University of Notre Dame Press, 1975), 10, 11. Frances Taylor Gench, by contrast, while he discerns wisdom motifs in these texts, does not believe they signal the presence of Wisdom Christology. Gench does not think it follows that Jesus is identitifed with Sophia. The Matthean Jesus, says Gench, appears not as Wisdom Incarnate, but as one who speaks and acts upon the authority of God, the preeminent Son of God who mediates God's revelation. *Wisdom in the Christology of Matthew*, (New York: University Press of America, 1997), 209.

34. Terence L. Donaldson, "Guiding Readers—Making Disciples: Discipleship in Matthew's Narrative Strategy," from *Patterns of Discipleship in the New Testament*, edited by Richard N. Longenecker (Grand Rapids, Michigan: William B. Eerdmans Publishing Company), 30-49.

35. These are conveyed both by short indicative wisdom sayings (proverbs) and by imperative sayings (admonitions) as well as by parables and other narrative portions. For preaching, each individual passage needs to be examined in its immediate context in the Gospel as well as this overview. The rich imagery used to convey many of these truths needs to be honored.

36. Lack of faith or failure to accept the gift of faith impedes Jesus' healing ministry (17:14-20; 14:31; 16:8). The disciples are rebuked for their lack of faith (6:30; 8:26; 14:31; 16:18; 17:20).

37. In most of the healings in Matthew, people had a confidence in Jesus' healing authority when they came to him. (Matthew 4:23-24). Examples include the

healing of the leper (8:2), the Centurion's servant (8:8), the paralytic (9:2), the woman with the flow of blood (9:20), and the two blind men (9:27).

38. Terence L. Donaldson, "Guiding Readers—Making Disciples," 30-49. According to Matthew's depiction of discipleship, doubts occur even in the presence of the risen Jesus. Unwavering faith is the goal of discipleship more than the prerequisite (28:17).

39. Daniel Patte, *The Gospel According to Matthew: A Structural Commentary on Matthew's Faith* (Philadelphia: Fortress Press, 1987), 61.

40. Dale C. Allison, *The Sermon on the Mount: Inspiring the Moral Imagination* (New York: The Crossroad Publishing Company, 1999), 13.

41. Ibid., 11,12.

42. Ibid., 15.

43. David Hill, *The New Century Bible Commentary: The Gospel of Matthew* (Grand Rapids, Michigan: Wm. B. Eerdmans Publishing Company, 1972), 110.

44. A. W. Argyle, *The Gospel According to Matthew: The Cambridge Bible Commentary on the New English Bible* (Cambridge: Cambridge University Press, 1963), 44.

45. Douglas Hare, Matthew: *Interpretation: A Bible Commentary for Teaching and Preaching* (Louisville, Kentucky: Westminster John Knox Press, 1993), 35.

46. Robert H. Schuller, *The Be (Happy) Attitudes: 8 Positive Attitudes That Can Transform Your Life!* (New York: Bantam Books, 1985), 16.

47. Hill, 109-110.

48. Hill, 110.

49. Thomas G. Long, *Matthew, Westminster Bible Companion* (Louisville, Kentucky: Westminster John Knox Press, 1997), 47.

50. Amy-Jill Levine, Matthew, *The Women's Bible Commentary*, eds. Carol A. Newsom and Sharon H. Ringe (London: SPCK, 1992), 255. For insights into reading Matthew in ways that acknowledge, yet move beyond its anti-Judaism and patriarchy, see two articles by women scholars. They are Amy-Jill Levine's "Matthew's Advice to a Divided Readership," and Elaine Wainwright, R.S.M.'s "The Matthean Jesus and the Healing of Women." Both articles appear in *The Gospel of Matthew in Current Study: Studies in Memory of William J. Thompson, S.J.* (Grand Rapids, Michigan: William B. Eerdmans Publishing Company, 2001), 22-41.

51. Allison, 45.

52. Hill, 110.

53. Hans Dieter Betz, *Essays on the Sermon on the Mount* (Philadelphia: Fortress Press, 1985), 35.

54. Allison, *The Sermon on the Mount*, 46.

55. Ibid.

56. Douglas Hare, *Matthew*, 37-38.

57. *The Interpreter's Dictionary of the Bible*, ed. George Arthur Buttrick. Four vols. (Nashville: Abingdon Press, 1962), 3:334.

58. Allison, 47.

59. Hare, 39.

60. Ibid., 40.

61. See Anthony J. Saldarini's "Reading Matthew without Anti-Semitism," in *The Gospel of Matthew in Current Study: Studies in Memory of William G. Thompson, S.J.*, edited by David E. Aune (Grand Rapids, Michigan: William B. Eerdmans Publishing Company, 2001), 166-184.

62. Hare, 41.

63. Ibid.

64. Ibid., 21.

65. Stephen Barton, *The Spirituality of the Gospels* (London: SPCK, 1992), 22.

66. Hill, 113.

67. Hill, 114.

68. Alyce M. McKenzie, *Matthew: Interpretation Bible Studies* (Louisville, Kentucky: Geneva Press, 1998), 45.

Chapter Nine

1. In each instance where the Baptist appears in John's Gospel there is a negative statement made by him or about him (1:20; 3:28; 1:27; 3:30). The term "the Jews" is used in the Gospel to designate those who reject Jesus (70 occurrences in John compared with five or six in the each of the Synoptic Gospels). In John's Gospel, "the Jews" is a technical term for the religious authorities, especially those in Jerusalem, who were hostile to Jesus. On three occasions the Gospel refers to the removal of believers in Jesus from the synagogue (9:22; 12:42; 16:2). Mellvyn R. Hillmer, "They Believed in Him: Patterns of Discipleship in the Johannine Tradition," *Patterns of Discipleship in the New Testament*, edited by Richard N. Longenecker (Grand Rapids, Michigan: William B. Eerdmans Publishing Company, 1996), 80-81.

2. Sharon H. Ringe, *Wisdom's Friends: Community and Christology in the Fourth Gospel* (Louisville, Kentucky: Westminster John Knox Press, 1999), 10, 11.

3. Ringe, 27.

4. See Raymond Brown, *The Community of the Beloved Disciple* (New York: Paulist Press, 1979) for a plausible account of the history of the group. For an account of the nuances of the theology of the Johannine Epistles, see Melvyn Hillmer's "They Believed in Him: Discipleship in the Johannine Tradition," 93-96.

5. Raymond Brown, *The Gospel According to John I-XII, The Anchor Bible* (Garden City, New York: Doubleday & Company, Inc. 1966). Brown is convinced that the Wisdom Literature offers better parallels for the Johannine picture of Jesus than do the later gnostic, Mandean, or Hermetic passages sometimes suggested. This is also the conclusion of Martin Scott's more recent treatment *Sophia and the Johannine Jesus Journal for the Study of the New Testament Supplement Series* 71 (Sheffield, England: University of Sheffield Press, 1992).

6. See John Ashton, *Understanding the Fourth Gospel* (New York: Oxford University Press, 1991), 167-174.

7. Ibid., 173-74.

8. Martin Scott, 90.

9. The figure of the Son of Man (Daniel 7:13-14; 1 Enoch 70:2; 71:1) in late Jewish writings represented the human being in whom God was revealed. In Daniel he

may well be a figure representative of the whole nation. He descends on the clouds of heaven and is given everlasting dominion over the earth. In Enoch, Enoch ascends and is identified with the Son of Man (1 Enoch 70:2; 71:1). In descending and ascending, the Son of Man is the human being in whom God reveals himself.

10. E. Earle Ellis, *The Gospel of Luke* (Greenwood, South Carolina: The Attic Press, 1977), 105.

11. John Ashton, *Understanding the Fourth Gospel* (Oxford: Clarendon Press, 1991), 358-363.

12. Ibid., 371-373.

13. Stephen C. Barton, *The Spirituality of the Gospels* (London, SPCK, 1992), 118.

14. Craig R. Koester, *Symbolism in the Fourth Gospel: Meaning, Mystery, Community* (Minneapolis: Fortress Press, 1995), Chapter 3: Symbolic Actions, 74-122.

15. Craig R. Koester, *Symbolism in the Fourth Gospel: Meaning, Mystery, Community* (Minneapolis: Fortress Press, 1995), 74.

16. In Matthew, the miracles underscore the authority of Jesus' teachings. In Mark, they represent the inbreaking power of the Son of God over against the power of Satan's realm. In Luke both Jesus' words and deeds are considered part of his preaching of the kingdom and signify the destruction of the kingdom of Satan.

17. Brown, John (1-XII), Appendix IV: "I AM", 533.

18. Proverbs includes references that characterize Wisdom and her gifts as light, way, food, gate, life, and fountain: light (4:18-19; 6:22-23), way (2:7-9, 20; 3:6, 17; 4:11-12, 18, 26; 6:22-23; 15:10, 19; 16:9, 17; 20:7; 28:6), food (9:5, 6; 31:15); gate (8:3), life (4:13, 22-23; 6:22-23; 8:35; 11:30; 15:4; 21:21), fountain (4:22-23; 10:11; 16:22; 18:4).

19. Koester, 138.

20. Ibid., 142-143.

21. J. Massyngbaerde Ford, *Redeemer, Friend and Mother: Salvation in Antiquity and in the Gospel of John* (Minneapolis: Fortress Press, 1997), 125.

22. Ibid.

23. Ibid., 127, note 172.

24. Karl-Gustav Sandelin, *Wisdom as Nourisher: A Study of an Old Testament Theme, Its Development within Early Judaism, and Its Impact on Early Christiantiy.* Acta Academiae Aboensis, Series A, Humaniora 64/3. (Abo. Abo Akademi, 1986), 184.

25. Ben Witherington, III, *Jesus the Sage: The Pilgrimage of Wisdom* (Minneapolis: Fortress Press, 1994), 375.

26. Hillmer, 92.

27. Ibid., 87.

28. James Charlesworth's *The Beloved Disciple* (Valley Forge, Pennsylvania: Trinity Press International, 1995). In Chapter 4 (pp. 225-287), Charlesworth presents evidence for his view that Thomas is the Beloved Disciple.

29. Ringe, *Wisdom's Friends*, 17.

30. Brown, *John XIII-XXI*, 1005.

31. Ringe, 67.

32. Barton, 116-117.

33. Ibid., 117.

34. Ibid., 121.

35. Hillmer, 84-85.

36. Hawkin, 68.

37. Ibid., 68-69.

38. Ibid., 72.

39. Ibid., 76.

40. R. Alan Culpepper, "The Plot of John's Story of Jesus," *Interpretation: A Journal of Bible and Theology,* October 1995, 353.

41. Jouette Bassler, "Nicodemus in the Fourth Gospel," *Journal for the Study of the Old Testament* 108/4 (1989): 638.

42. See Gail R. O'Day's treatment of this text in *The Word Disclosed: John's Story and Narrative Preaching* (St. Louis, Missouri: CBP Press, 1987), 19-27.

43. Witherington, 371.

44. Koester, *Symbolism in the Fourth Gospel*, 48.

45. Gail R. O'Day, *Revelation in the Fourth Gospel: Narrative Mode and Theological Claim* (Philadelphia: Fortress Press 1986), 47. O'Day is drawing on a classic article by Wayne Meeks in which he argued that the language and speech forms of John 3 create a "virtual parody of a revelation discourse," puzzling the reader rather than clarifying Jesus' identity. "The Man from Heaven in Johannine Sectarianism," *JBL* 81 (1972); 44-72.

46. Bassler, 635.

47. Ibid., 639. See especially John 7:13, 26; 12:42 and the fearless confession of the man born blind (chapter 9).

48. Bassler, 641-643.

49. Gail O'Day, *Revelation in the Fourth Gospel*, 59.

50. Koester, 48-51.

51. Judith McKinlay, *Gendering Wisdom the Host: Biblical Invitations to Eat and Drink*, 182-192.

52. Koester, 65.

53. Ibid.

54. Kathy Black, *A Healing Homiletic: Preaching and Disability* (Nashville, Tennessee: Abingdon Press, 1996), 66.

55. Brown, John 1-XII, 371.

56. In Luke 13:1-5 Jesus points out that misfortune does not strike because people are sinners. All humankind are sinners who will perish if we do not repent.

57. Brown, *John,* Vol 1, 371-372.

58. Black, 32-33.

59. Ibid., 58.

60. Ibid., 77.

61. Ibid., 37.

62. Ibid., 37-38.

63. Kathy Black in *A Healing Homiletic* includes a very helpful discussion of traditional rationales for disabilities in chapter one entitled "Healing and Theodicy."

Scriptural strands support many of these traditional interpretations. Misfortune and illness as punishment for sin underlies Exodus 20:5; 34:7, quoted in Numbers 14:18 and Deuteronomy 5:9,10. Illness as a test of faith seems to be implied in those healings in which Jesus attributes the healing to the person's faith. (Two prime examples are Luke 8:48 and Mark 10:42.) Disability or illness as an opportunity for character development is implied in Proverbs 3:11,12. John 9:3 and 2 Corinthians 4:7 indicate that one role of suffering is to manifest the power of God.

64. Black, 67.

65. Ibid., 77.

66. Koester, 64.

67. Ibid., 68-69.

68. *The Booker T. Washington Papers*, Vol. 3, page 496, January 1895, University of Illinois Press.